12,95

BOOKS BY RAOUL D'HARCOURT

L'Amérique avant Colomb, Paris, 1925.
L'argenterie péruvienne a l'époque coloniale, Paris, 1927.
Les textiles anciens du Pérou et leurs techniques, Paris, 1934.
La médecine dans l'ancien Pérou, Paris, 1939.
Archéologie de la Province d'Esmeraldas, Équateur, Paris, 1942.

IN COLLABORATION WITH MARGUERITE D'HARCOURT

La céramique ancienne du Pérou, Paris, 1924.
Les tissus indiens du Vieux Pérou, Paris, 1924.
La musique des Incas et ses survivances, 2 vols., Paris, 1925.
Chansons folkloriques françaises au Canada, Paris and Quebec, 1956.

TEXTILES OF ANCIENT PERU
AND THEIR TECHNIQUES

Edited by

Grace G. Denny and Carolyn M. Osborne

Translated by Sadie Brown

UNIVERSITY OF WASHINGTON PRESS *Seattle and London*

TEXTILES

OF ANCIENT

PERU AND THEIR

TECHNIQUES

BY RAOUL D'HARCOURT

Textiles of Ancient Peru and Their Techniques, first published in 1962,
is a translation, with revisions and additional material, of
Les textiles anciens du Pérou et leurs techniques, published in Paris in 1934.
The present edition was reproduced by photo offset, in a slightly reduced
format, from the 1962 edition and was first published in 1974. The complete
text, all text figures, and all black-and-white plates are included.

Second printing (paper), 1975
Third printing (paper), 1977

The 1962 edition was published with the assistance of a grant
from the Bollingen Foundation.

Library of Congress Catalog Card Number 62-17150
ISBN (paper) 0-295-95331-4

Printed in the United States of America

Preface to the American Edition

I WAS considering the publication of a new edition of my book *Les textiles anciens du Pérou et leurs techniques* (now out of print), and incorporating into it discoveries which I have made since 1935 and certain new analyses which I have conducted, when I received a letter from Miss Grace G. Denny, inquiring whether I would be disposed to publish this work in an English language edition and advising that, if so, she and her colleague Mrs. Carolyn M. Osborne would undertake its preparation. I accepted the offer gladly.

This second edition is now completed, thanks to the joint labors of Miss Denny and Mrs. Osborne, who have collaborated in bringing the task to a conclusion. Both of them are specialists in matters of textile technology and have thus been able to supply exact English equivalents for the French technical terms. They are more than mere translators, they have become my collaborators. My thanks also go to Miss Sadie Brown; I know how precious her help has been to Miss Denny and Mrs. Osborne.

Señor Rafael Larco y Herrera, now deceased, was the friend to whom I dedicated my book. He always showed great interest in my works pertaining to Peruvian Americanism. I had hoped that, in his great *hacienda* at Chiclin, Trujillo, he might establish hand-weaving studios where Indian women would resume the practice of, and once more delight in, the ancient techniques, which have fallen into complete oblivion. This is especially true of tapestry, which until the Incaic period maintained a high degree of perfection, and which contributed, during the seventeenth and even into the eighteenth century, very beautiful fabrics in which the Indian art was closely mingled with that of Spain. But that proved to be only a dream—the past cannot be revived.

Paris, 1959

Preface to the Original Edition

I SHOULD like, at the beginning of this work, to express my gratitude to all those who, either personally or as curators or directors of museums, have been kind enough to help me with their knowledge, or have allowed me to study and reproduce specimens in their collections. I wish to mention especially the Museo Nacional, Lima; Señor Schmidt-Pizarro, Lima; the Museum of Anthropology of the University of California, Berkeley; the Textile Museum of the District of Columbia, Washington; the Museum of Fine Arts, Boston; the Museum of the American Indian, Heye Foundation, New York; the American Museum of Natural History, New York; the Riksmuseum, Stockholm; the Göteborgs Museum; Professor Walter Lehmann and Herr Heinrich Hardt, of Berlin; the Museum für Völkerkunde, Berlin, Munich, and Stuttgart; the I. G. Farben-Industrie A. G., Ludwigshafen; Dr. R. Wegner, the University Museum of Archaeology and Ethnology, Cambridge; the Musée de l'Homme, Paris; M. Ratton, of Paris; M. Charles Hein, of Paris; and finally my friend, M. Fritz Iklé, of Saint-Gall, to whom I owe special gratitude for the great courtesy which he has never ceased to show me, and for the valuable advice which he has given me.

The figures in the text have been drawn in accordance with my rough sketches.

Paris, 1934

Contents

PART I
Woven Fabrics

Contents

PART II
Nonwoven Fabrics

Contents

PART III
Ornamentation and Trimming of Fabrics

Plates

Plates

TEXTILES OF ANCIENT PERU
AND THEIR TECHNIQUES

Introduction

In a previous study (Harcourt, 1924) I endeavored to show, with the aid of selected examples, the degree of perfection and decorative beauty attained in Peruvian weaving in pre-Spanish times. I wanted especially to draw the attention of artists to a human production then known to only a small number of people. I also added to the plates there reproduced an explanatory notice that could be understood by the general public. Here my purpose is different. I wish to describe in detail all of the ancient techniques that examination of Peruvian weaving, network, needle-made fabrics, and plaiting has revealed to me, as well as the techniques of embroidery, and to show to what extent they are connected with one another and can be grouped together. This study seems to have been neglected up to now. We shall see that, before the arrival of the Europeans on the new continent, the Indians had invented very intricate techniques, which gave their textiles an extremely rich and varied effect, often comparable, and sometimes even superior, to those obtained in the Old World in the days before machinery had developed the possibilities of spinning and weaving to their present extent. Thus, the inventions of an industry due solely to the skill of the Indians will be specifically described. This study will serve as a trustworthy foundation for later comparative studies which space does not permit me to develop in this work. I shall be satisfied if these pages may also serve to revive in Peru and Bolivia the remarkable techniques that today have fallen into complete oblivion.

I have chosen as the cultural region for my study the central and southern portions of the Peruvian coast because they are the ones best known today and are the areas where the techniques appear to be most numerous. However, all the people of the coastal sections

3

of this region were remarkable weavers; and their conquerors, the Incas, were certainly not inferior to them, as we know, thanks to a small number of specimens spared by man and time,[1] and thanks also to the evidence of the chroniclers. The excavations made at and to the south of Lima have been especially fruitful because of the protection afforded by the graves and because the particular dryness of the soil aided in their preservation. The specimens analyzed in this study came chiefly from the well-known archeological sites of Nazca, Ica, Paracas, Cajamarquilla, Ancón, Chancay, and Pachacamac.

Can the age of these textiles be determined? The specimens studied and used as examples in this work do not show any characteristics that can link them to the Inca period, which, strictly speaking, was a long one in the coastal area—from two hundred to three hundred years—and which came to an end with the arrival of the Spaniards. Furthermore, such diversified and perfected techniques could have been developed only by a civilization many centuries old. Some authors have tried to classify the fruits of their research in a relative chronology by studying the decoration of ceramics and textiles in the levels of excavated ground and correlating the more or less frequent uses of the same techniques. Others have gone even further and have attempted to fix the dates of the various periods. I shall gladly follow the first group but not the second, whose deductions, in the present state of our knowledge, contain too many hypotheses. The analysis of ancient organic matter containing radioactive carbon (C^{14}) has aroused great hopes of determining the age of archeological specimens. But the great diversity in the successive estimates of objects coming from the same place and the same stratum has caused the method to be considered insufficiently reliable up to the present time. It will be necessary to await the perfecting of the method before accepting without reservation the dates suggested by it. On the authority of Kroeber (O'Neale and Kroeber, 1930, p. 30), the variety and perfection of the textile techniques were almost as great in the most remote period he investigated, which goes back to the beginning of the Christian era, as in the period immediately preceding the coming of the Incas to the coast, which may be fixed as around the fourteenth century.[2] This single statement by Kroeber should make us cautious in assigning an age to a textile on the basis of its technique, or the degree of perfection of the technique. As to the persistence of styles, I have ascertained that the influence of the so-called Tiahuanaco civilization had not yet been extinguished at the time of the Inca epoch in the region of Lake Titicaca.

For complete information with respect to the quality of the textile materials formerly used in Peru, the method of obtaining the yarns, the structure of the fabric, and the methods of dyeing, I refer the interested reader to works already published.[3] I shall con-

---

[1] The damp climate of the highlands rarely permitted preservation of funerary articles placed in the ground, other than those of stone or ceramics.

[2] One epoch varies from another in the percentages of use of the different textile materials and techniques.

TEXTILE MATERIALS

fine myself to the following more general summary.

The aborigines had at their disposal as primary materials the subdivided agave fiber;[4] two kinds of cotton, natural brown and white; and the glossy wool of the llama and domesticated alpaca, as well as the finer and silkier wool of the wild vicuña. In rare instances they added human hair. An old chronicle mentions that the Incas sometimes incorporated gold and silver threads in their fabrics, but I have never seen a textile with these.

YARNS

The yarn, twisted by hand, without the aid of a spindle rotated or governed by a flywheel, was usually even and tightly twisted, often excessively so. Yarns were used in single form or in several joined strands, in conformity with the purpose for which they were required. Double or two-ply yarns predominated; of equal thickness, they were smoother and stronger than single yarns. According to Crawford, the fineness of the single Peruvian cotton yarns did not exceed No. 250, that is, either 210,000 yards to the English pound or 211,600 meters to 500 grams. These yarns are coarser than those of the delicate muslins woven in ancient times in India. On the other hand, according to the same author, the fineness of the two-ply wool yarns could reach No. 300, that is, 168,000 yards to the English pound or 169,250 meters to 500 grams, which is quite remarkable (Crawford, 1915, p. 81).

The intrinsic qualities of wool and cotton were recognized and used judiciously by the weavers of ancient Peru, and no errors can be pointed out in their use of fiber materials in the warp and weft of woven cloths. Such woven cloths might be made entirely of cotton or entirely of wool, but when the two fiber materials were used in the same fabric the warp was never of wool. There is no exception to this rule.

DYES

The ancient Peruvians had a very extensive range of colors. Their materials for dyeing and the method of their use are still, in part, unknown. In order to ascertain them, in addition to chemical analyses difficult to carry out in many cases and uncertain of result, research would be necessary in the localities where vegetable products or minerals are still used in the Andean highlands. I shall say merely a few words upon the obtaining of three essential colors: blue, red, and yellow.

[3] See especially the works of Crawford (1915) and of Ephraim (1905) as well as the anonymous work entitled "Tecnología indígena" (1923).

[4] American agave is commonly known in Peru as "*cabuya*."

The Peruvians knew how to prepare a bath of light or deep indigo, which was done by the more or less prolonged immersion and reduction by fermentation of the leaves of various shrubs which contained coloring matter. When a fabric is taken from an indigo bath, it is yellow; it is the oxidizing action of the air that later turns it blue. The Indians knew how to obtain a range of very fast blues, from celestial blue to deep blue.

The reds came from vegetable and animal sources. The principal one was the insect cochineal, which gave a beautiful slightly carmine red. The cochineal is gathered from the leaves of the *Opuntia*. It is not known whether this small insect was bred on the coasts of Peru, as it was in Mexico. Dyeing with cochineal produces red or black, according to the mordant used, and it is interesting to note that the Indians in the area of Cajamarca still dye their fabrics black with this product. This leads to the belief that it was also used in this manner in former times.

Yellow often came from the bark of the false pepper tree (*Chinus mollis*), but many other substances were also used which are unknown to us at this time.

Violet and green resulted from successive dyeings of blue and red or of blue and yellow. The yellow could be simply the natural fawn color often found in the fleece of the llama, and in this case only one dyeing was necessary.

Wool is easily dyed, and the richest colors were obtained in this fiber. Cotton, on the other hand, requires mordants that the Indians did not use. Although indigo can dye cotton a satisfactory blue, cochineal, on the contrary, lacks intensity without mordant and thus was but little used for dyeing this fiber.

LOOMS

The looms were quite rudimentary. They consisted basically of two parallel bars (Fig. 3, *a, a'*), between which the yarns of the warp were stretched. The bars were sometimes kept separated by four stakes driven into the ground, or, for more delicate pieces, were attached to a small frame (Schmidt, 1911, Fig. 7, p. 9; Fig. 49, p. 60), but usually one of the bars was attached by means of a cord (Fig. 3, *i, i'*) to the branch of a tree or to a beam or rafter, while the other was held firm by means of a strap (Fig. 3, *j*) passing around the lower back of the weaver, who, by a single bodily movement, could increase or diminish the tension of the warp. That this method was common in Mexico and Peru is attested by the old documents reproduced in Figures 1 and 2.[5] Peruvian looms generally belonged to the so-called horizontal type. The yarns of the warp were not connected directly to the bars, but to a small cord (Fig. 3, *c-c'*) running parallel to the bars and attached to them at intervals (Fig. 3).

The entire warp was exposed because the loom did not have a warp beam. The warp

[5] See also the reproduction of a drawing of Huaman Poma de Ayala (1936, p. 564).

6

yarn went from one of the cords to another in a regular lacing or wrapping movement. Because of this fact the woven pieces are all quite small in size. They possess four selvages, so to speak, but those at the ends,[6] to which the term "tape" should not be applied, have not the same appearance as those at the sides. It is only in rare instances that the direction of the weaving cannot be discerned by the practiced observer. This distinction is important when one wishes to reconstruct techniques and methods of work, and I have found

Figure 1. Reproduction of a scene painted on a vase from Trujillo (British Museum, London)

Figure 2. Reproduction of a scene from a Mexican manuscript (Kingsborough, 1831–48, p. 61)

that where one of the elements, warp or weft, was given a predominating role, there was a corresponding method of weaving in which the other element played this part. I shall demonstrate this in the course of the following pages.

Pieces of fabric two or three meters in length are not unusual in plain weaves, made of fairly coarse yarn, but in the fine fabrics, and especially in tapestries, these dimensions rapidly dwindle. The widths of the fabrics do not exceed the space within which a woman could freely pass the bobbin from hand to hand, which is generally 60 to 75 centimeters [23 to 30 inches] (exceptional maximum in joined plain-weave fabric 130 centimeters [51 inches]); certain delicate braids are less than 1 centimeter [⅜ inch] wide. When a very large cloth was required, either two pieces of normal width were sewed together at the selvages, or, by a more elegant method, a common yarn connected them, threading alternately the looped ends of the weft yarns of each cloth.[7]

In the course of making a plain weave, a stick—usually a large reed (Fig. 3, *b*)— separated, and kept separated, the yarns of the warp into two groups of leases, each comprising yarns of odd and even rows. By means of a system of convenient small loops (Fig. 3, *h*), a shedding stick (Fig. 3, *g*) permitted the automatic raising of the groups of yarns placed by the large roller under the other group (see Fig. 3, *b*). Thus the alternate cross-

[6] This relates actually to the ends in which the yarns of the warp are not cut, but form loops, as do the yarns of the weft on the side selvages.

[7] See also on this subject O'Neale and Kroeber (1930, p. 30, note 15).

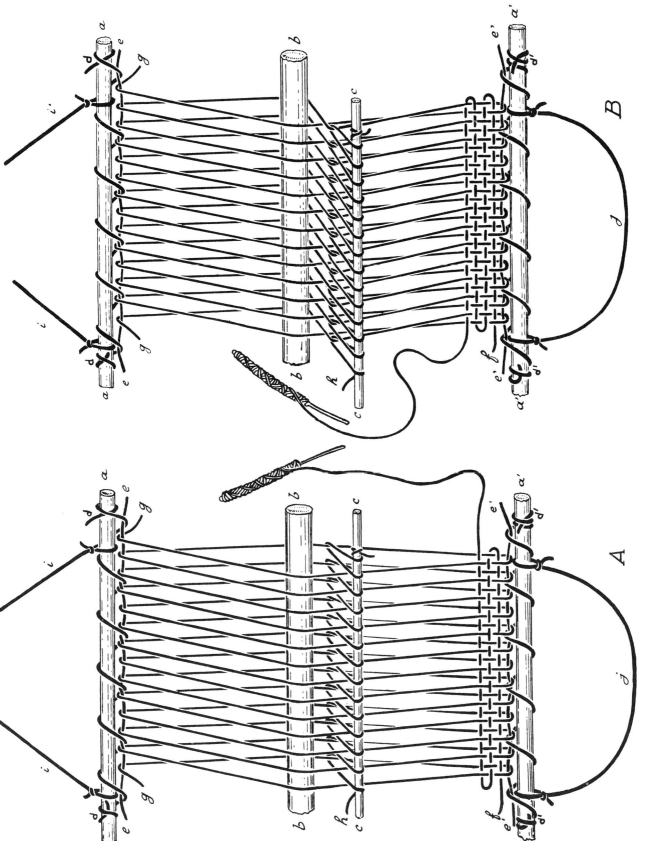

Figure 3. Common form of the ancient Peruvian loom. A: heddle lowered, odd yarns lifted; B: heddle raised, even yarns lifted. The parts of the loom are: *a*, *a'*, loom bars supporting warp for weaving; *b*, coarse rod or roller separating the two warp sections; *c*, small rod which, with the loops formed by yarn *h*, constitutes the only heddle of the loom; *d*, *d'*, cord that secures *e*, *e'* to the loom bars; *f*, weft yarn supplied by the bobbin; *g*, continuous warp yarn; *h*, heddle loops; *i*, *i'*, small cords used to attach the upper loom bar to a given position; *j*, girth passing from the opposite loom bar around the lower back of the weaver

ing of the sheds was achieved (Fig. 3, A and B).[8] A long, flat wooden blade helped the weaver to tighten the weft yarns against each other. I have never seen an ancient loom with two or more shedding sticks, but, since the principle of the automatic raising of the warp yarns was discovered by the Indians of Peru, it is very probable that the multiplicity of heddles had already been applied in intricate weaving; O'Neale (1946) is convinced of this. Furthermore, there has been found in an uncompleted narrow fabric a series of small heddle loops that permitted the automatic raising of the warp yarns for the making of the design (Wardle, 1936, pp. 35 f.).

When the work consisted of a fabric with an intricate design, the weaver usually worked with a model as a guide, which she kept before her. It is probable that the worker either copied the model or used her own interpretation of it, as circumstances required (Fig. 1). In examining Peruvian textiles, the fact that the loom gave the weaver but little assistance must not be overlooked. Manual skill, however, made up for the rusticity of the instrument. Because of this the worker had a good deal of liberty in the use of techniques, which were often varied in the course of the same piece of weaving.

Torn pieces of fabric, or garments that had suffered from wear, were undoubtedly stretched on a loom, or at least on a frame, in order to be repaired. Here they were not merely darned, but the fabric was actually rewoven in accordance with the original crossing of the yarns; numerous examples bear this out (see Garcilaso de la Vega, 1609, Book IV, chap. xiv).

To my knowledge, no archeological discovery, and no evidence contemporary with the Conquest, permits the assertion that the ancient Peruvians used any instrument other than a needle with an eye for joining yarns to each other or to a fabric. Crochet hooks and knitting needles seem to have been unknown. There were needles with eyes in both curved and straight shapes, of metal, of fishbone, of wood, and of thorns. Some of them must have been very fine, suitable for the close work that still arouses our admiration today.

Cactus thorn needles must have predominated. An examination of the eyes leads to the belief that these were obtained by simple lateral perforation of the thorn made with another thorn used as a bodkin. The eye must have been made by the worker at the moment she required the needle. In coastal graves, small plaited baskets containing weavers' or embroideresses' accessories sometimes contain boxes of carved pelican bone, filled with cactus thorns not yet transformed into true needles.

I, personally, have found only one fine cactus needle threaded with a yarn; this one was with cotton yarn. The threading must have been accomplished simultaneously with the perforation of the thorn needle by another thorn, that is, the yarn was simply forced into the thorn needle and was not truly put through an eye.

Eyed needles of copper, silver, or gold have often been described. To make the eye,

---

[8] See also Schmidt (1911, p. 7, Fig. 5).

the end of the needle opposite to the point was bent into a rounded hook, which was then caught between two flanges formed by flattening the needle stem near the end of the bent-over hook. These flanges were then hammered and closed around the end of the hook, making a coarse, round, closed eye. Metal needles are relatively coarse. I have never seen curved needles; however, they would appear necessary for certain types of work.

I shall not attempt to describe the harmony of color of the Peruvian textiles. As for the interesting decorative designs, the plates in this volume speak for themselves. An explanatory account of each of the specimens reproduced will be found preceding the plates.

The methods of weaving and knotting and the stitches that I am going to describe have all been reconstructed by me; I can guarantee, therefore, that their execution is feasible, without claiming, of course, that the weaver followed exactly the same procedures I did, and that she may not have used actions of the hands which were different or more practical.

To avoid uncertainty, I shall specify some definitions and also the meanings I attribute to certain words:

> *Woven cloth*: the product obtained by the intercrossing at right angles of yarns divided into at least two elements—warp and weft (muslin, tapestry, etc.).
>
> *Warp*: the assemblage of parallel yarns stretched between the two loom bars.
>
> *Lease*: the assemblage of warp yarns raised simultaneously to allow passage of the weft yarns; in plain weave, the assemblage of even or odd warp yarns.
>
> *Warping*: the operation that consists of placing and stretching the warp yarns between the loom bars, with a view to their being crossed by the weft.
>
> *Weft*: the yarn that crosses the warp perpendicularly.
>
> *Weft row*: section of the weft yarn comprised between the two side selvages.
>
> *Plaiting or braiding*: the product obtained by the regular interlacing of yarns originally arranged in the same way as the leases of warp, that is, with alternating odd and even yarns.
>
> *Draft*: planned preparation of the elements of woven cloth or braid.
>
> *Network or netting*: needle or single element construction, usually made of loops or knots.
>
> *Embroidery*: ornamental yarn incorporated by means of a needle into a woven, needle-made, or plaited fabric after it has been constructed.

10

In spite of the inconvenience that may result, I am refraining from using the names of current techniques to designate the ancient ones that merely resembled them, but were basically different, nor shall I use the name of a country in connection with a general technique of world-wide use. Thus, the words "velour," "knitting stitch," "Gobelins," and so forth will be avoided, as their use has already caused too much misunderstanding.

The assistance afforded the study of Peruvian weaving by the ancient chroniclers is negligible. Although some of them, such as Garcilaso de la Vega (1609, Book IV, chaps. ii and xiv), Cobo (1890–95, Book XIV, chaps. ii and xi), and Huaman Poma de Ayala (1936), did speak of weaving and woven fabrics, they touched only upon generalities and cast scarcely any light upon the problems required to be solved.

PART I

Woven Fabrics

ONE

Plain Weave

FABRICS WITH CONTINUOUS WARP AND WEFT, EQUALLY VISIBLE

THE SIMPLEST regular weave is formed in the following manner: parallel yarns, stretched between two rigid bars and composing what is called the warp of the fabric about to be made, are divided into two groups, of which one includes all the yarns of the even rows and the other all the yarns of the odd rows; these two leases are alternately raised, and

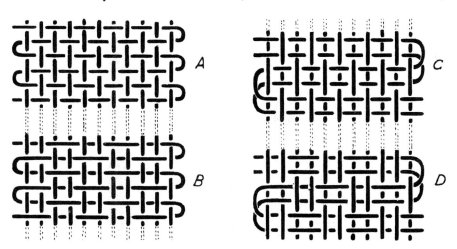

Figure 4. Plain weave. A: single wefts pass over and under single warps; B: single wefts pass over and under two warp yarns; C: double wefts pass over and under single warps; D: double wefts pass over and under two warp yarns

there is inserted between them, perpendicular to the yarn of the warp, another yarn called the weft. The passing of the weft through the lease is possible only if the warp yarns are kept level with one another.

Textiles of Ancient Peru and Their Techniques

If the weft yarns and the warp yarns are alike, and if the compacting of the weft yarns corresponds to the tension and spacing of the warp yarns, the fabric will have a unified appearance and will also have an equal number of warps and wefts (Fig. 4, A). Such are voile, taffeta, muslin, etc., which, except for the textile material used and the coarseness of the yarns, differ from one another only in the degree of density and compactness of the warp and weft. It is hardly necessary to say that the ancient Peruvians made fabric of this kind, ranging from fine muslin to the thick and coarse fabric that formed the protective armor for warriors or the external wrappings for mummies.

The plain weave of Peru shows several variants that modify its character somewhat: instead of passing over and under a single warp yarn, the weft may pass over and under two each time; instead of comprising a single yarn, the weft is sometimes formed of two adjacent yarns. Figure 4, A, B, C, and D, illustrates the four variants of plain weave produced by the techniques described above.

Striped and plaid fabrics

By varying the color of the warp yarns or the weft yarns at intervals, a striped fabric is obtained. If these changes of color are produced at equal intervals in the warp and weft, the fabric will show squares formed by the perpendicular crossing of the stripes. Many ancient fabrics have been found in Peru with simple or perpendicularly crossed stripes (Fig. 5; Pl. 1, A).

Figure 5. Plain weave of two colors, the stripes of which intersect each other and form squares

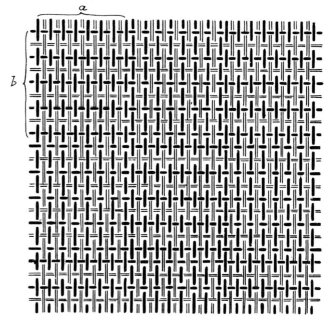

Figure 6. Arrangement of the yarns of plain weave of two colors, shown in Plate 1, B

16

The alternation, according to certain irregular rhythms, of yarns of two different colors in the warp and the weft results in varied patterns such as that shown in Plate 1, B, the scheme of which is set forth in Figure 6.

FABRICS MADE OF DISCONTINUOUS AND INTERLOCKED YARNS WITH VISIBLE WARP AND WEFT

In the preceding examples it has been stated that the warp yarns placed in a regular manner between the two loom bars before the passage of the weft were all of the length of the fabric intended to be woven, and that the weft yarns crossed the whole width of the fabric without interruption. The weaver did not always follow this plan, however; she might choose to work with discontinuous and interlocked yarns.

First example (grids)

Let us assume that a fabric of brown and white squares in the form of a checkerboard is desired (Fig. 7; Pl. 2, A). The warp, made up of a series of brown and white yarns in equal number in regular sequence, will be established at the top of the first row of squares. In order to form the second row of squares, a new portion of the warp, like the first, but with the order of the colors reversed (brown yarns under white yarns and vice versa), will be interlocked yarn by yarn to the short warps of the preceding squares. The succeeding rows will be prepared in the same manner, reversing the order of the colors each time. It may be asked how the worker, in order to make the weft pass through, could raise alternately the odd and even yarns of such short portions of the warp. It should be noted from the outset that this difficulty is by no means peculiar to this technique. It is encountered at the end of the weaving of fabrics of all descriptions. It was solved, undoubtedly, by means of very fine bobbins or more probably by means of needles, which, without the aid of the alternate raising of the warp yarns, passed regularly between them.

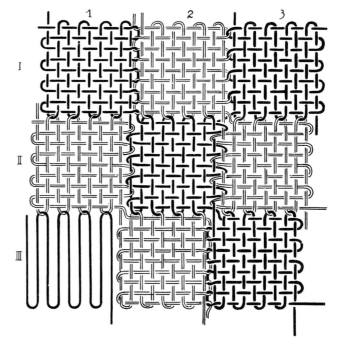

Figure 7.   Fabric in squares of two colors, having discontinuous warp and weft yarns interlocked according to different methods

With respect to the weft, it must have been of two colors, one brown and the other white, in order to cross the warp yarns with the corresponding color. The weaving consisted of passing successively a brown or a white yarn through as many small, independent passages as the material contained squares in its width. Upon changing direction, each sectional weft interlocked with its neighbor in the adjacent squares, in accordance with one of the methods indicated in Figure 8. The greatest difficulty of a practical nature, it would seem, must have been in setting up the portions of the warp in which the yarns had to be of strictly equal length. It may be assumed that the worker was helped by small, intermediate dividers or grids, actually made of small, tightly stretched cords around which the warp yarns were passed, and which the weaver withdrew after the interlocking of the following portion of the warp, before the weaving began.

Checkered fabrics of two or more colors arranged in grids have frequently been found in Peru. The method I have just described produces perfect checkered fabric, because it requires the interlocking of all the warp yarns and all the weft loops between adjacent squares. But there were two other methods, which were also in common use. In one, only the warp yarns were interlocked with one another, so that the weaving had to be done in the form of long, narrow bands, the width of a square; in order to form the fabric, these bands were joined laterally to one another by means of fine sewing. In the other method, numerous small squares of equal size (I have seen some of them less than two centimeters [¾ inch] across) were woven separately; each square was monochrome, but at least two colors were used in the finished fabric. These squares, which naturally had a selvage on each of the four sides, were placed side by side and then sewed together in such a way that their different colors formed a decorative motive (see Pl. 2, B).

Second example (complex design)

In the fabrics shown in Plates 3, A, B, and 4, discontinuous warp yarns and sectional wefts are to be found again, but the accomplishment of the weaving must have been ex-

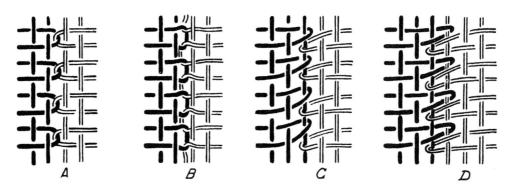

A   *B*   *C*   *D*

Figure 8.   Methods of interlocking the yarns in fabrics with discontinuous warp and weft yarns

ceedingly difficult because of the complexity of the design. The worker had first to arrange her warp yarns, which were to be joined to each other, following the main lines of the design to be reproduced and leaving intervening spaces by the omission of yarns. The difficulty was in maintaining the ends of the warp yarns in place, in view of the empty spaces. In this also the worker undoubtedly made use of small, transverse cords which were temporarily inserted and withdrawn toward the end of the weaving of the sectional wefts, when the passage of a certain number of wefts rendered the aid of the cord unnecessary. This type of weaving, by reason of its complexity, seems almost unbelievable today.[1] It was used, however, to produce textiles of large dimensions, such as that shown in Plate 4. In the filling in of the open spaces with plain weave, which must have been done by needle, the same yarn often served successively as warp, then as weft, as in true darning (Fig. 9; see also O'Neale and Kroeber, 1930, p. 40, Fig. 9).

REP; WARP AND WEFT CONTINUOUS, ONE OF THE TWO ELEMENTS CONCEALED

Up to this point the fabrics studied have shown their two elements, warp and weft, equally. If the yarns of these elements are unequal in thickness or in flexibility, if their spacing and their compactness vary, the appearance of the fabric will change completely (Fig. 10, A, B). One of the elements may even disappear from sight, being enveloped and concealed by the other. That is the principle of rep. The Peruvians used it extensively, making use of all the variations it permitted.

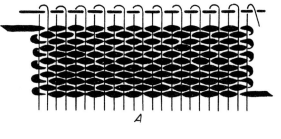

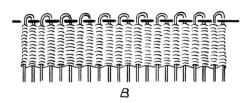

Figure 9. Method of filling in, with a needle, a space left open in the course of weaving; warp and weft made with a single yarn

Figure 10. Plain weave, rep. A: fabric in which the warp yarn is fine and the weft yarn is coarse; B: fabric in which the warp yarn is coarse and the weft yarn is fine and supple

[1] See the study made by L. M. O'Neale of this technique (1933).

Weft only visible

This type of rep is common. It is usually made with a cotton warp, the yarns of which are relatively coarse, firm, and well stretched, crossed by the fine and flexible weft yarn, usually of wool, in closely packed weft rows that completely cover and conceal the warp yarns (Fig. 10, B). It is frequently alternated with tapestry, the similar technique of which we shall study later.

Warp only visible

This other rep is also common. The warp and weft are generally of the same textile material, but the well-twisted yarn of the not too closely spaced wefts leaves only the warp visible. The result is a fairly dense but flexible fabric (Pl. 3, A). The method was used and is used to this day in the highlands, especially for making workers' pouches or bags, and for the square piece that is thrown over a woman's shoulder as a mantle or a carrying cloth for a baby or a bundle. Ordinarily, the fabric included lengthwise stripes of various colors. The rep with only the warp visible formerly often alternated with the technique for warp-design fabrics with two alternating colors, with concealed weft and construction subordinated to the design (see p. 31).

Warp only visible; formed with discontinuous and interlocking yarns

The special features of fabrics with discontinuous and interlocked elements, pointed out in plain-weave fabrics, are also found in rep where the warp only is visible (see Pl. 3, A). The rules for setting up the discontinuous warp are essentially the same. As in the case of the checkered brown and white fabric, the color of the weft yarn is generally the same as that of the warp yarns, and each sectional weft is interlocked to those that precede and follow it. But, since the weft is almost invisible, the weaver was allowed some license in changing the color of the sectional wefts (see Fig. 11). The specimen shown in Plate 6, A, presents these special features. In addition, since the warp yarns were intentionally omitted at intervals, the weft yarns crossed over empty spaces, where later they served as a foundation for the needle-made tapestry that filled these spaces.

The hypothesis that the transverse yarns intended to support the ends of the sectional warps were placed into position before the warping is confirmed by an examination of some reps of mixed colors. In these the warp yarns do not interlock, as we have just stated, but turn around a common transverse yarn, alternating either singly or by groups of three or four yarns of the same color (see Pl. 11, A). This singular technique produces a fabric very like tapestry (see next section). It may be called, with a certain degree of precision, "tapestry with visible warp and concealed weft." In addition to the appearance of the selvages, especially the terminal selvages, it can be recognized at a glance by the not too closely spaced wool wefts, which give the fabric a flexibility that true tapestry does not possess.

My hypothesis regarding the use of provisional transverse yarns for warping has been completely confirmed by an unfinished specimen from Ica belonging to the American Museum of Natural History in New York (see Pl. 5). These transverse yarns were placed at equal distance from each other, and their separation corresponded to the shortest length that the warp yarns reached in one color; a perfectly logical disposition.

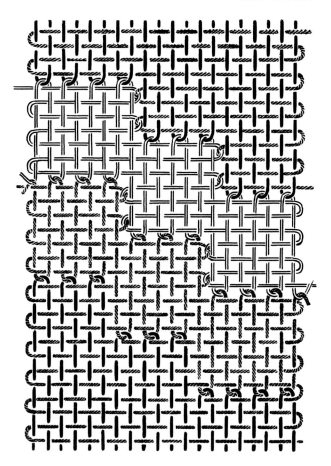

Figure 11.   Arrangement of warp and weft yarns in the fabric shown in Plate 3, A

If the same color had to extend to greater lengths, the intermediate transverse yarns were not used and simply remained between the two warp leases.

TAPESTRY; CONCEALED WARP, DISCONTINUOUS AND PREDOMINANT WEFT

The word "tapestry" has two accepted meanings, which unfortunately can lead to misunderstanding. It signifies embroidery done by needle, covering open-textured fabric, such as bolting cloth or canvas; it also signifies, and this is the only sense in which it is used in this study, a plain weave in which the warp, as in the reps studied above, is the passive element and is completely covered by the weft, but instead of one single weft crossing the entire width of the fabric, there are several successive yarns of different colors, each one of them crossing only a limited and variable number of warp yarns before returning upon itself. Stated differently, tapestry is like small, distinct, and adjacent pieces of weaving on the same warp (Fig. 12, A). By this method the weaver was quite free to reproduce most

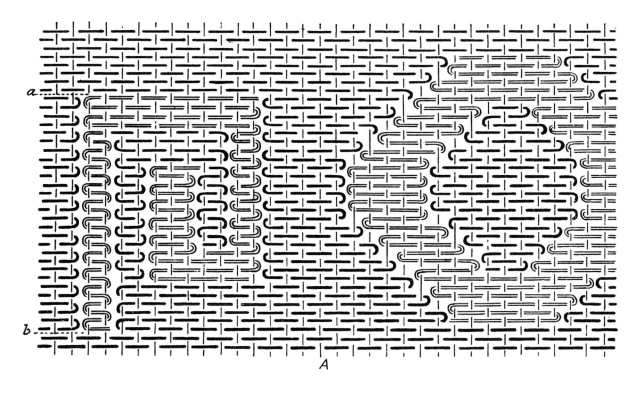

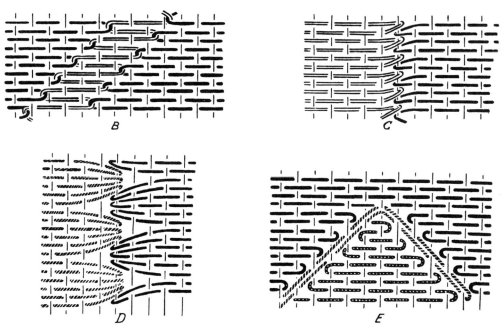

Figure 12. A: diagram showing the appearance of a two-colored tapestry (from *a* to *b* is an example of a perpendicular slit formed by sectional selvages between two adjacent warp yarns); B: sectional wefts interlocked; C: sectional wefts turning singly around a common warp yarn; D: sectional wefts turning by groups of three around a common warp yarn; E: tapestry motive in which the separation of colors is emphasized by two yarns that pass obliquely and form a border.

varied designs, for the special weaving could be extended to the entire length and the entire width of the textile, or diminished to the mere covering of two adjacent warp yarns and to the thickness of two wefts, that is to say, practically to one stitch.

Reversible fabrics (total or partial)

The ancient Peruvians brought tapestry to a degree of excellence seldom attained, and its use was very widespread.

In the colonial epoch, the seventeenth to the eighteenth centuries, beautiful tapestries were still being woven in which the European influence impinged upon the Indian decorative art (see Means, 1932). In our day, tapestry is almost forgotten. One has to go far to the south, to the Araucanians, to find it again.

Tapestry is nearly always made of a fairly strong warp of cotton yarn and a weft of fine, flexible wool, which covers the warp and completely conceals it (Pl. 7). Weft of cotton is quite rare. Wool warp is found only in the very fine tapestries of highland Peru (the Inca and even Spanish colonial periods). The two faces of the fabric have a similar appearance, and very often the same perfection of workmanship, the ends of the yarn where color changes occur being carefully hidden in the thickness of the tapestry. This is not always so, and the worker who neglected to conceal the end of the weft yarn on terminating a piece of sectional weaving sometimes crossed directly from one surface to the other, leaving the yarn exposed on the reverse of the fabric.

Number of warp yarns and of weft yarns to the centimeter

In tapestry, whereas the warp is usually quite coarse, the weft can be extremely fine. I have indicated elsewhere, without concealing my amazement, that Crawford counted, on a tapestry that he considered the finest he had examined, 42 warp yarns and 260 to 280 weft yarns to the inch, or about 16 warp yarns and 105 weft yarns to the centimeter (Crawford, 1915, p. 93). These figures astonished me. I have done personal research on the finest pieces of tapestry I possess, and on a piece from Cajamarquilla I succeeded in counting, to the centimeter, 15 warp yarns [39 to the inch] and 36 visible weft yarns counted on the same warp yarn. In tapestry one is counting in this way every other weft; therefore, the weft crosses the warp more than 72 times in the space of a centimeter [186 times in the space of 1 inch]. It is quite possible that, in a fabric finer than mine, Crawford may have found the figures he gives. They provoke admiration. How much time must the weavers have required to accomplish such pieces of work! It must be recognized that this extreme fineness is relatively rare. The tapestries of average quality range between 8 and

12 warp yarns and between 30 and 50 weft yarns to the centimeter [that is, between 20 and 30 warp yarns to the inch and between 75 and 125 weft yarns to the inch].

Sectional wefts not wholly perpendicular to the warp

Generally, sectional wefts in tapestry follow each other for the whole width of the fabric with great regularity. However, the independence of the individual sections of weaving permits a certain inequality in the number of yarns that may cross in order to maintain a regular weaving edge from one selvage to the other; thus, in one section the tapestry will be tight, and in another it will be less tight. The elasticity of the wool renders hardly visible this inequality, which facilitates the reproduction of a design; it also permits the insertion of oblique wefts or wefts in curved lines. But the Peruvians, with their preference for deep ridges and clear angles, made much less use of this technique than did, for example, the Copts. The tapestry shown in Plate 11, B, however, gives an example of great sinuosity in the passage of the weft. The obliquity of the wefts was especially used in Peru for the dark outline around decorative motives (see Fig. 12, E). Its use was extended, under Spanish influence, in the tapestries of the colonial epoch.

Slits

The principle of tapestry with its short weft yarns gave rise to a feature, most often considered a defect, which was sometimes used in Peru for decorative purposes: the adjacent surfaces of the woven sections were not joined to each other. If, for example, two of these surfaces, in which there is a rather long common frontier, parallel to the warp yarns, were not joined, the lack of joining appears as a slit and may spoil the beauty and solidarity of the fabric (see the slit in Fig. 12, A, *a–b*). When the design in geometric form is repeated with regularity and is not unduly long, these multiple slits are acceptable and have an ornamental function. In other cases, when a common frontier of two surfaces resulted in an undesirable slit, the worker connected these surfaces with each other at intervals by means of a needle-made stitch after the weaving was completed.

Means adopted to avoid slits

In order to avoid slits, the weavers sought means other than sewing. They conceived at least four methods.

The first consists of introducing during the weaving, every three or four rows, a very fine weft of the same yarn as the warp, which crosses from one selvage to the other. As it is covered over, absorbed by the sectional wool wefts, which form the design, this yarn remains practically invisible. This method can be used only if the level of the work is kept

strictly even across the whole width of the fabric during the course of the weaving (Pl. 8).
If tapestries with continuous, concealed cotton wefts were unquestionably woven in the
manner that I have just described, it would be unwise to pretend that this method was
unique. I believe that in cases where the cotton wefts are very closely set and are very regular, such a piece may be a tapestry embroidered on plain-weave cloth (see p. 120).

The second method, still more exacting than the first, also requires the worker to
direct the weaving of the fabric over the whole width simultaneously. It consists of interlocking each sectional weft with its neighbors on the right and on the left, at the weaving
edge, before returning upon itself. In this way, all the wefts are interlocked (see Fig. 12, B;
Pl. 6, B). The worker was sometimes content merely to interlock the sectional wefts at
intervals.

The third method, which was rarely used in the coastal area of Peru, consists of turning the yarns of the sectional wefts that face each other around a single warp yarn (Fig.
12, C; Pl. 9). This method has two drawbacks: it doubles the number of weft yarns covering the neighboring warp yarns, causing an irregular compacting of the wefts, and renders
less distinct the separation of the different colored surfaces, because the colors alternate
on the thickness of the yarn serving as a border. The textile shown in Plate 9 illustrates this
method in certain places. Plate 11, A (if the visible element were weft), also illustrates the
method, but instead of the facing wefts alternating one by one on the bordering yarn, as
in Figure 12, C, they alternate by groups of three (Fig. 12, D), and this produces the special aspect of the line that separates the different fields of color. The Arabs, in the loose
tapestry of their light wool decorated blankets (*bottaniya amara* or *ferrashiya amara*),
made constant use of alternation around a single warp yarn of partial weft passages that
faced each other (Bel and Ricard, 1913, Fig. 63). In the lowlands of Peru, this method
was especially reserved for reps with visible and discontinuous warps, which have been
studied previously (see p. 20). It was a commonly used method in the region of Cuzco
during the Inca epoch, and also at the beginning of the colonial period.

I was able to study the fourth method only in connection with a tapestry coming from
a grave in the region of Chachapoyas (Musée de l'Homme, Paris, No. 33–90–40). The
specimen must originally have consisted of a white cotton plain-weave fabric, broken by
decorative bands of tapestry. The plain section of the cotton is almost destroyed today; it
used two warp yarns and two weft yarns at the same time (Fig. 4, D). In the section in
which the tapestry commences, the cotton weft in a regular manner and at spaced intervals releases in each passage the warp yarns which are woven and covered by the wool
weft; a kind of double cloth is thus formed with tapestry on one face and cotton plain-
weave cloth on the other, joined together at intervals by a cotton weft, which weaves all
of the warp yarns, but which remains invisible on the tapestry side because of the covering
nature of the adjacent wool weft yarns. The slits in the tapestry, strengthened by a double

thickness of cotton, run no risk of opening, whatever their length may be. Careful examination of the specimen shows that the weaving of the plain cloth and the tapestry was accomplished simultaneously.

Border of decorative motives

In order to delineate more exactly the boundaries of the different fields of color, the weavers, in imitation of what was done on the mural frescoes and especially on painted ceramics in the southern and central coastal region, outlined their designs with a narrow border of black or a very dark color. This border was generally made of two adjacent warp yarns and was consequently of the same width as these yarns. Sometimes, in the short spaces, the weft merely wrapped itself around a single warp yarn. The elaborateness of so small a border greatly increased the complexity of the weaver's task, and sometimes she simply used a diagonal wrapping with the weft, as indicated above. The wrapping of the warp yarn for a certain length and the lateral spaces that resulted were also used for decorative purposes (see Pl. 10, A, B). In the Nazca tapestries, borders of designs sometimes contained shell beads threaded onto the warp yarns (see p. 131 and Pl. 117, A).

Mixed techniques: warp left partially exposed

Tapestry is alternated intentionally with other techniques in the same fabric. It is often found combined with concealed warp reps,[2] as well as in the technique of weaving in two colors of weft yarns with concealed warp, the plain weave being subordinated to the design. Tapestry is sometimes also alternated with the gauze technique (see p. 53). In this case, the crossing of the warp yarns is held in place by means of a supplementary weft yarn, which crosses the fabric from one selvage to the other. This yarn, which is of cotton, like the warp, is sometimes visible and sometimes overlaid by the sectional wool weft yarns, except in the spaces in which the warp is left exposed intentionally. The technique permits the making of open-work tapestry. Plates 11, D, and 12, A, B, contain some remarkable examples of this. It might be thought that these were cases of gauze being embroidered, one in cotton and the other in wool. As to the first, it is nothing of the kind. It is actually a tapestry woven in the usual way with the weft yarns passing across plain gauze for the whole width of the fabric, leaving the gauze uncovered at regular intervals. As to the second, the hypothesis of an embroidered gauze should not be entirely rejected.

The Peruvians sometimes left parts of the warp exposed or merely connected the widely spaced yarns of the warp to each other by tapestry over the weak surfaces; such is the case of the fabric reproduced in Plate 13. The warp yarns, in groups of sixteen, are

---

[2] Thus many of the specimens, chiefly the *cushmas*, are woven in rep and have only a decorative band in tapestry.

brought close to each other, so that they may be used as a support for a small tapestry design representing a pelican; they then separate into two groups of eight, each one of which will later be joined to the neighboring group of eight, with which it re-forms a new group of sixteen; this new group is likewise used as a base for a tapestry motive similar to the preceding one, and so on. The exposed foundation of the warp in this way forms a sequence of lozenges (Fig. 13).

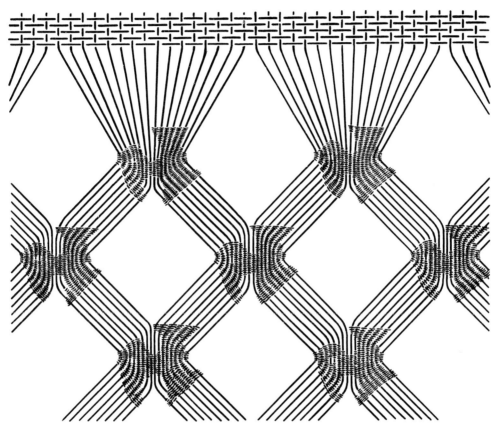

Figure 13.   Arrangement of yarns forming the warp of the open-space tapestry of Plate 13

There are also in existence open-work tapestries in which the warp leaves spaces at regular intervals, but with yarns entirely covered by the weft. I shall speak of these later (p. 54), when dealing with the subject of open-work fabrics.

LOOPED-PILE FABRIC

The looped-pile fabric of Peru had only an ornamental character. It is a simple type of tapestry, and for this reason it is described here. It seems that the Peruvians did not understand the practical utility of the fabric, which today is commonly designated "terry cloth" (Turkish toweling), and which resembles the decorative looped fabric so well developed in Coptic weaves.

Perpendicular loops in woven fabrics appear on the surface of rep (concealed warp) or tapestry. The looping is accomplished in rows, as required. The rows are separated from those that precede or follow them by one or several regular wefts. The very simple procedure consists of letting the weft yarns make a loop between each of the warp yarns successively, on one face of the fabric, during the complete passage of the weft between the two selvages

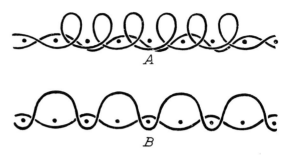

Figure 14.   Cross section, perpendicular to the warp, of tapestry with looped pile. A: usual arrangement of the yarns; B: exceptional arrangement of the yarns

(see Fig. 14, A); because of the compacting of the weft yarns the loops acquire a certain stability. Sometimes, instead of being formed between all of the consecutive warp yarns, the loops cover one warp yarn between their two ends (Fig. 14, B); the rows of loops is thus less decorative, and, to avoid this undesirable result, the return passage of the weft can make a second row in which the loops alternate with those of the first row.

It is possible that the worker, in order to facilitate the making of the loops and to assure their regularity, used a small rod in the form of a provisional "mold."

Sometimes the fabric is ornamented only with small groups (Pls. 16, B, E; 47, B) or isolated rows of loops (Pl. 16, C, D). In certain cases the rows of loops touch each other in imitation of a sort of fleece or fur, as in the beautiful specimen reproduced in Plates 15 and 16, A.

28

TWO

Fabrics of Varied Weave

TWILL

IN THE VARIOUS types of weaving previously discussed, plain-weave fabric results when the weft yarns of even rows regularly intersect the even warp yarns, and the weft yarns of odd rows intersect the odd warp yarns, or vice versa. But, instead of passing over and under every other yarn, the weft may pass over two and under two, or it may pass over two and under only one. Each weft yarn, in both cases, is displaced from the weft yarn of the preceding row at the right and at the left selvages. There are thus two types of construction for making the fabric at the present time called "twill" (see Fig. 15, B, C). The surface of twill fabric shows diagonal and regular ridges. Many other rules of crossing and intersecting can be planned and worked out. By extending the principle of twill construction to several warp yarns instead of two, and by substituting for the regular sequence of the weft yarns a sequence that breaks the regularity of the ridges, the complex structure of satin can be obtained.

The Peruvians knew these structures, but they used them very little for regular, monochrome fabrics.[1] For them the chief virtue of twill construction or irregular construction was that it could be used to develop a design. Furthermore, in order to make the design clearer and more attractive, they used a different color for the warp and for the weft when these two elements were to be visible, or they arranged the yarns of the visible element in alternating colors when the other element was intended to be concealed. Thus we have the two kinds of fabrics described below.

[1] See, however, the herringbone fabric reproduced by O'Neale and Kroeber (1930, Pl. 25, c).

29

FABRICS OF TWILL STRUCTURE 2/1 IN WHICH THE TWO ELEMENTS ARE VISIBLE

The Peruvians used the dissymmetry produced by the structure shown in Fig. 15, C, to form a design, either by passing over two yarns and under one or by passing over one and under two. For this purpose, the weaver first used a weft of a different color from that used for the warp; then, for the area required by the chosen design, she reversed the order of the crossing of the elements, leaving visible twice as many warp yarns as weft yarns, or vice versa (see the central part, in the form of a lozenge, of the diagram shown in Fig. 16). In this way, for example, were woven the decorated cotton fabrics in two colors of the coastal region of Pachacamac and of Chan Chan, showing a regular scattering of small motives, often of birdlike forms, separated by lines that crossed each other diagonally (Musée de l'Homme, Paris, No. 33–90–31). The method that has just been described is still utilized in an identical manner in many fabrics by the Indians of Peru.

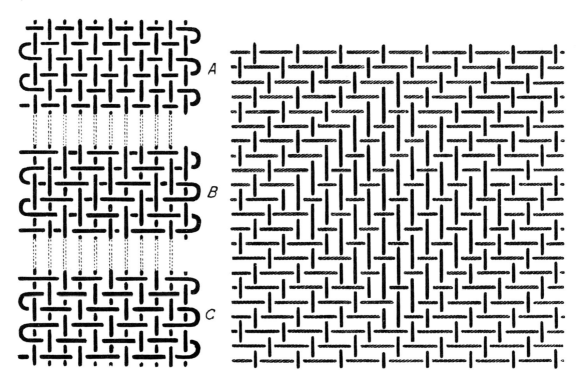

Figure 15.   Arrangement of yarns, A: in plain weave; B: in twill 2/2; C: in twill 2/1

Figure 16.   Twill 2/1; the order of the crossings is reversed in the central part, which is in the form of a lozenge

FABRICS OF VARIED STRUCTURE AND OF TWO ALTERNATING COLORS IN THE WEFT OR IN THE WARP, ONE ELEMENT ONLY BEING VISIBLE

According to the principle dear to the Peruvians, this technique presents two possibilities: it may use either the warp or the weft as the active element. The final results, however, can be identical.

Invisible warp

The first passage of the weft yarns, utilizing yarn of a chosen color and following the form of the design to be produced, crosses one, two, or three warp yarns, sometimes four, but rarely five, before passing under the warp; it reappears later crossing again one, two, three, four, or five warp yarns, and then it plunges once more, and so on. The second passage of the weft, utilizing a weft yarn of a different color from the first, goes over the same path as the first, but in reverse, that is to say, where the first passage is over the warp the second is under it, and vice versa. The third passage of the weft passes over the yarns of the first, and the fourth those of the second. The weaving continues according to this alternation, each passage of weft yarns crossing over the number of warp yarns necessary for the formation of the design and at the point where such crossing is necessary.[2] By this means a fabric of irregular structure is obtained; the weft only is visible, and the appearance and design are identical on both faces, but with the colors reversed. It can be seen that the structure of the fabric is entirely subordinated to the motives of the design; from this fact arises the name "true fancy weaving" given by Crawford to this technique. In order that the weft should not cross too large a number of yarns at a time and in the same place in several successive passages, as this would detract from the compactness and beauty of the fabric, the chosen design should allow for limited areas of one color. The weft yarn very rarely crosses more than five warp yarns at a time; in practice, its range is between one yarn and three yarns.

The technique requires the regular alternation of two wefts of distinct colors, but there is nothing to prevent the weaver, at the end of the weaving of one motive, from alternating two wefts of different colors for subsequent motives; in fact, these changes are frequent.

Weaving with two alternate weft yarns is usually done with strong cotton warp yarns, which are covered and completely concealed by the wool weft, as in tapestry, with which this technique is sometimes alternated in the same piece of weaving (see Harcourt, 1924, Pl. 3).

Invisible weft

In Peruvian weaving it must always be kept in mind that in the techniques in which one of the two elements, warp or weft, is in a way passive and covered, and the other element is active and covering, the roles of the warp and the weft can be reversed. We have seen this above in plain weave for reps (actually tapestry!), and we find it again here. The warp, in practice just as frequently as the weft, is the only visible and active element and forms the design. In this case it is made of yarns of two colors, regularly alternated so that

[2] Figure 17, looked at sideways, will immediately make this method of weaving understandable.

from the beginning the separation of the even and odd yarns into two leases makes each of them monochrome. The weft, which is generally of wool and a neutral color, is stronger and finer than the warp and remains completely concealed. Each weft passes between the warp yarns, but the crossing of these colored yarns, that is, the passage of one of them under and of the other above, or vice versa, occurs only when required by the design (Fig. 17;

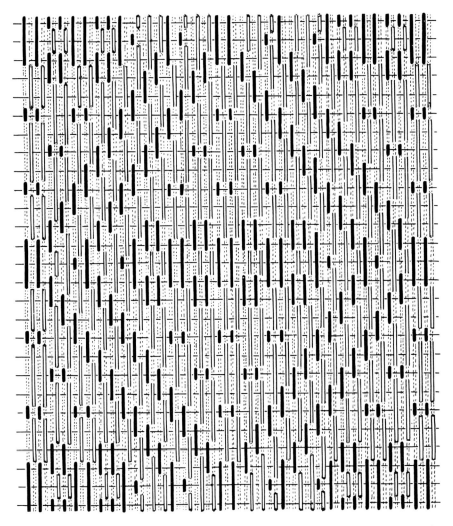

Figure 17. Arrangement of yarns of two colors forming the small decorative motive of the fabric shown in Plate 17, A, B

Pl. 17, A, B). Thus the warp yarn can remain visible for several successive wefts, if necessary. The appearance is in all respects similar to that obtained when the weft is the active element.

I cannot give better proof of the interchangeability of the roles of warp and weft than by referring the reader to Plate 44. At the lower edge of the fabric reproduced there is a band of tapestry intersected perpendicularly at intervals by tapes woven in accordance with the technique just described. As long as the tapes cross the tapestry, the active ele-

32

ment is the weft; beyond that point, because the support of the warp is lacking, the weft is transformed into warp, but it retains its active role. After completing each passage of the weft from the interior edge of the tapestry band to the outer edge, the worker let her yarn, at the point where she was using it in the return passage, form a loop of the length of the free part of the tape to be made. These adjacent loops formed the element of another small warp, woven later by means of different wool weft of neutral color, which was also invisible. It may be said that at the point where the weft becomes warp the appearance of the tape does not undergo any modification, either in fabric or in design, except a certain distortion of the motives due to the fact that the wefts are not sufficiently close to each other in the free part of the tape. It can also be seen that the two alternating colors are replaced by other colors at the end of a motive. What has been said with regard to the weft is equally applicable to the warp.

Despite the successive changes of colors, the worker could use only one color on the length of a warp or weft yarn, according to the type of weaving chosen. To obviate this inconvenience and to break the monotony, the Peruvians made use of methods that will be explained in detail.

Invisible warp, discontinuous weft

In this technique (invisible warp), one of the two weft yarns, instead of traversing the entire width of the fabric, crosses only a portion of it; it is then interlocked with a yarn of a different color which meets it at the design edge. A second weft yarn, which is of a single color, is passed through from selvage to selvage; this yarn conceals the interlocking

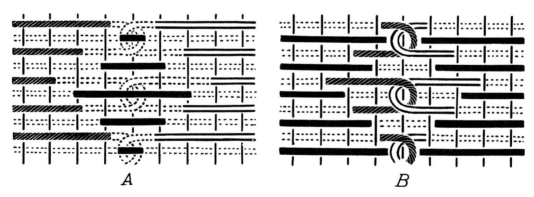

A   *B*

Figure 18. Method of interlocking sectional wefts of the fabric shown in Plate 18, C, D. A: right side; B: reverse

of the first wefts. Finally, the discontinuous wefts return in the next passage. This technique is related to the one that has already been explained in the discussion of plain weave with discontinuous weft. It is also related to interlocked tapestry. It permits variation of decorative color at given points on a plain foundation. The specimens shown in Plate

17, C, and Plate 18, C, D, were made in this way. The scheme in Figure 18, B, shows the progression of the yarns and their reciprocal interlocking on the reverse of the fabric; the loops and the passing over of the continuous yarn, which are barely visible on the face of the fabric, make the reverse less perfect (see Pl. 18, D).

Supplementary warp or weft yarns, three or four colors

The following is another method used in either of the two techniques of concealed wefts or concealed warps. If the warp was to constitute the visible element, instead of being of yarns of two colors it might include yarns of four colors, regularly alternated.

The weaving was accomplished in the manner that I have just explained above, with this one difference: the worker allowed the same two adjacent warp yarns of different colors to appear on the surface each time; these yarns were superimposed in the completed fabric, the one covering the other in the order chosen by the worker. Obviously, because of this superimposition the fabric became thicker, but twice the number of colors—four instead of two—were made available in this way.

Sometimes the colors were reduced to three; in this case, the worker allowed one yarn, then two, to appear alternately on the surface, producing a slight irregularity in the thickness of the fabric (Fig. 19, A). This involves a simple variant of the preceding method, used for example in making the decorative bands of the bag shown in Plate 20 (see also Harcourt, 1924, Pl. 11).

I have said that when the worker was using four colors of warp yarn she allowed two yarns of different colors to remain on the surface in each weft passage. One of these covered the other, in the order desired, at the point where the concealed weft held them firmly. This method has a rather elegant variant, the general principles of which will be discussed in the technique studied on page 36. When one of these two yarns was required to be visible on a surface equal to at least three consecutive wefts in length, the underlying warp yarn was secured not by the same wefts as the visible yarn, but by the following and preceding wefts. The fine quality of the fabric was thus enhanced and the covering of one color by the other assured (see Fig. 19, B).

If the visible element was the weft, two wefts of different color were used in exactly the same way as those just described for the technique in which only the warp is visible.

Supplementary warp or weft yarns forming floats on the reverse of the fabric

Instead of resorting to the method of covering yarns in order to use several colors at once, the Peruvians often sacrificed the beauty of one face of the fabric. The replacement of one color by another in the course of a particular passage of the weft or in the length of a particular warp yarn required the introduction of supplementary yarns of other colors, ready to take the place of yarns already in active use in the weaving. The worker had, therefore, to have at her disposal, either as warp or as weft according to the technique she was

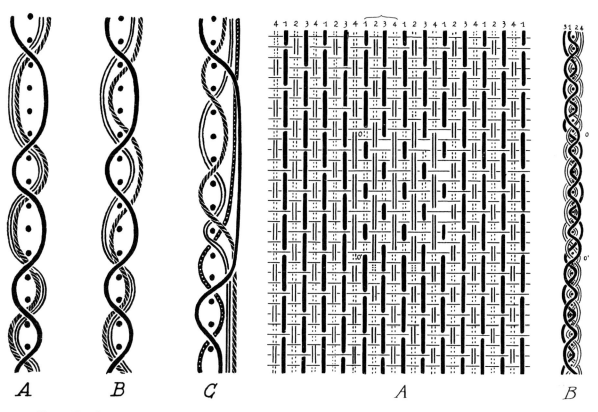

Figure 19. Cross section, perpendicular to the weft, of a fabric in three colors (A and B) or in four colors (C), in which the construction is subordinated to the design

Figure 20. Construction of fabric shown in Plate 21, A. A: right side; B: cross section perpendicular to the weft, showing how yarns 1, 2, 3, and 4, marked by bracket, are actually superimposed. At points o and o′ there is a reversal of colors

using, several adjacent yarns, which were introduced alternately into the fabric proper as required by the design. The unused portions of the supplementary yarns were left visible, forming floats on the reverse of the fabric. These supplementary yarns were all incorporated into the fabric, the weft yarns at the lateral selvages, and the warp yarns at the initial and terminal selvages. Plate 19, A, B, and C, shows examples of these two types of weaving which were very popular with the Indians of the Peruvian coast, especially in the central region (Fig. 19, C).

Finally, when a fabric with only the weft visible was involved, not only did the unused portions of the yarns form floats, but the wefts were sometimes reduced to sections and interlocked, as we saw above.

TWO-COLORED WARP FABRIC WITH CONCEALED WEFT, WITH DESIGN OF UNLIMITED
EXTENT IN ONE OF THE TWO COLORS PERMITTED BY SUPERIMPOSING YARNS

Applying general principles to the method that I have outlined above, which consists of elimination of one color and superimposition of two yarns, the Peruvians, by using the construction
shown in Figure 20, succeeded in producing a design of a single
color, unlimited in extent, which stands out on a background of
another color. The fabric is quite thick. It looks identical on both
faces, as does the design, except that the colors are reversed from
one face to the other. The warp consists of yarns of two colors
alternating regularly, as for example a white yarn followed by a
black yarn. The weft, of a neutral color, remains concealed. The
construction is as follows: yarn 4 (white) appears on one side for
the first three passages of the weft, disappears under the fourth
weft, appears again in the next three consecutive passages, and so
forth; yarn 3 (black) appears and disappears in the reverse order
of yarn 4; yarn 2 (white) appears and disappears like yarn 4, but
with a displacement of two wefts; yarn 1 (black) follows the
order of yarn 2 in reverse; the fifth passage follows the order of
the first; the sixth passage follows the second; and so on. After the
compacting of the weft yarns, which makes possible the superimposing of yarn 1 on yarn 4 for one face (yarn 4 on yarn 1 for
the other face), yarn 3 on yarn 2 (or 2 on 3), and so forth, the
fabric would, if the weaving were continued in this way, appear
uniformly white on one side and black on the other (see Fig. 20);
but the slight displacement indicated at points *o* and *o'* suffices to reverse the direction
of the colors, and thus as fine and extensive a design as may be desired can be obtained
(Pl. 21, A). This method, generally used by the Chinese in their patterned silk fabrics, is
very rich in application; the Peruvians knew of it but apparently did not develop it very far.

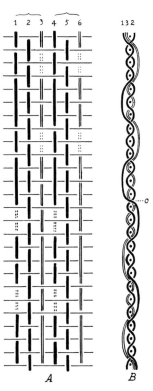

Figure 21. Construction of
a fabric in which the warp yarns
are alternately covered, forming
floats on one side of the fabric or
the other. A: right side; B: cross
section perpendicular to the weft.
At point *o* there is a reversal of
colors

*Additional warp fabrics of two or three colors, with concealed
weft and of varied construction*

I cannot describe all the classifications resulting from the method I have just explained. I will mention, however, a fabric of which a schematic drawing is shown in Figure 21. This technique often alternates with that of simple rep (concealed weft). It permits the construction on a plain-weave foundation of lines and horizontal rectangles in a

color different from that of the foundation, without interrupting its regular formation. For this it is necessary to insert within the warp, between every two foundation yarns, a yarn of a color different from that of the foundation. Figure 21 shows that yarn 3 follows a progression similar to that of yarn 1, but on the opposite face and with a displacement of three wefts, and that yarn 2 is taken up and left regularly by each passage of the weft; yarn 4 follows the order of yarn 1.

In brief, this technique makes use of the floats of the yarns, alternating on one face or the other, to form a design. At point *o* the color of the floats is reversed; this change can be effected as often as the design makes necessary.

THREE

Fabrics with Supplementary
Decorative Warp or Weft Yarns

SUPPLEMENTARY DECORATIVE WEFT, BROCADED FABRICS, TWO TYPES

Fabrics were made in Peru using two weft yarns in each passage. One of these, throughout the whole fabric, passes over every other warp yarn, producing plain-weave cloth; the other, which is intended to form the design, passes over a varied number of warp yarns in a less regular manner. By the use of this method, the regularity and compactness of the fabric are guaranteed by one of the wefts, while the other is free to appear or disappear or to cross at will the number of warp yarns required for the chosen design on the reverse side or on the right side of the fabric. This yarn, so to speak, is freed from the requirements of the weaving. In order that the decorative result may be fully attained, it is preferable that the decorative weft yarn should be of a different color or nature from that of the warp yarn, and that it should be more flexible and more enveloping. In fact, the Peruvian fabric was most frequently made by the regular crossing, warp and weft, of cotton yarns, to which was added a supplementary weft yarn of wool. This weft yarn was added not by means of a needle or similar instrument after weaving, but in the course of the weaving itself, row by row, and it was incorporated into the fabric in the regular manner at the lateral selvages.

The two faces of the fabric have a different appearance, and the value of the decorative motives is reversed from one face to the other.

The fabric can sometimes have a decorative weft over the entire surface (Fig. 22; Pl. 22). Often, however, the latter is used for an ornamental border only (Pl. 24). In both cases the technique is known as brocading selvage-to-selvage. The decorative weft may also extend not over the entire width of the fabric but over only one part of it, such as the center

38

or the corners of the piece (Fig. 23). Plate 24 shows two remarkable examples of this decoration, which, let me repeat, is accomplished not by embroidery after weaving, but in the course of the weaving by successive passages of the bobbin, which cover only a limited section of the width of the fabric. These, then, are brocaded fabrics.

It goes without saying that the decorative weft can change color at each row and thus introduce variety of color into the design.

This weft can also change color in the course of the same passage, a red yarn, for example, taking the place of a yellow yarn. In the return passage these yarns can either interlock or not (see Pl. 25, A, B). Interlocking of the supplementary decorative weft is dispensable; the fabric is rendered independent of this because of the regular weft.

SPECIAL FEATURES OF FABRICS WITH SUPPLEMENTARY DECORATIVE WEFTS

Here is a fabric (Pl. 21, B, C) in which the two faces are not alike: one is covered with adjacent floats whose arrangement in two colors forms a design, while the other has

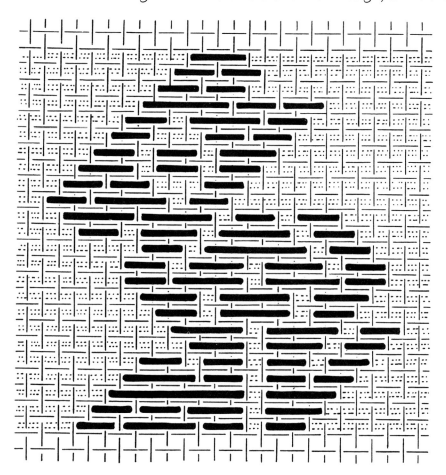

Figure 22. Arrangement of yarns in selvage-to-selvage brocade to form a decorative motive (small rodent) shown in Plate 22

39

the appearance of a plain fabric of somewhat loose texture. The fabrication is as follows. The two weft yarns (weft that is successively useful and decorative), of equal quality and thickness, differ from each other only in color. They pass one after the other in the usual way, but both, in rotation, form decorative floats and cross the warp yarns regularly. When color changes occur, the two weft yarns cross the same warp yarn on the plain-weave side (reverse), leaving the warp yarn visible and exposed on the float (right) side (Fig. 24). This type of weaving is quite uncommon. I have seen only four examples of it in specimens coming from the central coastal area of Peru.

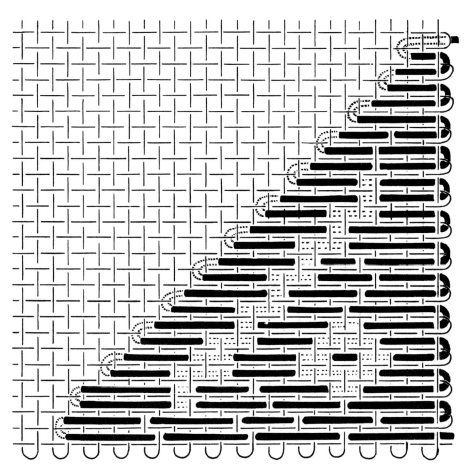

Figure 23.   Arrangement of the yarns in a brocaded fabric (corner)

Other special features of weaving with supplementary decorative wefts arise from the placing of decorative weft on rep, in which only the warp is visible. The nature of rep permits the decorative weft to be concealed in the same manner as the regular weft and with it, when so desired. These are, therefore, fabrics in which the design motive is not extensive and in which large expanses of the basic fabric are left exposed. In these the decorative weft, which otherwise might form long, straggly, and inelegant floats on the reverse, is crossed at intervals by the warp yarn, which fastens it invisibly on the right side (see Pl. 25, C, D). Conversely, if the floats are allowed to form the design on the right side, the points at which they are secured by the warp yarns are not visible on the reverse, and the two faces of the fabric, which are both perfect, have an entirely different appearance (see Pl. 25, E, F). In conclusion, rep can be woven with two similar weft yarns, which are, however, each of a different color. These yarns, used together, are concealed,

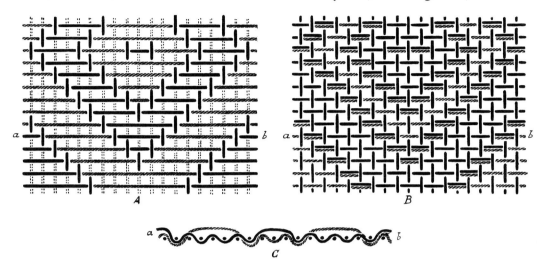

Figure 24.   Construction of fabric shown in Plate 21, B. A: right side; B: reverse; C: cross section perpendicular to the warp at *a–b*

except in the spaces where one of the two alternately forms small floats used in the formation of the design on the face of the fabric. Assuming one has a white warp and two weft yarns of yellow and red, the fabric will show one side (the reverse) to be entirely white, and the other side (the right side) to be white, but decorated with yellow and red motives. Such is the case of an elegant coca bag from the Nazca region, which I had an opportunity to examine.

SUPPLEMENTARY WARP YARNS

The Peruvians naturally applied the principle of decorative weft to warp yarns, that is to say, they added to the regular foundation, warp yarns of a different color from that of the basic fabric. The fabrics thus woven have a different appearance from those that have a decorative weft, because the supplementary warp yarns are most frequently of the same nature and the same thickness as those of the foundation cloth, and also because these yarns, when they appear on the right side, are incorporated into the plain-weave cloth and make the warp more compact in certain places. Thus, the plain-weave fabric is often changed into rep (see Pl. 26, B, C).

In a fabric in which all the changes of technique were combined, I found that the warp consisted of regularly alternated white and brown cotton warps, crossed by a brown weft. The work commenced with plain weaving, which resulted in a striped compact fabric (of the rep family); then the white yarns were eliminated for several rows, according to the order and frequency required by the design. By reason of the elimination of the white yarns, the less dense part of the weaving (plain weave) stood out on the right side of the fabric in pure brown, while the eliminated white yarns floated on the reverse. Later on, a second weft, added to the first, but in white, permitted the making of true double cloth for a certain distance. Finally, the first method of weaving was resumed until the work was completed.

SUPPLEMENTARY WARP AND WEFT YARNS

In other cases the Peruvians merely added to the warp yarns of the foundation cloth several yarns of colors that differed from the former and were inserted at intervals. These yarns were incorporated into the fabric when the design so required, thus making them appear on the surface where, with the supplementary weft, they formed more or less intricate geometric patterns. In Plate 26, A, will be found a simple specimen of this method of weaving. It may be noted that the decorative warp and weft yarns intersect at right angles, the yarns in each category (warp or weft) remaining parallel to each other.

Plate 27, A, B, shows a much more complex example of the same method. The numerous decorative warp yarns of white or beige in the vertical band of the fabric pass from onc facc of the fabric to the other, following the requirements of the design. These decorative warps are crossed and woven on the right side by the decorative weft yarns, which are likewise white or beige. The latter do not form rows from selvage to selvage, but are secured at each edge of the unit by the white or beige warp yarns. In this case, one may well question whether these weft yarns were really introduced during the weaving or after.

Supplementary warp and weft textiles form an introduction to the weaving techniques of double cloth.

DECORATIVE NONPARALLEL WARP OR NONPARALLEL WEFT YARNS

Up to the present time I have not found textiles with supplementary wefts, flitting and plunging at will from one row to another, as if carried by an imaginary shuttle. On the other hand, in Plate 28, A, will be seen a specimen of fabric with decorative warp yarns, where blue and white yarns in groups of two separate symmetrically to form ornamental lines on one of the faces of the fabric. The two warp yarns separate at a depth of four wefts to a width of eight warp yarns, where they are incorporated into the fabric. They come together at the end of three more weft rows and are again incorporated into the fabric. In this way they form regular sequences of lozenges, alternating on each face of the fabric.

Plate 28, B, C, illustrates another specimen of decorative warp yarn fabric; the design is likewise formed by a series of lozenges, but it is made only on one face of the fabric.

These attempts at design, made by warp yarns that regularly cut the fabric in an oblique manner, are quite tentative. I have found no other types than those just described. The technique may, perhaps, have been in its infancy.

FOUR

Double Cloth

WEAVING of varied construction and with two alternating colors of warp and weft, such as has been described above, had one defect. The beauty of the fabric might be impaired by unlimited floating of warp or weft yarns. To avoid this the surface to be covered by the same color was restricted in length or in breadth to the space of a few warp or weft yarns, crossed respectively by the other of the two elements. Peruvian weavers overcame this obstacle by the rare technique studied above (p. 36), as well as by double weaving, which afforded them the means of covering a surface of any dimensions whatsoever with the same color while leaving both the elements, warp and weft, completely visible.

TWO WARPS AND TWO WEFTS EQUALLY VISIBLE

The method, in its initial stage, consists of commencing simultaneously the weaving of two superimposed fabrics I and II in plain-weave cloth. The two fabrics differ from each other only in color, each having similar elements similarly arranged. In most cases, at the end of each row the two wefts interlock at the point where they make a return loop. If the weaving is continued in this way, the result will be two fabrics identical except in color, joined only at the lateral selvages (see Fig. 25, B, E). It is also possible for the worker, using this arrangement, to cross the assembly of the two warps and their respective wefts at will, and thus, for the number of warp yarns and for the number of weft yarns she requires, to use elements of Fabric II in Fabric I, while corresponding elements of Fabric I pass into Fabric II. In this way a double cloth is woven whose two visible faces have the

44

same appearance and the same design, but whose values are symmetrically reversed as to color (Fig. 25, C, D, F). The designs of the specimens shown in Plates 29, A, B; 30, B; and 31, B, have been formed in this way. In the first two the elements of warp and weft, which are of cotton, are equally visible; the third, which is of wool, approximates rep.

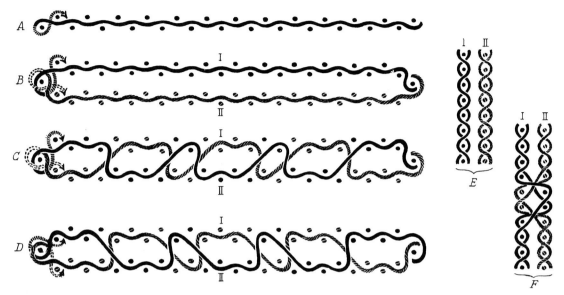

Figure 25. Schematic arrangement of yarns of double cloth. A: cross section, perpendicular to the warp, of a simple weave; B: cross section, perpendicular to the warp, of a double cloth before crossing of the elements; C and D: the same cross section after the crossing of the elements (first and second weft passages); E: cross section, perpendicular to the weft, of double cloth before the crossing of the elements; F: the same cross section after the crossing of the elements

One element only visible

We have seen that in plain-weave fabric one of the elements, warp or weft, can become, so to speak, passive, wrapped, or covered by the other element (as in the case of rep); the same situation occurs in double cloth. In this case there is simplification with respect to the colors because, since the passive element is completely concealed from view, it is not necessary that it should be of the same color as the active element. Instead of one warp and weft of one color and another warp and weft of another color, two warps or two wefts of different colors are used, the concealed elements in the two fabrics being of a neutral color. The arrangement of the weaving remains the same; in fact, there are generally two warps and one weft, the latter element being concealed and common to both parts of the fabric. After one row of Fabric I has been finished, the weft forms in reverse a corresponding row in Fabric II, then goes back to Fabric I, and so on (Fig. 26).

TUBULAR WEAVING

This method of weaving with a single weft can be used to obtain fabric in tubular form—also known to the ancient Peruvians—in which a continuous weft, visible or concealed, proceeds spirally to weave first the upper and then the lower of two double-cloth warps. The total number of yarns of the two warps must be uneven so that the successive weft yarns take up the same yarns only every other time.

Narrow fabrics, double straps and cylindrical cords

Where the two double-cloth warp yarns do not cross each other, the fabric is woven as a tube. At the point where the yarns cross each other, the tube loses its cavity, becomes flat, and its walls touch each other. Formerly, narrow fabrics such as carrying straps, undergirths for llamas, and so forth, which had to be of great strength, were made in this way in Peru. Even in our own day, this technique of tubular weaving is reserved for such uses. In these types of fabrics, which are very thick because of the double weaving and usually quite narrow, the weft, as I have said, is entirely concealed. The warp yarns cross only in the central section, where the design appears. The borders on the two faces of the fabric are of a uniform color. The yarns of each warp are generally arranged as follows: at the left, the required number of yarns of a single color; in the center, a series of yarns of alternating colors; at the right, the required number of yarns of the first color (Fig. 26, A). These yarns are then divided into two layers. The crossing of the different colored elements in the central part enables the weaver to form various patterns; the borders of uniform color, where the crossing of the yarn is unnecessary, continue to be woven in tubular form and permit the formation of a partial central cavity. The strap shown in Plate 30, A, was woven in this way.

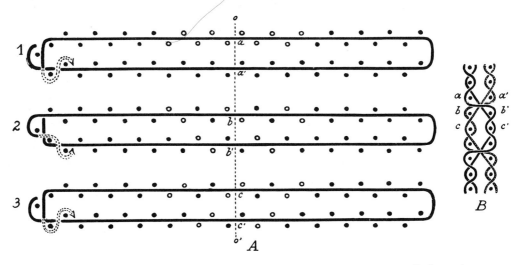

Figure 26. Arrangement of the yarns of tubular weaving. A: cross section perpendicular to the warp; 1, before the crossing of the warp yarns; 2, after the crossing (first passage); 3, after the crossing (second passage); B: cross section perpendicular to the weft showing the crossing of the warp yarns

This technique was also used in the weaving of fine, elegant little cords, with rounded sections. Their warp yarns of various colors are relatively numerous, making possible small decorative motives. These yarns are not all used at the same time, and they can exchange places. Those which for the time being are not used in the weaving form floats in the center, filling the cavity in the tubular fabric. The weft remains concealed. For example, a small wool cord 4 millimeters [⅛ inch] in diameter makes use of a total of forty-nine yarns; of these thirty-three yarns are used simultaneously in the circular weaving, and sixteen yarns remain idle in the center. Such fabrics, several meters in length, often encircle mummy heads like a turban and serve to hold the hair and its accessories in place. They are found, for the most part, in the southern coastal area (see the little cord in Pl. 58).

Application of the double-weave principle (with one element concealed)
to the two-color warp or weft technique with varied construction

Up to this point we have considered double weave of simple construction only, producing plain weave or rep. The Peruvians expanded the principle of double weaving to the technique studied above of using two colors of warp or weft, with the construction subordinated to the design.

They first applied the principle to the making of the thick straps that have just been described. The arranger   ᶠ the warps is the same; the crossing of their yarns is the same; so, too, is the passage   which remains concealed. Only the construction differs, certain yarns remai   ral consecutive weft rows (see the strap of the pouch bag in Pl. 20; al   ).

There i   ᴗuble-cloth weaving in which the visible element is not the v   , A, B, shows a particularly complex example.

ᴘ AND QUADRUPLE WEFT

ᴗe-cloth weaving the very special technique of specimens A, 32, because it implies knowledge of double-cloth weaving and These specimens form the central part of certain slings, no doubt ᴗn useful as weapons, in spite of their compactness. Lateral cords are ᴄtremities of this central part. They are made of rather coarse vegetable agave fiber) reinforced more or less by colored wool. All three specimens ᴄte because of the almost total destruction of their brown-black sections, which corroded by the action of the dye. As the gaps vary, however, from one specimen ᴏer, they can easily be reconstructed in imagination.

The specimens are made up of a varying number of separate narrow bands, joined two by two at the ends by weaving common to both. The plaiting of the round cords at each end of the slings (Pl. 32, A, C) was accomplished after the weaving of the section that unites the separately woven bands. These plaited cords are missing in specimen B. The bands are joined to each other by a knotted thread.

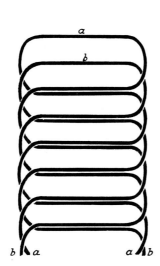

Figure 27. Arrangement of the yarns of one of the two weft systems in specimens A, B, C of Plate 32; *a*, first yarn; *b*, second yarn

Figure 28. Cross section perpendicular to the weft of one of the specimens A, B, C of Plate 32. A: regular and complete crossing of the warp yarns; B: the same crossing after destruction of the yarns of one color; C: erratic crossing of the warp yarns

I shall deal first with the passage of the weft and then with the method of crossing the warp yarns, because an analysis of the weave is extremely difficult to present clearly.

The weft is composed of four yarns, that is, of two identical systems, which are independent and composed of two yarns each. The two yarns in each system alternate regularly to form short, successive wefts. Furthermore, each yarn, which at the beginning of the weaving is used in its middle section, works through to its two ends, which cross each other in each of the rows they form. Figure 27 shows, under one system, the passage of the two yarns *a* and *b*, alternating and crossing each other at the selvages, as well as forming the double wefts. The completed weft, as I have said, comprises two similar systems arranged one over the other; but for reasons of clarity I have shown but one system in the figure. Each section is actually composed of twice two yarns, that is to say, of four yarns that are simultaneously enveloped by the warp yarns, just as if only an ordinary, simple weft were involved. But in this way is made a very thick fabric whose selvages appear to be plaited. If specimens B and C show exposed transverse yarns on one face or the other, but in alternating positions, it is because sections of the weft (of four yarns) have been left exposed by the destruction of half of the warp yarns, which were dyed brown-black.

The system of the warp is double. The two colored yarns of which it consists are arranged as for double-cloth weaving, but in that case there are two separate wefts, each crossing its own warp; here there is actually only one, because the four yarns of each section are in juxtaposition. In the specimens that I have had the opportunity to examine, each element, that is to say, each vertical band, consists of two warps, one light and one dark, each of twelve or sixteen yarns, and each divided into two groups of six or eight yarns. The lower ends of these yarns had to be free during the weaving. The work was carried on partly as in double-cloth weaving, in that the two groups of one single warp crossed each other, and partly as in fabric of varied construction with warp of two colors (concealed weft), in that the construction is not plain-cloth weave, and the crossing of the yarns is symmetrically similar in the light warp and in the dark warp. If the passage of the yarns in the four groups always followed the same rule, it would be as shown in the cross section indicating the weft, Figure 28, A, the yarns in each warp being taken up or left by two successive weft rows, but with a displacement of one row between the two groups of a single warp. This common progression recurs periodically. It is interrupted at intervals by an erratic crossing where the yarns pass over a varying number of wefts—one, two, or three at the most—as required by the design, but the paired warps always move symmetrically (Fig. 28, C). It must be remembered that specimens B and C are incomplete, as they show only the light warp; the dark warp is missing (Fig. 28, B).

The technique I have tried to explain is complicated by the presence of wool yarns in specimens B and C, which are incorporated in the course of the weaving as a simple decorative element on one face only and which, in specimen A, are either substituted for or superimposed upon the warp yarns and follow their crossings.

This type of weaving produces the same effect and the same design on the two faces of the finished fabric, but the position of the colors is naturally reversed on each face.

The preceding observations, although accurate, are not quite complete, as the ancient specimens studied could not be thoroughly analyzed. I have been able to continue my research on other specimens, and supplementary explanations will be found on page 96 of the present work. They show that the technique is, in reality, much more closely related to plaiting than to weaving. The reader is referred to this new analysis.

FIVE

Gauzes

IN THE Peruvian fabrics examined up to now, all the warp yarns were kept parallel during and after the weaving. This principle of parallelism of the warp yarns is not followed in gauze.

CROSSING OF THE WARP YARNS IN PAIRS (TWO-YARN GAUZE)

Let us assume that we have a warp set up ready to be woven. The first weft will be inserted in the usual way, passing under the warps of the odd rows and over the yarns of the even rows. The second weft will pass under the first two warps (odd and even), back over the odd yarn and under the even yarn, and then will return toward the following two warp yarns (Fig. 29, B). This movement of passing to and fro by the weft brings about, as a result of normal tension, a regular crossing of one warp yarn over another. The third row, in order to re-establish the parallel position of the warps, will have to travel the crossed passage of the second row in a reverse direction; the fourth passage will be like the second, the fifth like the third, and so forth (Fig. 29, A, b; Pl. 33, A).

It is in this way that the simple gauze of Peru must have been woven.[1] Ordinarily it was made with a cotton yarn of medium or exceeding fineness, usually overtwisted, which gives the fabric a very special crepe appearance.

[1] Editors' note: This paragraph, which gives the appearance of a simple gauze weave, is probably not a description of the actual method of producing a gauze weave. The sequence of movements of the weaving of gauze by modern Guatemalan women is given by O'Neale (1945, p. 75).

ALTERNATE CROSSING OF THREE WARP YARNS (THREE-YARN GAUZE)

By the application of the same principle, but carrying it further, the Peruvians worked out another gauze. The method consisted no longer of crossing alternately two warp yarns with each other, but of crossing alternately a warp yarn with its neighbors to the right and to the left, respectively, row after row. Numbering these yarns 1, 2, 3, 4, 5, 6, 7 . . . , 2 will cross with 3, 4 with 5, 6 with 7, and so forth in the course of the first passage, and 6 with 5, 4 with 3, 2 with 1, in the course of the return passage (Fig. 29, A, *c*; Pl. 52, A).

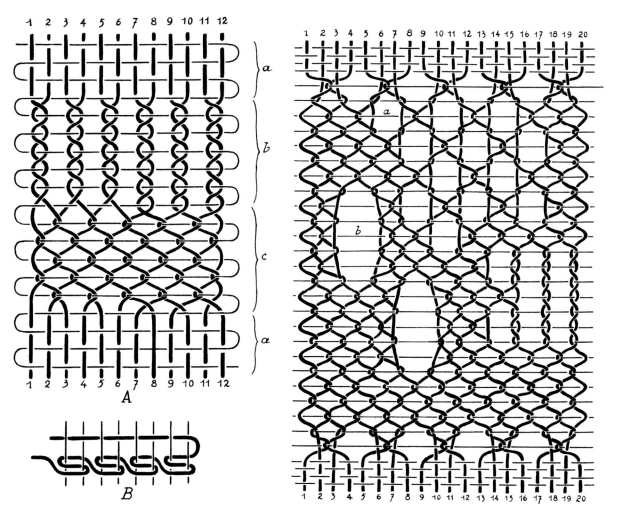

Figure 29. A: principal rules of crossing of warp yarns in gauze; *a*, plain weave; *b*, simple gauze (two yarns); *c*, complex gauze (three yarns); B: chart of the directional route of the bobbin in simple gauze (first and second passage)

Figure 30. Arrangement of the yarns in open-space gauze: *a*, open space formed by omission of a single crossing of two warp yarns; *b*, open space formed by omission of three crossings of the same two warp yarns

OPEN WORK

In order to elaborate gauze made with three warp yarns, the Peruvians conceived the idea of interspersing it with open spaces, which could be so arranged as to form a design.

If the open spaces were multiplied at their point of contact with each other, however, as in the upper central section of Figure 30, they formed a new type of regular gauze (Pl. 39, B, D). These open spaces were obtained by omitting in one passage the crossing of two yarns that, in accordance with the rule just indicated, would normally have had to cross each other. Either these two yarns were left free by the weft yarn, or they were grouped by it with the adjacent warp yarns, the warp on the left with the left-hand group, and the warp on the right with the right-hand group. Thus, let us assume that, at a point *a* in the fabric, yarns 5 and 8 (Fig. 30) ought to cross each other; either they will be disregarded by the weft (as shown in the figure), or yarn 5, superimposed on yarn 7, will cross yarn 10. It will be seen that by this method the warp yarns are separated and there is produced in the fabric an open part which is crossed only by the weft yarn. By increasing the number of open spaces and arranging them so that they follow each other in lines like a pattern, the most diverse effects can be obtained (see Pls. 33, B; 34, A; 35; 36, A; 37, A, etc.), but the principle outlined above is always the one applied. The technique is invariably as follows: the open space described above is obtained by the noncrossing of two warp yarns at a given point; this procedure can be extended to points in the upper and lower rows where the same two yarns should have crossed each other (Fig. 30, b). From these noncrossings a much larger open space results; specimen B of Plate 34 shows an excellent example of this.

The puckering of the supertwisted yarns frequently hampers the study of construction. By a forcible stretching of the gauze, the system that governs the crossing of the elements can be discerned.

IRREGULAR GAUZE

The principle of gauze was sometimes used in Peru for setting up complex constructions in which the simple alternation of the crossings of the warp yarns was replaced by crossings that vary as to direction, position, and number, in a given length.

In this way the fabric of the tiny bag shown in Plate 39, C, was made. The design of adjacent lozenges is charming. In Figure 31 appears the plan of crossing of its yarns. Its characteristics are as follows. The warp consists of a regular sequence of two white yarns and two red. The weft takes up two white yarns or two red yarns at a time. It is a simple gauze since the same four yarns always cross each other, two by two, but the direction of the crossing is regularly alternated from one column to another. In addition, the weft passes every other time between the yarns of two consecutive columns, without crossing them; finally, in every other group of two columns the crossing is delayed for two weft passages.

MIXED TECHNIQUES

The Peruvian taste for mixed techniques is found again here. Sometimes it is a matter of the alternation of two types of gauze, one more open than the other; sometimes a strip

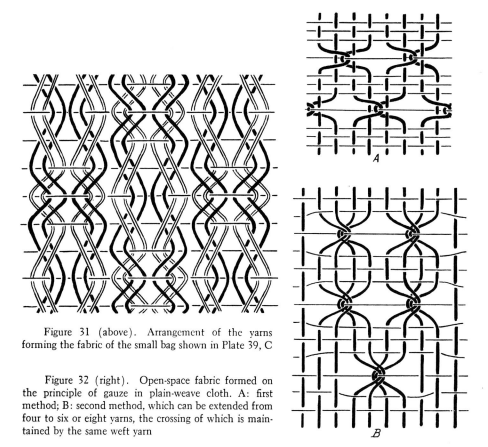

Figure 31 (above). Arrangement of the yarns forming the fabric of the small bag shown in Plate 39, C

Figure 32 (right). Open-space fabric formed on the principle of gauze in plain-weave cloth. A: first method; B: second method, which can be extended from four to six or eight yarns, the crossing of which is maintained by the same weft yarn

of plain-weave cloth follows a strip of gauze with or without decorative open spaces (Pls. 33; 39, B; 80, D, E). Sometimes the fabric is made up of solid squares and of squares of gauze arranged like a grid, the gauze section being intended to form the background for needle embroidery. I have already mentioned the use of crossed warp yarns in tapestry, where the warp is purposely left exposed (see p. 26).

In plain-weave cloth one often finds open spaces obtained by the application, at a given point, of the gauze principle: two, four, six, or even eight warp yarns are crossed at a time. The detail of the crossing is shown in Figure 32 (two and four yarns), and the effect produced can be seen in Plates 36, B; 37, B; and 39, A.

EMBROIDERY ON GAUZE

A needle embroidery is sometimes added to the decorative motives obtained by series of open spaces. The embroidery consists chiefly in outlining the designs with a thicker yarn, which is joined to the gauze by simple knots (see Pls. 35, 38).

It is regrettable that the overtwisting of simple cotton yarns too often gives Peruvian gauze a crepe appearance, which in some cases renders the design indistinct. This super-twisting even causes the formation of small loops in the yarn.

SIX

Open-work Fabrics

THE PERUVIANS had a pronounced taste for open-work fabrics and succeeded in making many very beautiful and varied cloths of this type. In addition to the special open work obtained by the crossing of warp yarns, as in gauze, with open spaces of very limited size which have just been described, there were open-work sections obtained by the methods analyzed below. These open spaces were never obtained by the technique of "drawing threads," and this is logical when one takes into consideration the fact that such a procedure presupposes a more or less industrialized production. Instead of partially unraveling a finished piece, it was more profitable to weave it directly, manipulating it so as to produce open spaces.

OMISSION OF THE WARP AND WEFT YARNS

In plain weave, by omitting a fixed number of yarns in the warp, at regular intervals, and by leaving the passage of the weft in abeyance for a similar number of intervals for a space equal to the width of the omitted warp yarns, one can produce a fabric consisting of woven squares with intervening spaces that are also square, arranged as indicated in Figure 33, A. The woven sections are joined to each other by warp yarns and exposed weft (Pls. 45, A; 47, B). By varying the relation of the woven sections to the omitted yarns in the warp and weft, one can obtain diversified effects. The technique can be applied to plain weave as well as to gauze and to tapestry. In the last case, the groups of warp yarns are usually entirely covered with sectional wefts, while the yarns of other complete weft rows (selvage to selvage) connect them at intervals (Fig. 33, B; Pl. 14, A; see also O'Neale and Kroeber, 1930, Pl. 35, b).

When spaces were left in a plain-weave fabric, the Peruvians, in order to avoid looseness in the woven surfaces and separation of the yarns at the unwoven edges, usually secured them with a yarn, probably run through with a needle, which fastened the warp to the weft with a knot. In Plate 45 will be found two examples of this edge in which one (specimen A) is very compact and has caused the bound sections to frill, completely changing the appearance of the fabric. Specimen B may be compared with the very beautiful material reproduced by Howard (1920, Fig. 80).

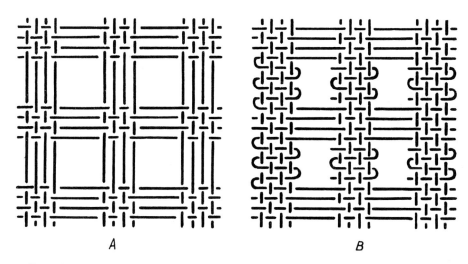

A   B

Figure 33.   Arrangement of yarns in an open-space fabric. A: plain weave; B: tapestry

OPEN WORK IN LOZENGE FORM

Certain plain-weave fabrics are decorated on given surfaces, such as edges, corners, central sections, and so forth, with open work in the form of adjacent lozenges, the effect of which is very attractive. The method of obtaining these lozenges must be explained with great precision, for it has already been described, but very inaccurately (Barnett, 1909). I am assuming the simple case of a fabric made of horizontal borders of plain-weave cloth and open-work fabric (Fig. 34). Let us take as our point of departure the last weft row of a regular plain-weave section: the warp yarns are distributed in groups of twelve; two adjacent weft yarns, peculiar to each group, join them to each other in plain-weave technique for a space of three or four weft passages; then the group is divided into two subsections of six yarns, each woven separately by one of the two weft yarns. Usually the warp is stretched very little; the weft, on the contrary, is well stretched, but the weft rows are not very close together, so that the weft yarn is hidden, covered by the warp. After the passage in each subsection of a number of wefts constant in each specimen but varying from specimen to specimen according to the size of the lozenges, the two subsections derived from the same group are joined on the right and on the left to the neighboring subsections by means of their weft yarns, which cross each other following one of the methods shown in Figure 34, *a* or *b*. Then the subsections, thus joined, are separated, their independent weaving is resumed, and a little later they re-form their original group. The work proceeds with this alternation until the plain-cloth weaving is resumed for the full width of the fabric or for a partial section, as required by the design. When the lozenges form a lateral border of a solid surface, they are rejoined to this surface by means of the weft of the latter, as though two lozenges were being joined to each other. The lozenges are never joined by means of stitches made with a needle.

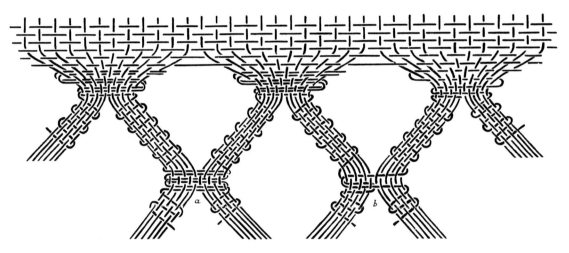

Figure 34.   Arrangement of yarn in a fabric with lozenge-shaped open spaces; *a*, fastening secured by the reciprocal crossing of two weft yarns; *b*, fastening secured by a single weft yarn

If the warp of the fabric is made of two alternating colored yarns, the open-work portion, in which the weft is hidden, is made up of small areas whose color is reversed at the passage of each weft, as the even or the odd warps come to the surface.

The procedure I have just described is not exceptional. I know of many specimens woven in this way. They come from the central coastal region. I refer the reader to Plate 46, A, B; also to Plate 29 of my work, *Les tissus indiens du Vieux Pérou*, which shows a more decorative specimen.

FABRICS WITH SQUARE AND TRIANGULAR SPACES (RESEMBLING KNOTTING)

The Peruvians conceived the idea of a special fabric with large square spaces, which at first glance looks like knotting. Actually it is a fabric and not network; the method of its construction shows this plainly. The fabric is generally white and is always made of quite fine cotton. It serves as a base for embroidery. The size of the open spaces varies according

56

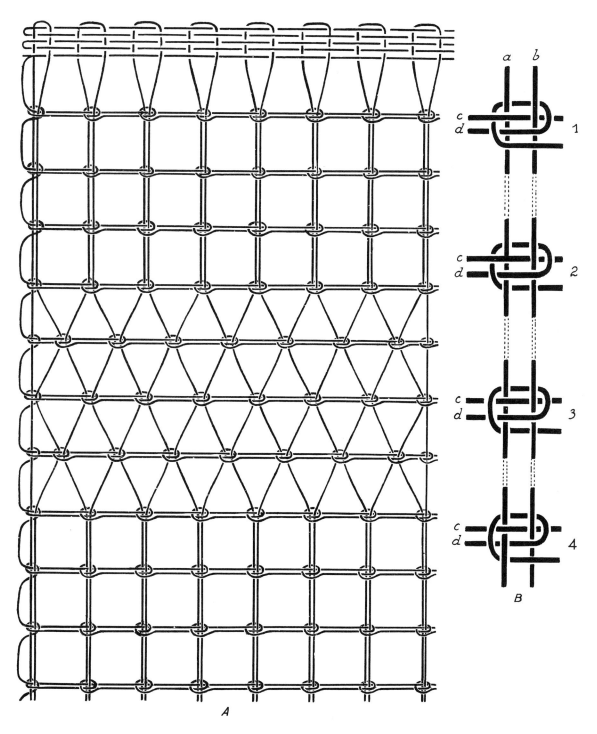

Figure 35. A: arrangement of yarns in a fabric with eighty-one square open spaces (in imitation of filet) and with triangular spaces; B: principal types of knots

to the specimen, ranging from half a centimeter [3/16 inch] to about two centimeters [3/4 inch].

Square spaces

First of all, the pairs of warp yarns are spaced according to the size of the mesh desired. Several weft rows are placed in regular fashion and more or less compacted in order to maintain the width of the fabric; the subsequent weft rows are spaced. The first isolated row crosses the warp yarns regularly, passing over every other one; the return row passes under two adjacent yarns (even and odd) every time and interlocks these two yarns, as well as the outward-passing weft, by means of a knot whose most usual forms are shown here (Fig. 35, B). The third row passes like the first at a distance from the second corresponding to the separation of the warp yarns, in order to form square open spaces. The fourth yarn follows the same path as the second row, and the weaving continues in this way (see Pls. 40–44). Thus a fabric is woven in which double warp and weft yarns form square open spaces. The knotting of the weft yarns is not firm and slips easily, detracting sometimes from the regularity of the open spaces.

The framing of a group of open spaces

In order to break the monotonous appearance of the open spaces, and also perhaps to give more strength to the fabric when it is made with very fine yarns, the Peruvians sometimes introduced a plain, tight weave of a dozen weft yarns with a corresponding number of warp yarns between every ten or twelve open spaces. From this resulted a sort of square framework enclosing a group of open spaces. Examination of Plate 44 will immediately make this special technique clear. The weft rows forming the solid upper and lower parts of the framework pass over and under, in plain weave, both the paired warp yarns and the warp yarns forming the lateral parts of the framework, while the double weft yarns that knot the paired warp yarns of the open spaces knot the grouped warp yarns in the same manner.

Triangular open spaces

The weaving of square open spaces, such as has been explained, can be varied in the following manner: instead of the return weft rows always interlocking the same warp yarns, they can, on the return row, separate them every other time by interlocking them with their neighbors on the right and on the left. In this way, two triangular open spaces are formed (Fig. 35, A, in the center section), each one occupying half of the surface of the square space (see Pl. 43). This method is employed to cover the surface with a design

58

that will stand out clearly on the basic fabric. In addition, the boundaries of these triangular spaces are made more distinct by the threading of a rather coarse cotton yarn of three or four strands along the line of the border after weaving; this yarn is secured at intervals by a simple knot, as in embroidered gauze.

Embroidery

For an analysis of embroidery on a base of square or triangular open-work fabric, the reader is referred to page 130.

FABRICS WITH DISCONTINUOUS WARP AND KNOTTED WEFT

I am including among open-work fabrics the specimen illustrated in Plate 47, A. Is it true weaving? It certainly has a warp, but it is not made of continuous yarns; it certainly has a weft, but it interlocks with its neighbor on the right and sometimes with its neighbor on the left, much in the same manner as the fabric with triangular spaces, which we have just been studying. There is thus formed a kind of light network, with triangular meshes or lozenges (Fig. 36). The specimen shown in Plate 47, A, makes use, both in the warp and the weft, either of a yellow or dark violet wool yarn, or of a much finer cotton yarn, formerly white, the two elements being of the same color and of the same nature in the parts where they cross each other. It will be noticed that the terminal loops of the warp yarns of one color are completely interlocked with the initial loops of the adjoining color, as in Fabric A of Plate 2, or the fabric shown in Plate 4. The design formed by the yellow and violet wool yarns stands out clearly upon the light cotton background: it forms wide bands that intersect obliquely the elements, warp and weft, of the fabric. The manner in which the worker arranged the warp yarns and rejoined these to each other remains hypothetical. It is here that the operational and artistic difficulty of this method of weaving lay, since the warp formed the design. The passage of the weft and the making of the knots could easily be accomplished

Figure 36. Arrangement of yarns of the open-space fabric shown in Plate 47, A

with the aid of a small shuttle, or even with a needle, after the assemblage of the warp yarns.

SEVEN

Fabrics with Wrapped Warp (Decorative Method)

I HAVE twice had the good fortune to observe this type of weaving. One specimen is the passementerie from Nazca (Pl. 59, F). The other is the fabric that forms the center of the remarkable specimen from Paracas shown in Plate 88: of this I have made a reconstruction.

This is a plain-weave cotton of the muslin family, the design of which is achieved by localized wrapping of warp yarns in wool, after warping, with yarns of suitable colors, but only in the areas required by the chosen design. When the task of wrapping the warp yarns was completed, that of the weaving, strictly speaking, began (Fig. 37). The difficulty of this method lay in the fastening of the wool yarn wrapping at the required points when beginning or ending. It may be said, too, that in spite of the skill of the worker some waviness in the lines of the design parallel to the weft does exist. The two elements—warp and weft—appear equally; the two faces of the fabric are identical (Pl. 104).

The nature of this technique may be said to approach that of *ikat*, where only the warp is dyed in pattern, that is to say, is dyed after warping and before weaving (see p. 70).

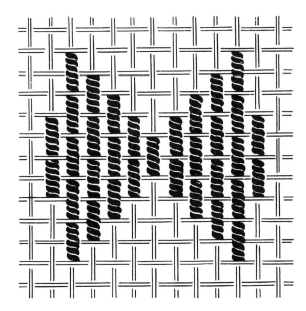

Figure 37. Plain-weave fabric in which the warp yarns are wrapped locally prior to the passage of the weft

Fabrics with Wrapped Warp (Decorative Method)

Instead of localized dyeing, there is a wrapping of warp yarns with a suitable color. The wrapping of the warp yarns before weaving may also have been used by Oceanic peoples. The methods used by the Mohawks to decorate their carrying straps may also be recalled here; they wrapped the weft of these straps with yarns of a particular color for a given length as the two wefts were twined together (Orchard, 1929, Fig. 106, p. 356).

EIGHT

Fabrics Made of Twisted Warp
or Weft: Passementerie

Decorative bands and edgings are for the most part only long, narrow fabrics, the techniques of which are borrowed from one of those that we have already studied, notably tapestry, tubular weaving, weaving with two colors of warp yarn (concealed weft) with the weave subordinated to the pattern. The following technique seems to be set apart more especially for such decorative bands and edgings.

BANDS WITH TWISTED WARP YARNS

Up to the present, I have found this technique used predominantly on quite narrow bands or ribbons; there is theoretically nothing to prevent its use for wider pieces. The appearance of these bands is that of lines of adjacent chain stitches. The method of procedure is as follows. The warp yarns are twisted around each other in pairs, with regular alternation of the direction of twisting; that is to say, a pair twisted from right to left is followed by a pair twisted from left to right. At each spiral the weft glides between the two yarns, thus holding the crossing firm and fastening the pairs of yarns to each other (Fig. 38). It can be seen that the procedure and results are very closely related to those of "card weaving," but the Peruvians do not seem to have known the potentialities of this weaving technique; they did not proceed beyond this initial stage. Moreover, no small boards with holes or similar articles used in card weaving have been found among the material taken from graves.

Weaving with twisted warp can also be compared with the Arab technique known under the name *rbib* or *borshman* (Bel and Ricard, 1913, p. 181). The only difference is that with the Arabs the braid thus formed is joined to a fabric by the weft, which, at the end of each little row, comes back to its starting point across the fabric, while with the Peruvians the braid is independent, the weft being manipulated as in ordinary weaving. Among the braids I have been able to examine, several include three double twists of two yarns (that is, twelve yarns). It is possible that they may have been woven with the help of a second worker who manipulated the warp yarns by passing the six terminal loops of the yarns around three fingers of each hand. In this case, each double twist (four yarns) would have been formed as indicated in Figure 38, by passing the two loops through each other alternately and always in the same direction (which twists the yarns), and by insert-

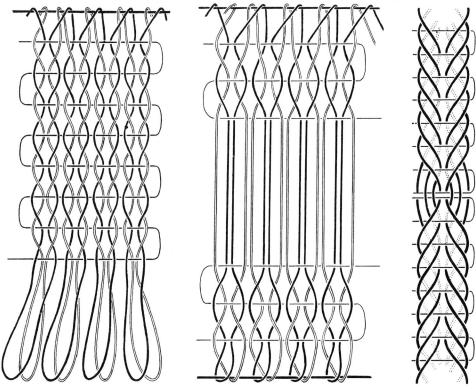

Figure 38 (left). Arrangement of yarns of a band in which warp yarns twisted in pairs are held by the weft; warps left free at one end during weaving

Figure 39 (center). Arrangement of yarns of a band in which the warp yarns are secured at both ends; weft yarns hold the twisting of the warp pairs at both ends simultaneously

Figure 40 (right). Central part of the left column of a band made with warp yarns twisted four at a time, in accordance with the methods shown in Figure 39

ing the weft at each spiral between the yarns, first from right to left, then from left to right, or vice versa. The presence of the loops at the ends of the two specimens D and E, shown in Plate 49, would lead to the belief that the method of manufacture was that which has just been explained, but this is only hypothesis.

On the other hand, in order to obtain wider braid, with more colors in each twist, the method employed must necessarily have been the following. The warp yarns were arranged as in ordinary warping and consequently made fast at their two extremities; the twisting of the pairs of yarns was done simultaneously and in the reverse direction in the upper part and in the lower part of the warp; each twist was held by means of a weft, as shown in Figure 39. The two twistings (the upper and the lower) approached each other and met in the center where the pattern underwent a slight irregularity, due to the fact that the direction of the twists was reversed. I had the good fortune to find a completed specimen in which the yarns were not cut at the ends, and which showed at the center the irregularity peculiar to the technique (see Pl. 49, A, B). In this example, each twist was no longer made with only two pairs of yarns, but rather with four pairs of different colored yarns (eight yarns); the method of twisting was the same, but instead of using a simple alternation of two pairs of yarns, the worker, before the passage of the weft, was careful always to bring back to the center of the double twists the two uppermost outside yarns (or the two lowest for the other end of the weaving) (see Fig. 40).

The flat sections belonging to the sling shown in Plate 64, which appear to be plaited, were formed by using the method just described, but with the following special features: the direction of the twisting of the yarns varies periodically in the same pair; it may be the same as, or opposite to, that of adjacent pairs, as the design requires.

The fabric shown in Plate 48, A, in which the technique of warp yarns twisted around each other in pairs was used, appears to be less perfectly made; on the other hand, it is much wider than the braids of which I have just been speaking. The yarns are of two colors, regularly alternated. The direction of the twisting of the yellow and brown yarns is sometimes reversed, producing small lozenge-shaped motives; however, in many cases these are the result of mere negligence on the part of the weaver. The work must have been done in the manner shown in Figure 39, taking into consideration the fact that we have only one half of the specimen (the other half would show the same small motives and the same irregularities, but in a reversed direction).

Soles of sandals; twisted warp

The soles of sandals were often of llama skin. However, vegetable fibers, most commonly agave, were fabricated into soles by at least two methods, one of which falls into the present category. This first technique consisted of twisting warp strands around each other in pairs; each twist was secured by one or two perpendicular weft yarns of the same fiber (Fig. 41, B). It is the same principle as that of twining used in basketry (Fig. 41, A), but with the twisting applied to the warps instead of to the wefts. However, because the shape had to correspond to the sole of the foot, that is, be rounded at the heel and toe ends, the twisting was delicate to manipulate. Work began at the toe; the spun fiber strands, fastened in their central length in pairs, were curved to the right and left. As the warps were twisted in pairs, they were secured by two yarns of the same fiber, crossing simultaneously from opposite directions. This practice of a shoemaker or harness maker permits the two yarns to be pulled against each other by their ends and greatly compacts the warp yarns. When the pairs of warp strands curved in a semicircle were so close to each other as to become parallel (after having formed the toe of the sole), the twisting continued using two yarns of the weft, which then crossed the entire width of the sole (Fig. 41, B). In order to form the round part of the heel, the worker abandoned use of half of the strands, at points *a* and *b* (on the left or on the right), and continued the twisting of the strands of the other half by curving them as was done in the beginning. The abandoned strands were picked up and united with the active warp strands as work progressed. These unions were made gradually so that the smoothness of the sole would not be impaired, and the

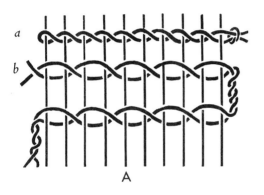

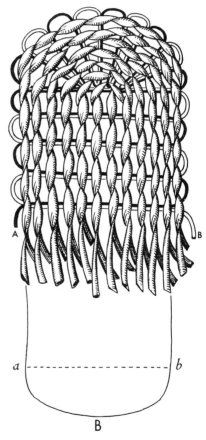

Figure 41. A: Warps secured by two weft yarns twisted in pairs (twining); *a*, wefts twisted around individual warp yarns, each row ending in a knot and the ends cut; *b*, weft yarns twisted around two warp yarns at a time, twisted together several times at the selvage, and continued in the next row. B: Method of construction of the sole of a sandal with two warp yarns twisted in pairs (see Pl. 60, A)

work was accomplished so skillfully that the points of junction can hardly be observed. The weft yarns, for this part of the work, must undoubtedly have been inserted with the aid of a coarse needle (Pl. 60, A). The second method of sandal-sole making falls under a different technique and will be discussed on page 99.

FABRICS WITH TWISTED WEFT; TWINING

There exists a method of weaving similar to that which has just been described, but in which the role of the elements is reversed, that is, the warp yarns are joined to each other singly or in groups of two or three, in simple or complex weaving, by means of two weft yarns that twist around each other in each row (see Fig. 41, A). This method descends in a direct line from basketry and must have preceded historically that in which the warp yarns are twisted around each other.

The ancient Peruvians knew twining, and examples of it have been found in the very early periods in Peruvian archeology. These strata contain what appear to be the first hesitant attempts at weaving (see Pl. 48, B). Recent excavation in Peru at sites which are believed to be preceramic have uncovered numerous fragments of twined textiles. Some of the fabrics display great complexity and expert use of technique in an already mature esthetic development. One such cotton specimen, from the Rio Seco, eighty-seven kilometers north of Lima, on the coast, introduces a series of open spaces arranged in regular oblique lines, which outline a pattern of fine concentric lozenges (Pl. 48, C). Twining subsequently was supplanted by fabrics with regulated crossings of the warp and weft yarns, although as a technique it survived in the fabrication of baskets. Some Amazonian tribes still use it, and its use by the Mohawks of North America has resulted in the production of very beautiful specimens (Orchard, 1929, Figs. 104, 105).

PASSEMENTERIE MADE OF EIGHT YARNS
(THREE COLORS)

Figure 42 shows the schematic design of a very elegant passementerie. This type of passementerie has been found several times in the course of excavations made in the Paracas-Nazca region (see Pl. 69, C). It is made with eight yarns and usually is of three colors, two of which predominate, one on one side and the second on the other. The operations of looping and crossing are initiated by three pairs of yarns around two vertical yarns, in accordance with the method indicated in Figure 42. The fragment of passementerie shown in Plate 69, C, has been enlarged four times.

Figure 42 (left). Passementerie of three colors made by six yarns interlacing two warp yarns

Figure 43 (right). Simple braid (soutache) made of six yarns crossing each other around two vertical warp yarns

SOUTACHE BRAID WITH SIX OR EIGHT YARNS OF ONE OR SEVERAL COLORS

I mention at this point a rather simple soutache braid made of a flat four- or six-strand plaiting around two vertical yarns. The yarns of the braid are usually of different colors (Fig. 43).

On page 78 will be found the description of another passementerie using a special technique.

NINE

Dyed or Tie-dyed Woven Fabrics

Designs on fabrics were not always accomplished by the judicious crossing of different colored yarns. They could also be produced by painting or dyeing monochrome yarns, either before or after weaving. Obviously, these methods are quite distinct from weaving, but they are of such interest and are so closely related to certain weaving operations that they must at least be mentioned.

PAINTING

Paint was applied locally to one face of the fabric by means of a brush or a tuft of wool or hair. Sometimes the brush was used to produce free-hand sketching on one face of the fabric, as appears on the tablets of split reeds covered with cotton fabric, large numbers of which have been found in graves in the Ancón region. Sometimes the painting was extended over larger design areas which might or might not adjoin (see Pls. 50 and 51). Up to the present I have formed no definite conclusion as to whether or not the Peruvians made use of incised stamps to impress the painted design on the surface of the fabric. In all the specimens I have examined where the same motive is used as a decorative theme, I have found that there is variation in the dimensions of the motive and in the arrangement of its parts, and that such variation cannot be attributed to the distortion of the fabric.

Painting with reserves

In Peru painted fabrics are sometimes found in which light, ornamental lines appear on a dark surface—veritable negative pictures. One may assume that this effect was obtained by one of the following methods. The fabric was covered by a uniform layer of paint; then lines were marked upon it with a brush soaked in a liquid that chemically discharged the paint following the lines of the design, so that the natural background fabric reappeared. The use of such a method, which might lead to blistering, remains hypothetical and doubtful. The other method, the more probable, would consist of tracing the design with a substance that would either chemically or physically prevent the paint from "taking." The paint would then be spread uniformly. Finally, after drying, the protective substance would be removed. This method would be closer to those which will be examined in connection with dyeing with reserves. It will be clearly seen from the specimen in Plate 51, A, that the color has been applied without reference to the lines which were to remain white, and which had been previously covered and protected; the brush strokes in this respect are significant.

DYEING WITH RESERVES

Paint applied by means of a brush or even by a stamp does not penetrate deeply into the fibers of the fabric and is confined to one face only. Dyeing is quite different; it requires a more or less prolonged bath, and it penetrates the fabric in its entirety. In order to obtain a design by means of dyeing, it is necessary to reserve certain of the yarns, before or after weaving, either in order to preserve their natural color or to dye them later a color different from that of the first. There are two methods of dyeing with reserves.

Dye applied after weaving (planghi)

Some of the surface of the fabric to be dyed is reserved by a layer of clay, or by wax, or even by the simple constraint of a tight binding like a ring, which ties the rolled fabric at regular intervals; or the fabric may be spread out and the reserves formed by bindings arranged at chosen points. After dyeing, drying, removal of the protective material or the ties, and unwrapping, the fabric will show design motives or simply a series of stripes or circles, as the case may be, which stand out in light tones against the dark dye of the background color. Such is the principle of *planghi* used in the East Indies. *Batik* is the name especially given to the technique in which reserves are made by means of a layer of protective material, such as wax, which adheres to the fibers, and which is finally dissolved when the dyeing operations are completed. Reserve dyeing was not elaborated in Peru, where the *planghi* [or tie-dye] technique was chiefly used. Simple examples will be found in the specimens shown on Plate 52, A, B; the light circles that appear on the gauze in A

69

were obtained by bindings tied around the ends of rods on which the fabric to be dyed had probably been placed. Specimen C of Plate 49 is more complex. It must contain, in its entirety, at least four similar separate fabrics, each dyed independently twice (with or without reserves), then joined and "remeshed," so to speak, since a common yarn secures the ends of the yarns on each surface, loop by loop, on the terminal selvage, which is made like the treads of a staircase, seen in profile.

Dye applied between the warping and the weaving (ikat)

We have seen that the warp yarns, before the passage of the weft, can be wrapped at given points with wool of different colors. Dye applied locally can be substituted for wrapping. The assembly of warp yarns is immersed in the baths, after some sections of them have been carefully reserved at various points of the length by being covered with a waterproof material. The yarns are then dried, the protective coverings are removed, and the restretched warp is woven.

The method just described was used in Peru only for dyeing warp yarns. In the East Indies and in certain Asian countries dyeing is likewise done on the weft yarns. For this, the yarn is stretched between the two opposite sides of a frame—as a warp would be—in the same position as it will be in the fabric to be woven. The tying and dyeing are then accomplished. After drying, the yarn is removed from the frame and the worker proceeds with the weaving in such a way that the weft rows retain the design, which was laid out when the weft was stretched on the frame. By means of successive baths of different colors and appropriate reserves, a rich and varied design can be obtained, whose slightly indecisive edges add greatly to its attractiveness.

This method of partial dyeing of yarns before weaving is known as *ikat*. The ancient Peruvians knew it and applied it. Plate 53, A, B, illustrates cotton fabrics whose warps were dyed locally by a method similar to that just described. It seems that before the arrival of the Spanish the process of *ikat* was not very widespread in America. At the present time, only five or six specimens of *ikat* have been described in the literature relating to ancient Peruvian textiles. These belong to a pre-Incaic period and have their provenience in the central coast of Peru (Pachacamac, Viru, Pacasmayo). Only in the warp and only in localized areas were dyes of one or two colors used. The weft was of a uniform color. The specimens show simple geometric motives as well as forms of birds and human figures (Bird, 1947; VanStan, 1957). Future researches on this subject may, however, hold surprises in store for us.

In our own day, the Araucanian Indians of Chile use this method commonly in the making of their ponchos and blankets. No doubt it represents the survival of an ancient technique of Peruvian origin. Ikle has given us a chart of the world-wide distribution of the *ikat* technique (1928).

PART II
Nonwoven Fabrics

TEN

Plaiting or Braiding

FLAT BRAIDING or plaiting is formed by the regular intersecting of two sections of warp in a chosen plan; these warps, separating from the perpendicular, proceed first in opposing directions, and then meet to form an angle, usually in the neighborhood of forty-five degrees from the perpendicular (Fig. 44, *a*). The yarn sections cross each other, therefore, at approximately right angles. The sections, in relation to each other, have the reciprocal functions of warp and of weft. Because of their oblique direction, the yarns reach the lateral selvages successively; there they are folded over and begin once more their course, making an angle with the perpendicular that is complementary to the first one. The simplest form of plaiting is represented by the flat plaiting with three strands that everybody knows.

The oblique progression of the two sections and their interchangeable character in the plaiting make possible the locking of the yarns be-

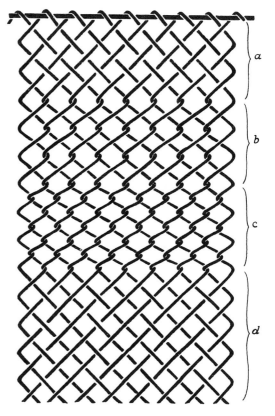

Figure 44.   Draft of ordinary plaiting in which the yarns cross each other (*a, d*) or interlock (*b, c*)

73

tween each other in a manner that cannot be accomplished in weaving; thus, instead of two yarns each belonging to a different section crossing each other and continuing their progress, they can lock around each other and substitute for each other in their further passage (Fig. 44, *b*, *c*). This special method leads to multiple combinations, according to the intervals and order of the interlocking. Because of its simplicity, plaiting often precedes weaving with two elements, warp and weft, and it is known to have been used by many primitive peoples. Basketry is no doubt one of its first forms. In the course of centuries, however, plaiting among the Peruvians developed complex forms whose techniques were often derived from weaving. With this explanation, it will be understood why weaving has been studied first.

The methods of plaiting can be grouped under two different headings, depending upon whether or not the lower ends of the yarns are left free in the course of the operation. These methods will be studied successively.

PLAITING OF YARNS WITH THE LOWER ENDS LEFT FREE

It is almost certain that the worker, to facilitate the weaving operations, rolled each yarn into a small ball or wrapped it around a reed to serve as a bobbin. This was particularly necessary for fabrics of large proportions, requiring work over a long period of time.

A

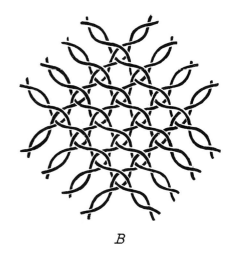

B

Figure 45. Method of weaving of the specimen shown in Plate 54, B; the yarns in each passage twist around each other by twos. A: general appearance of the plaiting; B: arrangement of the yarns in crossing

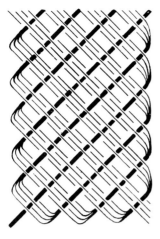

Figure 46 (left). Schematic plan of the yarns of the braid shown in Plate 55, B

Figure 47 (below). Detail of arrangement of the yarns of the band shown in Plate 55, C

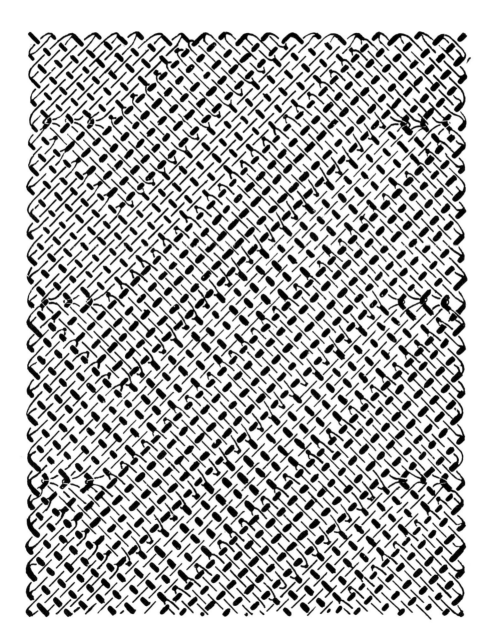

The specimen shown in Plate 56, A, enables us to advance this theory without fear of error.

Plaiting, like weaving in this respect, can be of plain construction or of irregular construction. Figure 44 shows the simplest plan of plaiting, upon which I shall not dwell further.

Plaiting with twisted yarns

Plaiting can be accomplished by a method of twining the yarns of the two warp sections around each other, in pairs, always in the same direction (as opposed to the principle of gauze). The rule for crossing the yarns is clearly shown in Figure 45, B, while Figure 45, A, demonstrates precisely how the work as a whole was carried on. It is similar to the principle applied to the making of bobbin lace. By plaiting with twisted yarns, very open fabrics can be produced that are delicate but cannot be distorted. Plate 54, B, shows a simple example (see also O'Neale and Kroeber, 1930, Pl. 7, *a*). A more compact fabric can be made when the yarns contact each other. This method was also used in plaited specimens in which the yarns were held fast at their two extremities.

Plaiting with only one element visible

As in woven cloth with only one element visible—reps—plaiting may also have one of the warp sections covered and concealed by the other section, with the special characteristic that the roles are reversed at the point where the oblique yarns, reaching the selvage, start out in their new direction. This principle is applied to fabrics of quite diverse appearance. Following are some of the types which I have had the opportunity to study.

First type (braid B of Pl. 55). The braiding is commenced with two groups of equal numbers of yarns (twenty-four in the braid in question); one group is light and the other dark. The group beginning in the upper left-hand corner will have the function of the covering group, which will proceed obliquely toward the right, and these yarns, like those in rep, will then "weave" (one yarn above and one yarn below); in so doing they cover the passive yarns of the other group, which have been arranged in two subgroups [of twelve yarns each], and which progress obliquely toward the left. Thus, in the specimen shown, each group has twenty-four yarns, and each is divided into two subgroups of twelve yarns during its passive role. The first two subgroups, which are passive, upon reaching the left-hand selvage, re-form their original group of twenty-four yarns and, progressing in a new direction (to the right), become an active and covering group; the second of the original groups, reaching the right-hand selvage, divides into two passive subgroups and progresses in its new direction (to the left). The plaiting continues according to this rhythm and results in a fabric formed of different-colored, oblique, parallel bands. Figure 46 has been simplified in the interest of clarity: the twenty-four yarns are reduced to four, and in their covered parts they are all joined without being divided into subgroups. The method of plaiting shown in the figure is not any less exact because of this simplification.

Second type (specimen C of Pl. 55). The Peruvians succeeded in plaiting pieces of fabric likewise made of different-colored oblique bands, but which were crossed; each of them, after having crossed the fabric diagonally from right to left, in such a way as to be visible at all times, crossed again from left to right in such a manner as to be visible only at intervals. To achieve this result, it was necessary to maintain the arrangement of alternately "covering-separated" yarns and "covered-grouped" yarns, and to pursue it in a still more complex fashion. It was necessary also to be able to reverse the direction of the crossing of the yarns in each of the sections. This is shown in Figure 47, a scheme by which the groups of yarn are reduced to a thick line in the covered parts and to two light lines in the covering parts.

Third type (braid A of Pl. 55; see also O'Neale and Kroeber, 1930, Pl. 17, *f*). In this type of plaiting, the yarns of the two sections are arranged in pairs of the same color, which are always used together. The yarns of the left half of the first section are passive and covered in pairs during half of their passage, that is, up to the middle of the braid, while the corresponding yarns of the second section, during the same passage, are active and covering, like the twined or twisted warp yarns of the fabric studied on page 62. These yarns are twined in pairs, one around the other, taking up in each crossing the pairs of the passive yarns. The direction of the twisting of the pairs of yarns alternates regularly. In the second half of the braid (at the right), the yarns of the two sections have a reverse role, that is, upon reaching the center of the work all the passive yarns become "covering," and all the active yarns become "covered." At the selvages the roles are again reversed. Two special features may be noted in Figure 48. First, the yarns of the right and the left halves cross each other

Figure 48. Arrangement of the yarns of the plaited braid shown in Plate 55, A, central part

at right angles, but they form, respectively, a lower and an upper angle of forty-five degrees with the perpendicular. The passive yarns, at the point in the center of the braid where they change their role and become active, modify their direction in order to cross the newly passive yarns of the second half of the braid at right angles. Second, to introduce variety into the appearance of the braid, the weaver, at intervals, maintained the passive character of two of the pairs of yarns in the second half of their passage; these yarns cross each other in the form of an **X**, while the active yarns continue their covering role after having changed their direction, as shown in the center of Figure 48. The concentric lines that appear in the central part of specimen A of Plate 55 were obtained in this way.

In plate 60, D, will be found a braid of wool in four colors which combines the second and third types of plaiting discussed above. It makes use of the principle of yarns alternately covering as separated yarns and being covered as grouped yarns according to the requirements of the design and the principle of yarns twisted by pairs. Thus, in their covered section, the yarns of one color are joined in groups of four; in the section where they are covering, these yarns are twisted around each other in pairs, taking up in each spiral the four grouped yarns; the direction of the twisting of the yarns is reversed from one pair to the other.

Plaited passementerie

A passementerie from Nazca (Pl. 59, F) makes use, with some modification, of the third type above. It consists of two plaited bands placed parallel to each other, joined in the center and bound on the exterior edges by a small decoration in regular zigzags, likewise plaited (Fig. 49), which can also be seen in specimen B of Plate 67.

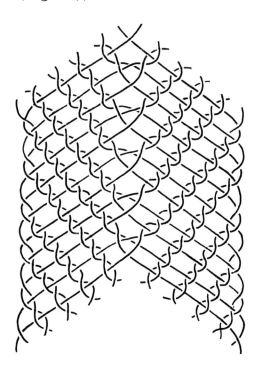

Figure 49. Method of plaiting of the narrow braid shown in Plate 59, F

Figure 50. Method of plaiting the yarns joining and bordering the braids of the passementerie shown in Plate 59, F

The yarns of the braids and those of the decorative zigzag use local wrapping of the yarns in order to effect color changes (see p. 60).

The method of plaiting of the two braids is very similar, as I have said, to that described above. It differs, however, in two particulars that completely change its appearance. The pairs of yarns intended to twist around each other all turn in the same direction for each half of the width of the braid, instead of changing direction one after the other; and these pairs of yarns, in their successive twists, cover only one yarn at a time instead of grouped yarns in the parts in which they function as hidden weft (Fig. 50). The plaiting is very close.

Double plaiting

The Peruvians applied the principle of double-cloth weaving to plaiting. Specimen E of Plate 55 gives an interesting example of this application (see also Pl. 31, A). For double plaiting one system of suitably colored yarns (as in all plaiting divided into halves with alternately active and passive roles) is superimposed upon a second system of differing colors, which is simultaneously fashioned in the same manner as the first. As in double-cloth weaving, the two systems are substituted for each other by interpenetration when change of color makes this desirable. The use of the double systems does not render this type of plaiting especially difficult, as only simple crossing of yarns or their twisting by pairs is involved.

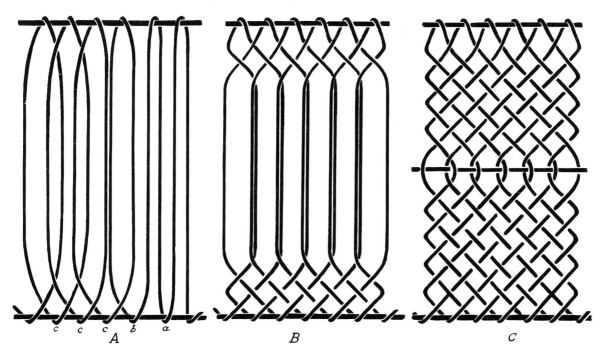

Figure 51. Detail showing the successive steps in the making of a braid whose elements are secured at their two ends (plaiting by crossing of yarns). A: the beginning of the plaiting; *a*, yarns not yet crossed; *b*, first stage of yarns crossing each other; *c*, second stage; B: plaiting in process; C: plaiting finished and transverse yarn in the center to hold the plaiting

79

PLAITING OF YARNS HELD FIRM AT THEIR ENDS

Simple plaiting

There is another method of plaiting in which the yarns are arranged in the beginning like those of an ordinary warp (Figs. 51, 52) and are kept stretched during the plaiting operation, but in a sufficiently elastic manner to allow for the progressive shortening of the yarns resulting from their oblique passage. The yarns are crossed or twined by taking them between the fingers, or with an instrument, at the center of their length. Because they are secured at the ends, each crossing or twining that is produced in the upper part of the yarns is likewise reproduced in the lower part, but in a reverse direction. The plaiting is thus carried on at the two extremities of the yarns, and the successive rows gradually draw near to each other at the center (Figs. 51, C; 52, B). A point is reached at which the fingers can no longer function because the yarns are too short, and a finer instrument must be substituted for the fingers (hook, small wooden or bone rod, or the like). In the last operation, a yarn is passed like a weft through the center of the fabric to prevent the disintegration of the crossing and twistings.[1]

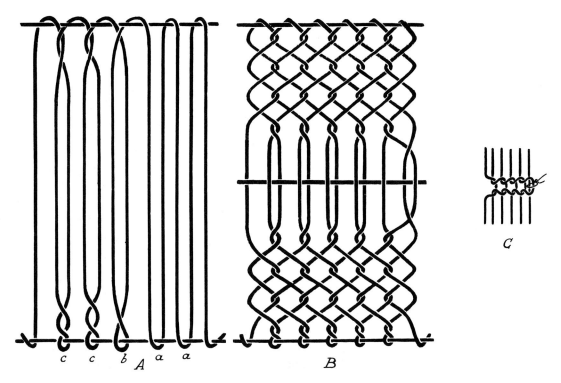

Figure 52. Detail showing the successive steps in the making of a braid whose elements are secured at their two ends (plaiting by interlocking of yarns). A: the beginning of the plaiting; *a*, yarns not yet interlocked; *b*, first stage of yarns interlocking; *c*, second stage; B: plaiting in process; C: chain of self yarns securing the center of the plaiting

[1] For explanations concerning this type of plaiting (still well known in Sweden under the name of *sprang*) see Reesema (1926).

The small bag shown in Plate 54, A, indicates clearly the reversed direction of the crossings where the transverse yarn just mentioned passes.

In the case of plaiting with intercrossed yarns, the fastening of the work in the center may also be achieved in another way; when the successive loopings of the upper part and the lower part have almost met, the yarns, in the short space in which they are still free, are made to overlap each other and to form a little chain, which is shown in Figure 52, C, and Plate 56, B. Finally, it is only necessary to join together the last loop of the little chain and the yarn at the edge of the fabric, to keep the whole plaiting in position.

Plaiting with yarns fastened at their extremities was known to the Peruvians. It permits of most diversified construction. By the intentional omission of intertwining among certain yarns it is possible to form open spaces, which can be arranged as designs (see Fig. 53; Pl. 56, B).

Double plaiting

The making of the specimen reproduced in Plate 57 presupposes the complete mastery of a technique that is in this case particularly complex. We have just seen that double plaiting with yarns left free at the lower edge was a technique used in Peru. Plaiting was also done, and perhaps with greater facility, with the yarns fastened at both extremities—a veritable warping of yarns, like the two superimposed warps in double-weave cloth. Decorative neck coverings were made in this way, especially in the Nazca region. These neck coverings consisted of two similar sections, which were fixed to the sides of the head by means of little cords; a sample showing only one of the two parts is reproduced in Plate 57. Two systems, each made up of the usual two sections, one red and the other yellow, arranged like those in Figures 51 and 52, were superimposed, and the plaiting of the two was pursued simultaneously at the two extremities, as I have just explained, but with the substitution of one system for the other in order to obtain a design. When the central part of the still unplaited yarns was reduced to about 8 centimeters [3⅛ inches], the plaiting operation was discontinued and the piece of work, separated from its supports, was folded in half in the middle of the unplaited yarns. The lateral selvages were sewed together. The unplaited center yarns, which formed the top of the neck covering, were pressed against each other, then joined together by lines embroidered in loop stitch. Examination of the piece of work, the interior as well as the exterior, leaves no doubt as to the method used. Finally, it may be remarked that the rules of the crossings of the yarns vary in the course of operations: the respective systems at the beginning and at the end of the plaiting are different, and the yarns in each of them intercross by fours, but in the whole central area, where the yellow and red sections are substituted for each other, different and varied construction will sometimes allow simple crossing of the sections, and sometimes the intertwining of the yarns from one system to the other. The specimen shown in the first plate of *Art of Old Peru* (Lehmann and Doering, 1924) was made with a technique similar to that which has just been described (see also O'Neale and Kroeber, 1930, Pl. 21).

Double plaiting can be still more complex. Instead of two superimposed sections, some neck coverings use four. Double plaiting takes place between the two paired sections, but at intervals all the yarns cross each other at the same level, so that the two lower sections take over the uppermost position and vice versa. Let us assume that the first two sections are red and yellow, and the other two green and blue; the piece of work will be composed on one face of a plaited red and yellow band, followed by a green and blue band, then a red and yellow band; on the other face the order of the bands will be reversed. Such is the case with the specimen shown in Figure 54. As the method produces a quadruple

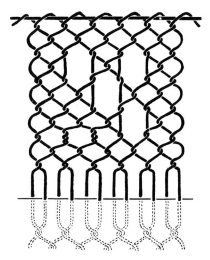

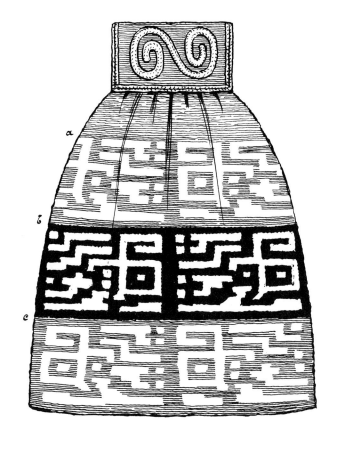

Figure 53 (above). Arrangement of the yarns of a braid made by interlocking of the yarns, resulting in open spaces and double interlocking. The figure shows only half of the specimen

Figure 54 (right). Part of an ornamental neck covering made by the superimposition of two double plaitings made of yarns twisted in pairs, one blue and green, the other yellow and red, which reverse their elements at points *b* and *c*. Above point *a*, the specimen consists of four thicknesses of simple plaiting

plaiting, that is, four superimposed thicknesses, the fabric will be of sufficient density and thus will not require the folding and lateral sewing of the specimen reproduced in Plate 57. Here the worker merely cut the fabric in two at the center, after having firmly tightened and secured to each other the nonplaited yarns that were to form the top of the two parts of the neck covering; thus the worker obtained at one step the two similar pieces that together formed the complete neck covering (Pl. 58).

82

PLAITED CORDS AND PLAITED COVERINGS OF CORDS

In addition to the straps and narrow bands plaited in simple structure (Pl. 31, B) or in complex structure (Pl. 55, D), the Peruvians made cords with round or square cross sections by plaiting together four, eight, sixteen, or more strands. The plaiting of these cords, which no doubt had multiple uses, is chiefly revealed in the slings taken from graves. Contemporary Indians of the highlands continue to use many of the ancient methods in making their slings.

Plaiting with square cross sections using eight strands can be done in several ways. It may be assumed that it was done in the following manner. At the beginning the strands are divided as shown in Figure 55, into two equal groups; in each of these the strands are numbered 1, 2, 3, and 4 from the exterior to the interior. Strand 1 on the left passes under its group, emerges in the center of the right-hand group, and returns on top of strands 3 and 4 to take up its place as 1' in its own group at the side of 4. Strand 1 of the right-hand group describes a similar movement, and then it is the turn of strand 2 on the left-hand side and strand 2 on the right-hand side, and so forth, the plaiting being carried on by the alternative crossing in each group of the strand that is on the outside.

Round braid of four strands can be obtained by a method similar to that which has just been explained, with the sole difference that, instead of the strands being divided into two groups of four, they are divided into two

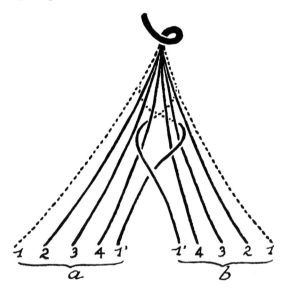

Figure 55. Arrangement of the strands of plaiting with square cross section (eight strands), showing the method of crossing of the first two yarns

groups of two; the movements remain the same. This method can also be used for plaiting with twelve strands, which are divided into two groups of six.

The rules of crossing of the strands obviously become more complex as the decorative motive to be obtained is more intricate.

It was interesting to me to study these rules of crossing in the motives that are most frequently met; they show the inventive genius of their makers. To make them comprehensible, I shall accompany the figure of the design being considered with a sequence of diagrams numbered in order and showing, in a cross section perpendicular to the axis of plaiting of the cord, the successive positions taken by the strands (represented by small disks designated by numbers or letters) in the course of their crossings until the cycle of the movements, producing a complete motive, leads the strands back to their initial position.

Textiles of Ancient Peru and Their Techniques

Darts in each diagram indicate the path traveled by the strands in order to reach their new position, which is defined in the following diagram.

In accordance with the general plan of this book, I shall proceed from the simple to the complex.

Plaiting with four strands in two colors

This plaiting, one of the simplest when it is carried out with strands of two colors, permits two different patterns depending upon whether or not the two strands that cross each other are of the same color. In the first case, the pattern shows a regular spiral (Fig.

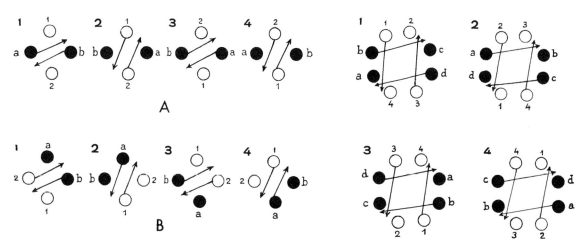

Figure 56. Plaiting with four strands of two colors. A: yarns of same color crossing each other; B: yarns of different color crossing each other

Figure 57. Plaiting with eight strands in two colors with square cross section

56, A); in the second, the pattern of the cord is divided into four longitudinal bands of alternating colors (Fig. 56, B).

Plaiting in square cross section with eight strands in two colors

Plaiting with eight strands requires sixteen movements before the strands return to their initial position. Figure 57 groups these movements into four diagrams and provides that the strands are of two colors, four white and four black.

When the strands are crossed as indicated in Figure 57, a cord with square cross section is obtained, divided on the four sides into two equal parts, one white and the other black. If the plaiting is done with the strands held in the hands as shown in Figure 55, it is necessary in the beginning to place the four white strands on one side and the four black strands on the other.

Instead of the strands being arranged across from each other, the white across from white and the black across from black, as in Figure 57, the white strands and the black strands can be regularly alternated in such a manner that a white strand will always be across from a black strand. When the yarns are then moved as indicated in Figure 57, there will be produced on each face of the cord a sequence of simple motives in the form of a **V** of alternating colors (one white and one black). When the strands are held as shown in Figure 55, it is necessary in beginning the plaiting to alternate the color of the strands in each group of four strands (one white, one black, one white, one black, or vice versa, in each group commencing with the outside).

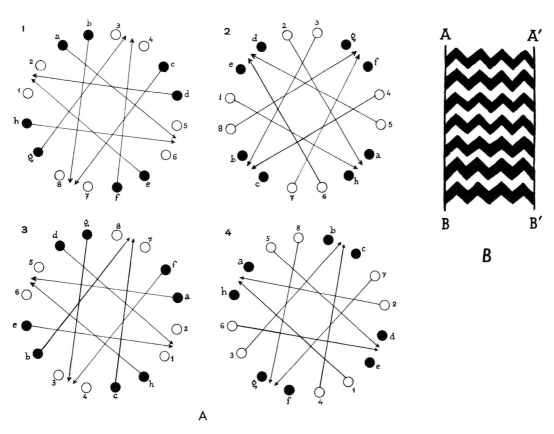

Figure 58.   Plaiting with sixteen strands in two colors with round cross section producing zigzag pattern. A: 1–4, successive positions of the strands; B: pattern produced by these movements

Plaiting in round cross section with sixteen strands in two colors

The number of strands becomes too great for me to continue to indicate with any degree of accuracy the manner in which the worker would hold the strands in her hands. I shall, therefore, use diagrams indicating the passage of the strands in order to form a certain pattern. Plaiting with sixteen strands requires at least thirty-two movements in order

85

that the strands may resume their original position. With eight strands of one color and eight strands of another, varied designs can be formed, of which the following three types are frequently encountered in Peru on both ancient and modern specimens.

Regular zigzag lines. The strands are distributed as shown in Figure 58 in groups of two strands of the same color, with regular alternation of the colors (here called black and white). The black strands *a* and *h* are placed between the white strands 5 and 6, then the two symmetrical black strands *d* and *e* between the white strands 2 and 1; the black strands *b* and *c* are placed between the white strands 7 and 8, then the strands *f* and *g* between strands 3 and 4. When these movements are completed, the strands are in positions shown in Figure 58, A, 2. From this position the white strands are now manipulated in the same manner as the black were previously, and so on. If a fifth diagram had been made, the strands would have resumed their initial position and the cycle would thus be completed. The cycle can then be repeated as many times as desired. The pattern formed is of regular small zigzag black and white lines arranged one under the other (Fig. 58, B).[2]

Chevrons. In order to form this pattern (Fig. 59, B), the strands are first arranged in four groups of four strands of the same color set opposite each other; that is, a group of four black strands is placed across from a group of four other black strands, and the adjacent group of four white strands across from a group of four other white strands (Fig. 59, A, 1). The strands of one color cross successively with the strands of the other color in the order and at the points indicated by the eight diagrams (Fig. 59, A); each diagram contains four movements (two crossings). Thus, in diagram 1, strand 8 crosses with *b*, 4 with *f*, and so forth. After the thirty-second movement is accomplished, the strands have returned to their original places and the cycle is completed and may be repeated (Pl. 59, A).

Lozenges. The initial arrangement of the strands in the lozenge pattern (Fig. 60, B) is the same as for that of chevrons: four groups of four strands of the same color are set opposite each other. But the movements are carried out successively between two strands of the same color according to the order indicated in Figure 60, A: *a* changing place with *e*, *c* moving to 5, *g* moving to 1, and so forth.

As in the preceding case, the cycle requires thirty-two movements before the strands return to their initial position (see Pl. 59, B). The initial arrangement and its periodic resumption allow easy change of the pattern from lozenges to chevrons and vice versa. The cord seen in Plate 59, A, shows this occurring.

In the plaiting of modern slings with sixteen strands there are other patterns, more or less derived from the motives above mentioned, which were perhaps used in former times.[3]

---

[2] In this and the following diagrams, the motive is illustrated as if the cylinder of the cord were opened and laid flat, the original A′ and B′ meeting in fact with A and B.

[3] I have described one of them in "Tressage de frondes au Pérou et en Bolivie" (Harcourt, 1940b, p. 115).

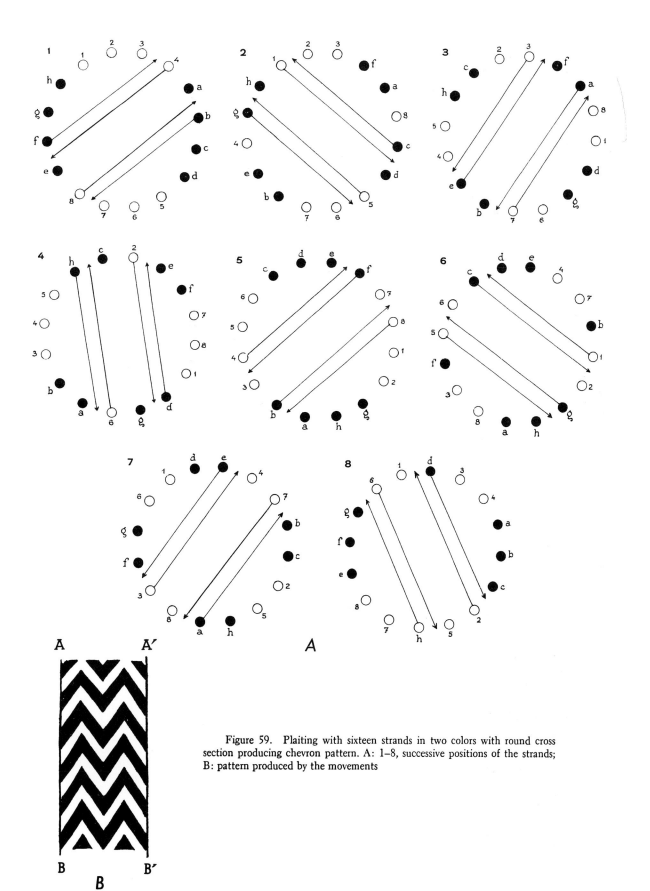

Figure 59. Plaiting with sixteen strands in two colors with round cross section producing chevron pattern. A: 1–8, successive positions of the strands; B: pattern produced by the movements

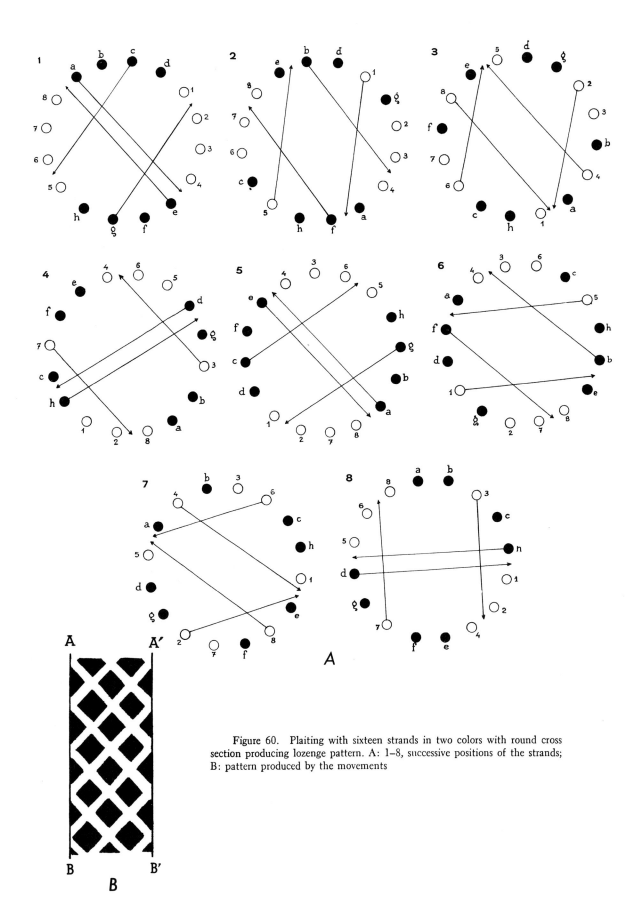

Figure 60. Plaiting with sixteen strands in two colors with round cross section producing lozenge pattern. A: 1–8, successive positions of the strands; B: pattern produced by the movements

Plaiting with twenty-four strands of three or four colors producing a round cross section and regular relief

This pretty plaiting (Fig. 61, B; Pl. 59, D) was especially in vogue at Nazca. It requires twenty-four strands of diverse thickness and of three colors. These varying thicknesses produce heavy relief symmetrically arranged, resulting in a special esthetic effect: twelve yellow strands consisting of two elements, eight gray strands of twice the thickness of the yellow strands, and, finally, four red strands consisting of four elements, each as thick as the yellow strands. The purpose of the yellow strands is to outline the motives and the pattern formed by the red and gray strands. The pattern is obtained by forty-eight movements, which have been illustrated in eight diagrams of six movements each; the strands in each diagram cross in a perpendicular direction those of the diagram that precede or follow it (Fig. 61, A).

Diagrams 1 to 8 of Figure 61, A, illustrate the exact arrangement of the crossings and the displacements of the strands, which are represented as follows: the eight gray strands by small letters and a white disk; the four red strands by capital letters and a half-white, half-black disk; the twelve yellow strands by numbers and a black disk.

The following is the order of the crossings and displacements: *b* and *f*, *2* and *6*, *8* and *12* cross each other to alternate positions; *c* and *g*, *3* and *11*, *5* and *9*, then *1* and *e*, *7* and *a*, and *A* and *C* move to take positions on the opposite side of the circle; then *10* and *d*, *4* and *h*, *B* and *D*, and so forth. It will be noted that diagrams 5 and 6 are not repetitions of 1 and 2, nor are 7 and 8 of 3 and 4; in the latter diagrams, the strands cross each other respectively within the group, *but in a reverse direction*, which permits them to resume their original position before commencing another cycle of forty-eight movements.

In diagrams 1 and 2 the four red strands have not yet moved. In 3 and 4 they change positions, and later in the plaiting they occupy a position ninety degrees from the original one. In diagrams 5 and 6 they do not move either, but in 7 and 8 they change positions again in order to resume their original place in the cylinder that forms the cord. These red yarns, in addition to being four times thicker than the yellow, frequently come together as pairs in the design, and this accounts for their great prominence.

Once the cycle has been finished, it can be repeated as many times as the length of the cord necessitates.

The plaiting I have just described has a variant in which an additional color supplements the three others. The decorative lozenges in semirelief, instead of being in a single color (red in the case mentioned above), can be of two different colors: the sling shown in Plate 61, C, is dark green and yellow (part of the cord included between the center of the sling and the slender terminal cords is of one color only). If strands A and C are green and yarns B and D yellow, the small lozenges they form will be half green and half yellow.

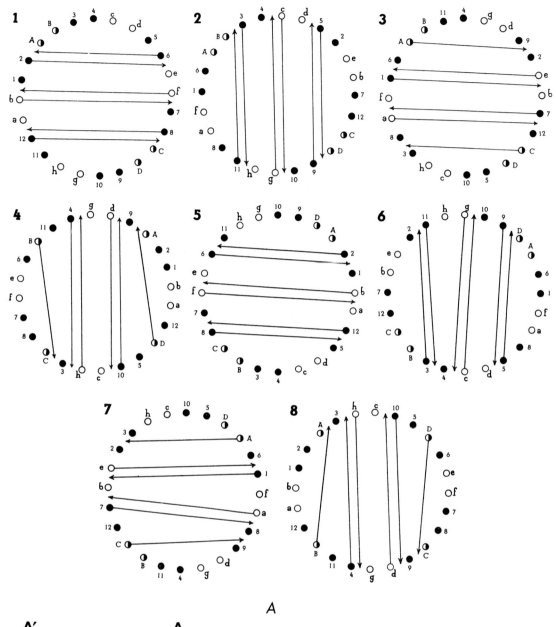

A

B

Figure 61.   Plaiting with twenty-four strands of three or four colors producing round cross section and regular relief in pattern. A: 1–8, successive positions of the strands; B: pattern produced by the movements

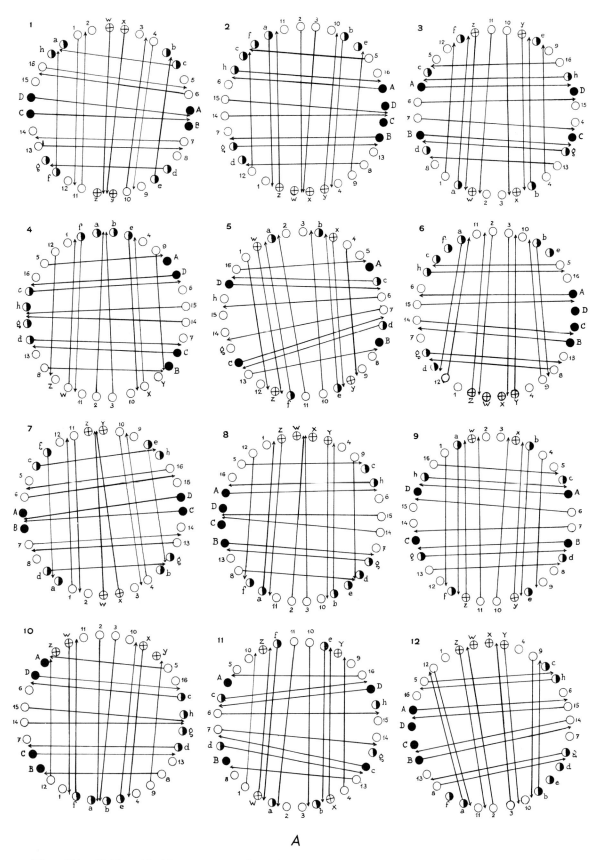

A

Figure 62A.   Plaiting with thirty-two yarns in four colors producing round cross section. 1–12, successive positions of the strands. Symbols: ○ white, ⊕ yellow, ● black, ◐ brown

Plaiting with thirty-two strands (sixteen plus sixteen) in four colors
producing a round cross section

This plaiting might well be called plaited-weaving, for the strands are divided into leases that alternately act as warp and weft in relation to each other. The strands are divided into four leases of eight strands each, placed opposite each other as if they formed the quarters of a circle (i.e., in Fig. 62, A, proceeding around the circle clockwise, strands *a* to *b* make up the first quarter; *c* to *d*, the second; *e* to *f*, the third; and *g* to *h*, the fourth; the first and third quarters constitute one set of two leases; the second and fourth, the second set of leases). The alternate crossing at right angles of the leases permits the strands of two leases to perform the office of weft for the crossing strands of the other two leases. Under these conditions, one might expect the plaiting to have a square cross section, but the elasticity of the wool, combined with slightly increased twisting of the strands that cross each other close to the edge of the lease, produces an almost cylindrical form. It is always the same sixteen strands (i.e., eight on each quarter of the circle) that constitute the two facing sections that intercross. There is never any interchange between the two sets of sixteen strands. Each set of sixteen yarns consists of eight white strands, four brown strands, four yellow strands in one set, and four black in the other.

Each strand, whether it belongs to the first or to the second set of leases, makes six crossings before returning to its place. The plaiting is done in the following manner: (1) eight strands of the first set of sixteen cross each other (Fig. 62, A, 1): *c*, 16, 6, D, C, 7, 13, *d*; (2) eight strands of the second set perpendicular to the first set intercross (Fig. 62, A, 1): 1, 11, W, X, 10, 4, *e*, *f*; (3) the still unused eight strands of the first set intercross in their turn (Fig. 62, A, 2): 5, *h*, A, 15, 14, B, *g*, 8; (4) the still unused eight strands of the second set do the same (Fig. 62, A, 2): 12, *a*, Z, 2, 3, Y, *b*, 9.

The pattern produced is that shown in Figure 62, B. It is obtained by 192 movements, which will be found in the twelve diagrams of Figure 62, A, each number containing two complete series of perpendicular movements. Although this plaiting with thirty-two strands is much more intricate, it is a development of many of the methods described previously, and a knowledge of the simpler techniques must be assumed. The pattern, too, is only a variant in four colors of the patterns already described (see Pl. 59, E).

Figure 62B. Plaiting with thirty-two yarns in four colors producing round cross section. Pattern produced by the movements in A

Figure 63. Plaiting with thirty-eight strands of four colors and varying thickness producing square cross section. A: 1–9, successive positions of the strands; B: pattern formed by the movements

Plaiting with thirty-eight strands of varying thickness in four colors (grouped twenty-six and twelve or twenty-four and fourteen) producing a square cross section

The plaiting of the cord producing the pattern shown in Figure 63, B, is extremely complex. The specimen comes from Nazca and is of four colors. As in the case of plaiting with twenty-four strands described above, the strands, for esthetic reasons, are of diverse thickness. Furthermore, the method of plaiting applies the same principle as that which produces cords with plain sections of two alternating colors (see the sling in Pl. 62), in that certain of its surface strands change regularly with those which, in the center, comprise the core of the cord (see p. 99). Its cross section is definitely square; the corners of the square coincide with the vertical lines AB, CD, EF, GH, which in Figure 63, B, pass through the center of the lozenges (see Pl. 59, C) (as in preceding patterns, Fig. 63, B, is pictured as though the braid were cut along the line A–B, A'–B', and laid out flat).

The plaiting requires thirty-eight strands in all: two coarse white strands, consisting of six elements, designated by the capital letters Y and Z and represented by a white disk; eight red strands, less coarse, consisting of four elements, designated by capital letters A to H and represented by a black disk; sixteen yellow strands, thinner than the red, consisting of three elements, designated by numbers 1 to 16 and represented by a half-white, half-black disk; twelve yellow brown strands, consisting of a single element, designated by small letters a to l and represented by a white disk quartered by a black cross.

Because the cord has a central core, the strands of which share only momentarily in the crossings of the plaiting that is in progress on the periphery, the plaiting is accomplished with only twenty-four strands at a time (or with twenty-six when the two white ones are visible), while the core is made with twelve strands (or fourteen when the two white ones are hidden in the center). These twelve strands, whose position with respect to each other is immaterial, are alternately either all yellow or eight yellow and four red. The four red strands are always the same: A, B, C, D. The yellow yarns, on the contrary, change by groups of four. There are three series of changes made through the length of the plaited lozenge (Fig. 63, A), that is, six series for the entire cycle of the pattern, which equals the length of two lozenges. The following are the movements of the red and yellow strands from center to periphery and vice versa: in diagram 1, strands 5, 6, 7, 8 go to the outside, and strands A, B, C, D reach the center; in diagram 3, A, B, C, D go to the outside, and 5, 6, 7, 8 reach the center; in diagram 7, 13, 14, 15, 16 go to the outside, and 1, 2, 3, 4, reach the center; in diagram 9, 9, 10, 11, 12 go to the outside, and A, B, C, D, reach the center; diagram 11, which is not depicted, would show A, B, C, D moving to the outside, and 9, 10, 11, 12 reaching the center; diagram 15 would show 1, 2, 3, 4 going to the outside, and 13, 14, 15, 16 reaching the center; diagram 17 would repeat diagram 1.

The twelve yellow brown strands remain always on the periphery and do not cease working; their role consists in outlining the various areas of the pattern and separating them from each other.

Until the momentary disappearance of the four red strands is required by the decorative motive, the intermingling of the two groups of four yellow strands seems justified only by the desire to make the core and its covering more compact, and thus the cord more attractive.

Diagrams 1 to 8, Figure 63, A, give the crossings and changes that are necessary to form the design of a completed lozenge, that is, half of the entire cycle. It seems unnecessary to give the movements of the strands for the second lozenge since these movements follow the rules of the first exactly. To diminish the number of schematic diagrams, from four to eight crossings, as well as the changes between the center and the periphery, have been grouped in each drawing. It will be noticed that the movements are symmetrical (one in each half of the circle). The following is the order of the movements of the brown and yellow brown strands shown in the diagrams: (1) *b, f, i, j* move; then the changes from center to periphery and vice versa of the other colors occur; (2) *e, d; 5, 8; a, h; 6, 7;* (3) changes of strands from center to periphery and vice versa of the other yarns; then *b, f; l, k;* (4) *G, H; 2, 4; c, g; 1, 3;* then *Y* and *Z* move to the periphery; (5) *E, F; h, a; e, d; C, A;* (6) *D, B; b, f; k, l;* then *Y* and *Z* return to the center; (7) *c, g; H, G; i, j;* then movements from center to periphery and vice versa of the other yarns; (8) *E, F; d, e; a, h;* (9) *i, j; k, l;* then movements from the periphery to center and vice versa of the other yarns.

The complete cycle is executed in 156 movements: the fine yellow brown strands make sixty crossings; the yellow strands make thirty-two changes from center to periphery and vice versa and sixteen crossings; the red strands make sixteen changes and twenty-four crossings; and the white strands make eight changes.

Plaiting-weaving with sixteen strands having the role of warp and with four or eight strands having the role of weft

This method, by means of which a thick flat braid is formed, partakes of weaving in that it uses two different elements, a warp and a weft, and of plaiting in that the strands of warp yarns, which have been arranged in groups of four of the same color, pass by and around each other, moving always in the same direction, between the passages of the cross strands or weft yarns. The four successive positions that are occupied lead to the assumption that the warp yarns are either free at the end opposite the plaiting or are freed periodically so that they can be untwisted. If the yarns were fastened at their two ends, plaiting would have to be accomplished with periodic reversals of the direction of the twisting of the yarns; this will be found in the third example that follows.

I have already given a preliminary analysis of this technique among the special methods of weaving (pp. 47–49). With the complete analysis of additional specimens, there is here given a new description of the technique with drawings; these will, I hope, make the preceding explanation simpler and clearer (see the slings in Pl. 32, A, C).

In the example used, the warp consists of the sixteen strands used to form the cords of the sling. They are divided into two leases of eight strands each. Theoretically, however, the warp can have a much larger number of strands, in which case a wider braid will result. The weft consists of four strands used, to begin with, at their center (as in Fig. 27), that is, with eight strands formed by their two free ends. These eight strands, generally of two colors, alternate row after row, making groups of four crossing together, two from right to left and two from left to right. The four yarns that do not move as weft are concealed between the warp yarns and in consequence are invisible, but at the edges of each row they appear in the border of the braid. By their alternation of crossing with the other four weft yarns that formed the preceding row and will form the following row, as well as their arrangement in two colors, they share in the formation of the pattern on the edges of the braid. The pattern in the central part will vary with the arrangement of the colors in the warp yarns and the rule of crossing of these yarns. Three examples of patterns are set forth below. In the first two, the yarns, in groups of four, always turn in the same direction around each other, maintaining successively four adjacent positions, two in the upper lease and two in the lower lease. In the third example, the direction of the twisting of the

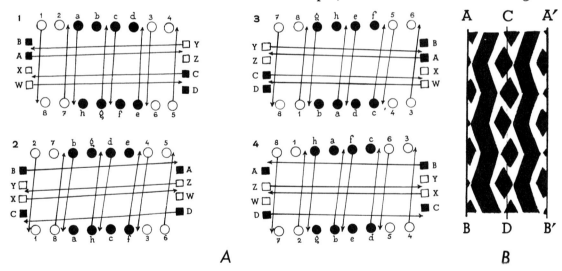

Figure 64.   Plaiting-weaving with sixteen strands as warp and eight strands as weft. A: 1–4, successive positions of the strands; B: pattern formed by these movements

yarns is reversed after the fourth movement; their twisting is thus suspended periodically. In each movement and weft passage there will be only eight yarns out of sixteen that cross, the other eight yarns crossing with the following row. This results in a simple twill 2/1 construction.

First example. The warp yarns are arranged in the following manner: four white yarns, eight black yarns, four white yarns; each group is divided into two leases that are opposite each other (Fig. 64, A, diagram 1). The pattern will be a black vertical band between two narrower white bands; actually this band zigzags a little toward the right, then toward the left (Fig. 64, B)[4] because it is displaced alternately to the right and left by the crossings on its edges of four weft yarns, which form small lozenges. This zigzag

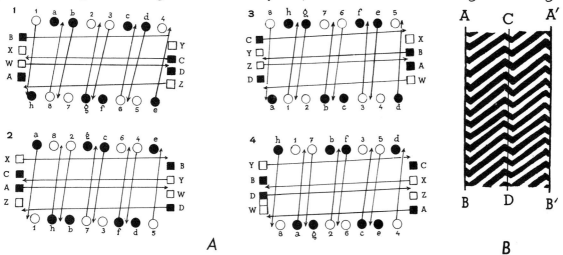

Figure 65. Plaiting-weaving with sixteen strands as warp and eight strands as weft. A: 1–4, successive positions of the strands; B: pattern formed by the movements

tends to disappear when the tightening of the weft yarns lessens. The order of crossing of the yarns is as follows: (diagram 1) wefts A, C, Y, W; then warps *1, 7, a, g, c, e, 3, 5*; (diagram 2) wefts B, D, X, Z; then warps *2, 8, b, h, d, f, 4, 6*, and so forth.

Second example. The warp yarns are arranged as follows: one white yarn in a lease across from a black yarn in the opposite lease; two black yarns across from two white yarns; two white yarns across from two black yarns; two black yarns across from two white yarns; one white yarn across from one black yarn. By this arrangement, the color of the braid is displaced after each weft passage, and consequently parallel diagonals in two tones are formed (Fig. 65, B); near the edges the weft yarns intervene in order to form a hook at the ends of the diagonals. The order of crossing of the yarns is as follows (see Fig. 65, A): wefts B, C, W, Z, then warps *1, 8, b, g, 3, 6, d, e*; wefts X, Y, A, D, then warps *a, h, 2, 7, c, f, 4, 5*, and so forth.

Third example. The warp yarns are arranged as in the second example above, but the movement of the warp yarns is such that the eight left-hand yarns turn around each other from the left to the right, and the eight right-hand yarns turn in reverse direction. After four movements, the direction of rotation is reversed for the two sides (Fig. 66, A, diagrams 4–8). The number of weft yarns, instead of being eight, is here reduced to four

---

[4] In this and the two figures that follow, the two faces of the braid are shown set out one after the other. Actually, the pattern should be folded at lines C-D; A', B' would thus join A, B.

(two white and two black). The rule of crossing of the strands is as follows: wefts *A* and *B*, warps *1, 8, b, g, f, c, 5, 4*; wefts *Y* and *Z*, warps *a, h, 2, 7, 6, 3, e, d*.

The handsome sling of Plate 64 is plaited in this method, but the order of crossing of the yarns is a little different, giving it a pattern that is a slight variant of Figure 66, B.

The examples of plaited cords that I have just given will suffice to show the ability and inventiveness of the workers who did the plaiting, to which the number of strands and the complexity of the crossings bear witness. In Plate 56, A, will be found a plaiting in the course of construction, in which can be seen, rolled into small balls, more than forty-two strands of wool (of a single color in this case) used in the plaiting of the braid.

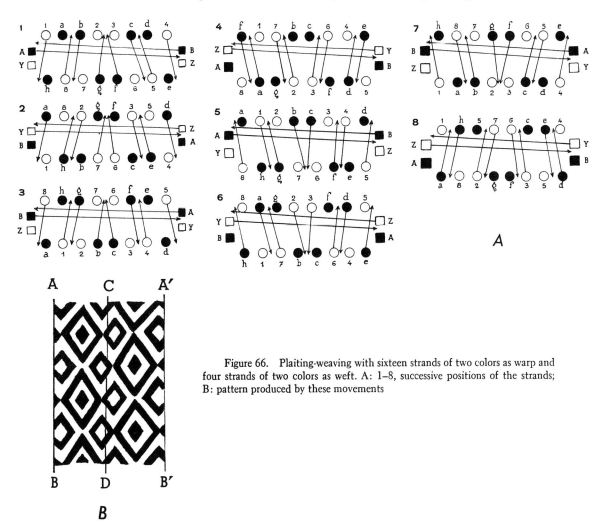

Figure 66. Plaiting-weaving with sixteen strands of two colors as warp and four strands of two colors as weft. A: 1–8, successive positions of the strands; B: pattern produced by these movements

Ordinary cords made of twisted fiber are sometimes wrapped or covered with plaiting quite comparable to that of modern drapery cords. The yarns of this covering are arranged around the central core in an even number sufficient to cover its surface, and they are fastened in this position by a circular tie. Plaiting is begun by moving alternately one yarn to the right and one yarn to the left, and proceeds by the method of simple crossing already described (see the cords of slings B and C in Pl. 61). In ceremonial slings, after the cover is plaited the central cord may be withdrawn, leaving only the tubular covering (see the sling in Pl. 63).

I mention again a special feature of this technique: the core of the cord, instead of consisting of yarns that are momentarily inactive in the plaiting, exists independently, and the strands not used in the plaiting are placed between the core and the wrapping.

Cords are found in which the wrapping is plaited in two colors, for example white and brown (Pl. 62), which succeed each other alternately for the length of the braid. They are made in an ingenious manner: the central core is made of a number of brown or white adjacent strands, which correspond to the number of yarns required for the plaiting of the wrapping. After the plaiting has been carried to a certain length, the yarns in the center are substituted yarn by yarn for those of the wrapping, which in its turn re-forms the core, while the new yarns, on the periphery, resume the plaiting of the wrapping. The operation continues with the regular alternation of the yarns of the central core and of the wrapping in their exchange of roles. This principle of substitution between the elements of the core and of the wrapping has already been applied in the plaiting with square cross section in four colors with thirty-eight strands of diverse thickness (Fig. 63, A, B).

Plaiting of soles for sandals

The first method of plaiting of sandal soles was discussed on p. 65. The second method (Pl. 60, B), which is quite different from the first, consists of superimposing one braid of three strands upon a second (with reversed direction of plaiting). The work is begun in the center of the sole by folding the braids back upon themselves at a distance of 7 or 8 centimeters [3 inches] from their ends; from this fold, the braids continue building the sole by wrapping the plaits in tight spirals. Thus there is obtained an elliptical surface whose shape is maintained by means of two yarns passed, as in the preceding method (p. 65; Fig. 41, B), through the thickness of the warped braids with long needles; hence these soles are sewed. By the tightening of the two yarns the sole is given a definite shape and firmness. This method corresponds to that which was used in Europe since neolithic times to make the soles of espadrilles. This was not a borrowing by the Peruvian Indians, for many pre-Columbian specimens attest its antiquity. It is a matter of independent invention.

Both these sandal soles and the ones discussed earlier are finished with a needle-made edge, described on page 136.

ELEVEN

Network

WE HAVE now completed a discussion of woven fabrics requiring two elements, warp and weft, and of plaited fabrics, requiring two systems of warps. Network is made with only one element, which interlaces or is knotted to itself.

NETWORK WITH ROWS OF SIMPLE LOOPS JOINED TO EACH OTHER

The simplest network used in Peru is that shown in Figure 67, A. The yarn first forms a series of loops or twists around a fixed support other than itself, usually merely another yarn. Having reached the end of the passage, it returns on the reverse side, forming a new series of loops, which this time are threaded through the corresponding loops of the first row; the third row will be threaded through the second, and the making of the network will continue in this way. The network is usually made in successive bands of quite narrow width, which are joined to each other laterally. This explains the thicker lines that can be seen in specimen B, Plate 65; they arise simply from the fact that in the bands other than the first, at the end of the rows of meshes, the yarn crosses the corresponding terminal mesh of the preceding band before returning on the reverse side to form a new row of meshes. If the width of the band is reduced to one single mesh, the appearance of the work will be as shown in Figure 67, B. In network with threaded loops the color of the yarn can be changed and consequently a design can be obtained (see Pl. 65, D). It is used impartially with yarns of agave, cotton, or wool. Comparison of Figure 44, C, with Figure 67, B, will show the similarity between the result of this technique and that of simple plaiting with interlocked yarns, but the method of obtaining it is different.

NETWORK MADE WITH SIMPLE LOOPING

This network differs from the preceding type in one particular, which completely changes its aspect. After having formed a loop, the yarn crosses it, then forms the next loop, which it crosses in turn, and so on, this looping is clearly shown in Figure 68. In order

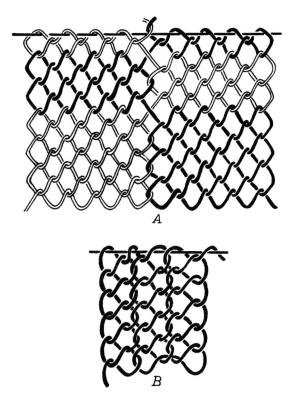

A

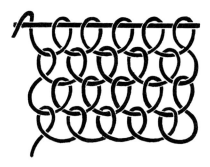

Figure 68. Network made with simple looping

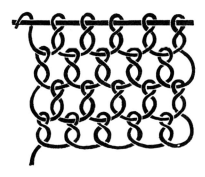

Figure 67. Network with loops threaded through each other. A: ordinary network in two colors; B: network in which each row consists of one loop only

Figure 69. Network made with simple looping in which the yarn makes a twist around the side of the mesh it has just formed

to prevent the network from curling, when a plain surface is desired, the direction of the loops is reversed for each new row. When the network is made in tubular form, spiraling around a central point, this special procedure is obviously not found. Network made with simple loops serves for many purposes. In the central coastal region and in the south, it was used either for a cotton skullcap intended as a foundation for the hair of a wig (Pls. 65, C; 78, C), or to form ornaments and borders on the bottoms of garments (Pls. 84, B; 107, A), or to form the interior reinforcement for embroidered motives, such as may be seen on the frieze of the Paracas textile (to be noted especially in 50 of Pl. 97).

NETWORK MADE WITH COMPLEX LOOPING

This is a variant of the above-mentioned stitch. The yarn, after having threaded the mesh of the upper row in the opposite direction to that of the network of simple looping, turns around one of the sides of its loop (Fig. 69). The little bag, specimen A of Plate 65, gives an example of the use of this stitch. Near the upper edge of the bag may be seen a new variant of the network: the yarn turns not only once but two or three times around one of the sides of the loop that has been formed. This lengthens the mesh and changes the appearance of the network.

NETWORK MADE WITH VENICE STITCH

Venice stitch is closely related to the simple looping stitch. There is the same inter-looping, but under each row is stretched a yarn that is taken up by each loop of the new row simultaneously with the corresponding upper loop (Fig. 70, A and B). Venice stitch is related to lace and by its nature can be used to fasten the ends of the stretched warps in a fabric, or to fill a space that requires decoration, or for mending. The face of the little

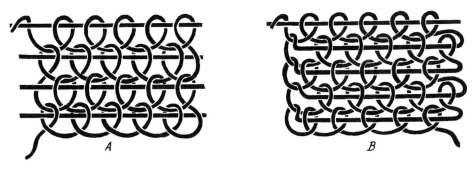

Figure 70.   Network made with Venice stitch. A: the transverse yarns are independent; B: the transverse yarns are made with the yarn of the network itself

figure shown in Plate 80, C, which comes from a specimen shown in Plate 17 of *Tissus indiens du Vieux-Pérou*, is done in Venice stitch, like those of similar figurines often found in graves in the central coastal area of Peru.[1]

NETWORK MADE WITH OVERLAPPING LOOPS

I have been able to study this network in a very pretty little bag belonging to the Museum für Völkerkunde of Munich (see Pl. 69, D). I have also seen it used in the making of solid articles (wrappings, carrying bags) with a yarn of vegetable fiber, which is coarse and unyielding (Pl. 79, C). Its appearance differs, depending upon whether or not the network is tightly pulled. The two specimens shown in Plates 69, D, and 79, C,

[1] See also Izikowitz (1932, Fig. 11, C).

demonstrate this clearly. When closely netted, as in the small wool bag in the Munich Museum, it has the appearance of plaiting with loops that cut back through the small horizontal chain after two crossings of the yarns have been completed. In fact, the network is made with loops which overlap spirally and which the yarn crosses and joins (cutting through two back loops) in accordance with the progression shown in Figure 71, A and B. The horizontal yarn in the center of Figure 71, B, is not indispensable and may be omitted.

NETWORK MADE WITH SUPERIMPOSED LOOPINGS

I have had the opportunity to examine a rare needle-made network (see Pl. 69, A, B), and for this privilege I am indebted to Professor Kroeber. The special nature of the technique of this network—which in a measure is related to the preceding one—lies in the fact that the rows of loops are not added to each other, but are superimposed upon each other in successive layers, each mesh of the row that is being formed being joined at one side, always the same side, to the corresponding mesh of the underlying row. Figure 72 shows the progression of the yarn, not in the general plan of the network, as, for example,

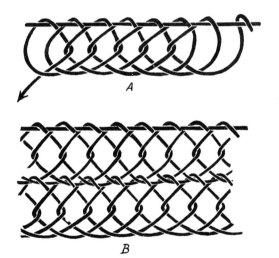

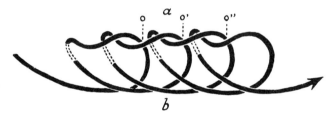

Figure 71 (left). Network made with overlapping loops. A: first row; B: two rows joined to each other

Figure 72 (above). Network made with rows of superimposed chains (seen as a cross section): *a*, reverse; *b*, right side

in Figure 71, but in a perpendicular plan. It is, then, the appearance of the network seen in cross section that is shown by the figure. It will be seen that the design formed by the loops is dissymetric. The side marked *a*, where the yarn is joined again to the row immediately below (the section indicated by dots), forms the reverse of the fabric; the side marked *b*, where the yarn remains visible, forms the right side. The next row will be formed over that which is shown in the figure, the yarn being joined as it passes under the crossings marked *o*, *o'*, and *o''*. The network thus made gives the impression on one face of a sort of plaiting, while on the other appear parallel and adjacent ridges (Pl. 69, A, B). Since the worker can change the color of her yarn when she so desires, there is an opportunity to make a design. It can be seen that the specimen reproduced in the plate was made in spirals. It may be assumed that meshes were added at intervals to the width, because each circle is larger than the preceding one.

NETWORK MADE WITH LOOP STITCH (WHICH HAS THE APPEARANCE OF KNITTING)

In other publications I have called this stitch "needle-knitting," and I regret it. This denomination can mislead the reader. It is not a question of knitting, but of a stitch that resembles it. The network made with this stitch has neither the supple qualities nor the defects of unraveling of true knitting.

The construction is similar to that of the first network above described, but the yarn, after the second row, instead of threading through each loop separately, forms a loop that takes up two adjacent loops at once (Fig. 73, II, A and B). The appearance of the stitch, and consequently of the network, differs according to the face of the fabric being considered. The regular alternation of the direction of the rows (one on the right side and the other on the reverse), when it is used, balances the general aspect of the two faces. When the meshes have been normally tightened, this network, made by needle, does not differ in appearance from knitting done with a hook or knitting needle. There is, however, a very important difference between the two which can be observed by firmly pulling the fabrics. In the true knitting stitch (Fig. 73, I), the yarn forms a loop that is open at the base; in

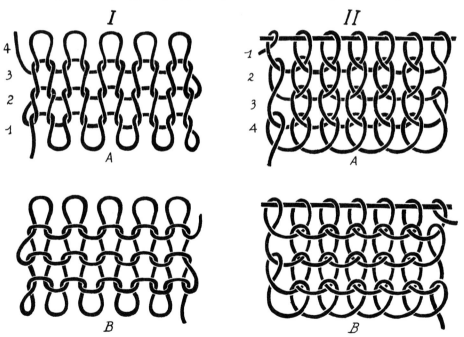

Figure 73. I. Network made in true knitting stitch. A: right side; B: reverse. II. Network made in loop stitch. A: right side; B: reverse

the Peruvian stitch that I shall call "loop stitch" (Fig. 73, II), a loop is formed that is closed by the crossing of the yarn, which passes back over itself. This closed loop tightens the corresponding loop in the preceding row, which cannot make the open loop of knitting. The practical consequences of this construction are that, if the yarn happens to break at some point in the network, the damage remains localized in the single mesh in which the yarn is broken, whereas in knitting the column of the broken mesh will open and the loops will slide and disintegrate one after the other. On the other hand, looped network is far from having the suppleness and elasticity of true knitting. Another difference from the point of view of construction: knitting is made in the reverse direction of that of looped network (see the numbers of the rows of meshes in Fig. 73, I, A; II, A). I do not know of any ancient knitting done in Peru by means of a hook or knitting needles, nor has any instrument comparable to a crochet hook been discovered in any archeological excavations.

Looped network can be made with a plain surface or in tubular form; it can be wide or narrow. Changes of color can be made, but in such cases the reverse of the network shows floats formed by the unused portion of the yarns (see Pl. 71, B). I do not believe that this network has often been used to make pieces of substantial size, in which no other fabric was combined. I can, however, mention some caps, like those shown in Plate 71, as well as a bag with a double pocket, made of quite strong wool, belonging to the Museum für Völkerkunde of Hamburg, the form of which approximates that of bags still used by the Indians of the Peruvian highlands to carry their provisions.

I shall not speak further at this point of looped network as far as network which is self-supporting is concerned. I shall speak of it at greater length when considering it as embroidery covering a reinforcing fabric in whole or in part.

NETWORK IN WHICH THE MESH IS HELD BY A SIMPLE KNOT

The common netting knot used in Peru is an unstable one. It is a simple (overhand) knot joining the yarn that forms the new mesh row to the center of the corresponding mesh of the preceding row (Fig. 74). It is in this way that fish nets, carrying nets, and the more delicate nets that are suspended like little bags from the beam bars of scales (Nordenskiöld, 1930, Pl. N), and so forth are made (see Pl. 66, C). This knot does not prevent slipping of the cord or yarn it entwines, and this defect can cause a distortion of the network.

With this simple knot fabrics can be made in which the meshes are reduced to practically nothing, for all the knots touch each other. In this case it is evident that no slipping need be feared. When all of the knots are made on the same side and in the same direction, the appearance of the network is not identical on both faces because of the dissymmetry of the knots that form it. In the technique of simple knots the worker can change the color of her yarn as often as she wishes, and this enables her to obtain fine and varied designs. Plate 67 shows three important examples of this network. It can be seen in specimens B and C of the plate that on the surface the visible parts of the knots, which generally appear in the form of small parallel lines, face each other at right angles; analysis shows that at this point the network has been recommenced in a direction perpendicular to that of the general progression. It can also be seen in specimen B, which is remarkable for its fineness and perfection, that the visible parts of the knots, in certain places, follow an oblique progression in the form of a V with their axis on the same diagonal. This effect arises from the fact that the worker has made the consecutive knots in opposite directions in the same mesh; the same network covers and completely envelops the large fringed tassel that completes the specimen. It is difficult to realize, at first glance, that there, too, a similar tech-

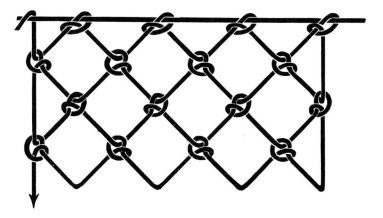

Figure 74. Netting with uniform meshes fastened with a simple knot

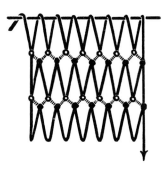

Figure 75. Netting with irregular meshes fastened with a simple knot. The plain lines indicate the rows executed from left to right; the striated lines indicate the rows of the return passage executed from right to left

nique is involved. In specimen A, the rows of knots are all parallel to each other, but in every second row the meshes have the dominant role, and from this results a network with regular open spaces (see Fig. 75).

NETWORK IN WHICH THE MESH IS HELD BY A KNOT IN THE
FORM OF TWO HALF HITCHES (SQUARE KNOT)

There is still another more solid and more elegant knot. It consists of two adjacent half hitches made in opposite directions (Fig. 76) (square knot). It is to be found made of agave, cotton, or wool, depending upon the purpose for which it is required. Like the simple knot studied previously, it has three distinct forms. Sometimes, after each knot, the yarn forms quite a large mesh, the dimensions of which remain constant, and which gives the work the appearance of true netting (Pl. 66, A, D). Sometimes the meshes exist in certain places only, while in other places the knots touch each other, permitting the

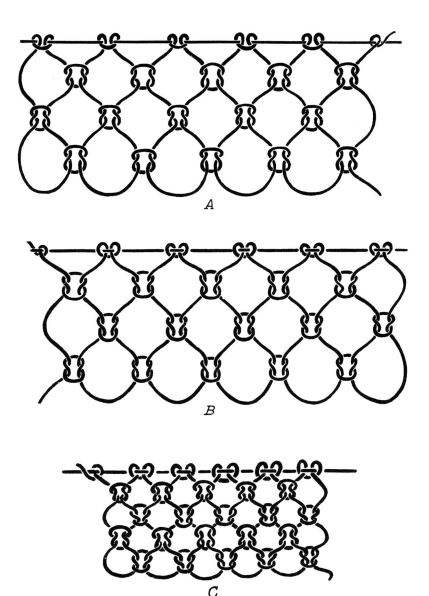

Figure 76. Network made with square knot. A: netting with uniform meshes seen on the right side; B: the same netting seen from the reverse; C: network made with closely placed knots executed in rows in alternating directions

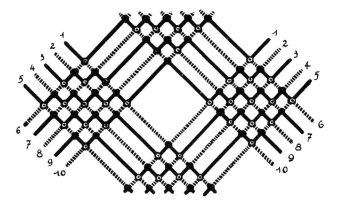

Figure 77. Network with meshes of unequal size executed in square knot (Pl. 66, B). The plain lines indicate the rows executed from left to right; the striated lines indicate the rows of the return passage executed from right to left

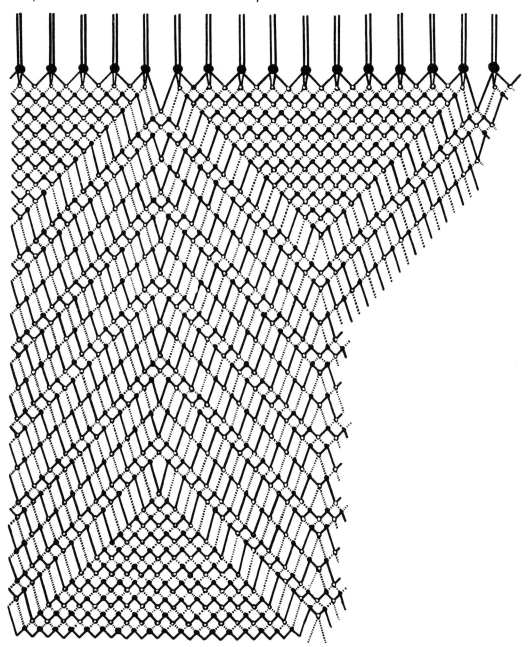

Figure 78. Arrangement of meshes of the network of the cap shown in Plate 70, B. The meshes of this network are not uniform and were executed in square knot. The plain lines indicate the rows executed from left to right; the striated lines indicate the rows of the return passage executed from right to left

making of a design that may be very graceful (Pl. 66, B; Fig. 77), or the meshes of varied size may themselves form the design by their arrangement (Pl. 70, B; Fig. 78).[2] Finally, sometimes all of the knots touch each other, the yarn passing directly from one knot to another without forming appreciable meshes; the tightened network that results does not

[2] These networks of unequal mesh are usually intended to be completed by needle embroidery. They were in common use in Peru until the nineteenth century, especially in fabrics intended for altar use and for priests' vestments, communion cloths, albs, rochets, and so forth.

show, at first glance, any resemblance to the others, even though the knot itself is identical. It is used in the making of fine articles, particularly caps, which most frequently are of wool.

The appearance of the knot formed by the two half hitches differs, depending upon which face of the fabric is being considered (Fig. 76, A, B). When the knotting is done with a coarse yarn and large meshes, the network usually shows alternating rows of knots on the right side and on the reverse. In this case, the worker always proceeds in the same direction, merely turning the work over at the end of each row, and from this fact arises the alternation we see. In fine work with close knots, the knots seem to be made on the same side except when the difference in the two faces is used for a decorative purpose. It is as easy to make the knot in one direction as in the other. Schematically, it can be represented with some exactitude by a short horizontal line for the right side, and by a **U** for the reverse face. I have used this method of representation to indicate the different aspects shown by the network when it is executed on the right side, on the reverse, in alternate rows, or in knots made in opposite directions (Fig. 79, A, B, C, D, and E). Finally, the figure shows at F the ornamental arrangement of the knots in the bonnet reproduced in Plate 72, B: lozenges are formed on the bandeau, and oblique lines, which meet each other, are formed on the upper part. The other bonnet in Plate 72 is made of rows of knots formed

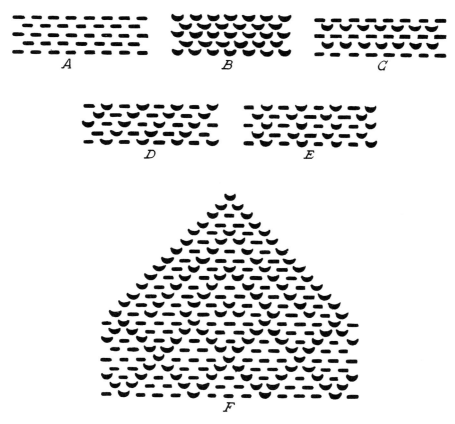

Figure 79. Schematic appearance of a tightly made network executed in square knot. A: right side; B: reverse; C: rows with alternating right and reverse sides of knots; D and E: with knots in alternate directions, right side and reverse; F: order of knots in the cap shown in Plate 72, B

in alternate directions; its bandeau is made of rectangular pieces worked on the four sides, which are then joined to one another. It may be noted that, whatever may have been written on the subject, as far as I know there has been no discovery in Peru of a network made with the dissymmetric knot used in modern netting (see Fig. 80).[3]

NETWORK MADE WITH LOOP OR CUT PILE (WITH THE
APPEARANCE OF VELOUR); "FURRED" CORDS

This network resembles velour; it is, however, essentially different from it in structure. Velour normally requires one warp, one weft, and a third element (usually a second weft), the small loops of which, when cut, form the "pile" of the fabric. In Peru we find a network made with a single yarn into which the element forming the pile was incorporated. The technique can be explained very briefly: it is simply the Chinese or square knot, made with two half hitches by the method that has just been examined. The special feature of the technique consists of incorporating an independent wool yarn along with the yarn of the network while making the two half hitches. The yarn of the network is usually cotton. The independent wool yarn, caught between two consecutive knots, will form a loop (Fig. 81, A); if the network is continued in this fashion, it will present a somewhat fleecelike appearance (Pl. 75, A, B); if the loops are cut and the two free ends untwisted, the yarn ends will, strictly speaking, be the equivalent of the cut pile of *"simili-velours"* (Fig. 81, B). In the figure, the cut pile is incorporated only in every other row of knots; in this not unusual case, the network is made with rows of knots formed alternately on the right side and on the reverse. The knotting is carried out easily; the wool yarn forming the loop or, later, the cut pile is placed in the form of a **U** on the lower part of the mesh, which is itself curved downward and through which the needle will pass to form the knot. The two yarns, mesh and loop, are then tightened simultaneously by the knot. When the wool yarn is added in all the rows of knots instead of in every other row, the *"simili-velours"* is thicker and more beautiful.

Network with closed loops or cut pile seems to have been used only in the southern region and for fine articles, chiefly bonnets and bandeaux; at least no larger specimens are known up to the present. This technique permits the making of many varied designs, with as frequent changes in

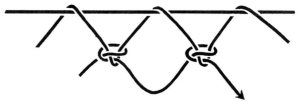

Figure 80. Network executed in the modern dissymetric knot (sheet bend)

color as the worker desires. The monochrome surface can be reduced to the two ends of the wool yarn passed through a knot. This yarn is firmly secured to the network; its single

---

[3] After re-examination of the specimens I have available, it does not seem that the knot (sheet bend or modern netting knot) shown in Fig. 1, *a* and *b*, of the article by Singer (1936, p. 16) was used in any of these specimens.

110

strands can be pulled without the risk of seeing any of them slip and become loose. Crawford has assigned to this network (1916c, p. 150) a schematic plan in which the yarn forming the cut pile seems to follow a progression not very well defined. This author refers to a specimen similar to those which I have studied and which are shown in Plates 73 and 74, and it is for this reason that I take the liberty of making the above comment. Furthermore, if the supplementary yarn were to be incorporated in the simple manner indicated by Crawford, it would lack security and the least pulling on one of its ends would easily displace it.

There is another type of procedure in which the knots are all made on the same side, the right side, and each one contains the cut pile yarn. In it the appearance of velour is more uniform and the cut pile is more compact. This type is used especially when trimming a tubular article with a "furred" decoration. In this case, the network turns in spirals, always in the same direction, thus forming a very small central cavity. The cord shown in Plate 76, B, was made in this way.

Those cords of the "chenille" family were made by two other methods. One of these methods, which has been described perfectly by Crawford, consists of arranging the cut pile around three small central cords by means of another yarn, which turns spirally around them, taking them up successively in a loop (Fig. 82). In this method there is thus no central cavity. The pile owes its firmness to the extreme tightness of the yarn that binds it (see Pl. 76, C).

The third method, used particularly in "furred" monochrome wrapping, is much simpler. First a long fringe, composed of four cotton warp yarns crossed by a wool weft, is formed as shown in Figure 83, A. After weaving, the terminal loops of the short wefts are cut along line *a–b*. The fringe thus made is then wrapped in tight spirals around the cord to be decorated, care being taken to leave the strands of the fringe free. The "furred" part of the fringe shown in Plate 61, A, was made in this way. The fringe can also be set up as shown in Figure 83, B. In this case the cotton yarns are reduced to two, and they are twisted around each other; they are no longer warp yarns, but rather weft yarns (Pl. 74, C). This method also permits the wrapping, one against the other, of two separate fringes of different colors around the same cord at the same time.

NETWORK MADE WITH PERUKE STITCH

There is still another manner of arranging yarns, pile, or hair in a network. The Peruvians no doubt thought that this independent element, since it had to be kept long and was of a slippery nature, must be attached in a particularly firm manner. They were thus inspired to invent another knot, a more complex descendant of the one we have just studied, but a knot that defies displacement of the independent element, however slippery it may be.

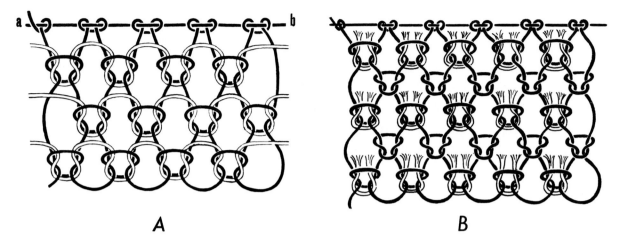

Figure 81.   Compact network executed in square knot with loop or cut pile. A: decorative wool yarn caught in each knot; B: decorative wool yarn caught in every other row of knots; ends cut to form the Peruvian *"simili-velours"*

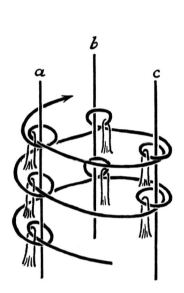

Figure 82.   Method of fastening around three vertical yarns the elements that form the cut pile of certain furred cords. Actually, the three yarns *a, b, c* touch each other

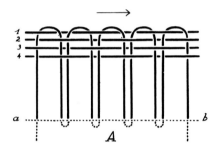

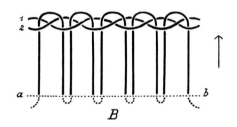

Figure 83.   Fringes intended to be wrapped vertically around a cord in order to produce a furred effect. A: warp made of four yarns; B: weft of two yarns (*1* and *2*) twisting around each other. The short warps are to be cut along line *a–b* in order to form the cut fringe

Figure 84.   Network executed in peruke stitch

This is the technique: it is commenced by making a knot with the yarn of the network in the form of two half hitches, which lock the yarn of the preceding row of knots and the independent element, as in network with cut pile. Instead of passing immediately to the following knot, however, the yarn of the network forms two loops (in certain specimens only one loop) around the apex of the angle formed by the independent element. Finally, a last loop has to be made, the progression of which can easily be followed in Figure 84. The normal tightening of this loop, which renders the independent element a twofold prisoner, gives the knot the double effect that can be seen in Plate 76, D, at the point where the independent yarn, partially worn away, leaves the network almost bare.[4]

The knots of peruke stitch are extremely firm, but coarse; they are used only to hold in place rather long, independent elements that can cover and conceal them. They are easily made in spite of their seeming complexity. The Peruvians used them for making small cases (as for needles and the like), which were wrapped with multicolored wool (Pl. 76, A); for headdresses (which often included simulated wigs); and for true wigs of wool and hair. The network for the wigs takes the form of a skullcap and is made by spiral turns around a central point. The strands of wool or hair taken up in each knot are overlapped and spread around the head, as in a real head of hair. There are also highly decorated wigs made of llama wool, which are in the form of a cylindrical turban composed of rows of knots turning in circles, like the knitting of a stocking. From each knot emerge coarse double or quadruple yarns, actually little wool cords, which, untwisting when they leave the network or a little later, look like long red or blond hair (Pl. 77). Three human figures in the frieze of the Paracas mantle are shown wearing wigs of this type (10, Pl. 90; 24, Pl. 93; 74, Pl. 101; see also the wig in Pl. 78, B).

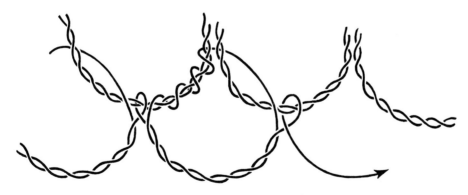

Figure 85.   Network with double twisting of the yarns

In other wigs, the complex knot that I have just described is not used, as for example specimens A and C reproduced in Plate 78. The hair was incorporated in a large braid (specimen A), or in a network with a simple loop stitch (specimen C), but after the making of the braid or the network. Here there was no fear of the slipping of the hair,

[4] The schematic plan of peruke stitch given by Izikowitz (1933, Fig. 5) is not accurate.

which was firmly attached to the network in tufts, or which, after its passage through the network, was braided, thus obviating the possibility of any displacement.

NETWORK MADE WITH DOUBLE TWISTING OF THE YARN OF EACH MESH

It was on an archeological specimen from the Cajamarca region that I found this network (see Pl. 79, A, B). It consists of a very compact bag or pouch made of somewhat coarse and stiff vegetable fiber. The network was spirally formed around a central point; the rows of meshes placed one below the other become successively wider to conform with the dimensions of the specimen. The progression of the yarn in the construction of a mesh can be followed in Figure 85. After having described the curve required for the formation of the new mesh, the yarn passes through the mesh of the preceding row, returns behind it joining it to the adjacent mesh, wraps around this mesh, then twists around itself before forming the following mesh, and continues its progression in this manner. This produces a very compact and sturdy network.

NETWORK MADE WITH SMALL RINGS ARRANGED IN ROWS OF FIVE AND JOINED TO ONE ANOTHER

This is a needle-made network of brown and white wool which covered the body of an Indian exhumed in the desert of Atacama (see Pl. 75, C). The worker first made a series of small separate circles of equal size with her yarn, making two turns for each circle. These rings or circles were covered and joined to each other with the knot already studied, formed of two half hitches (this knot when pulled as shown in Fig. 86 and Pl. 75, C, is

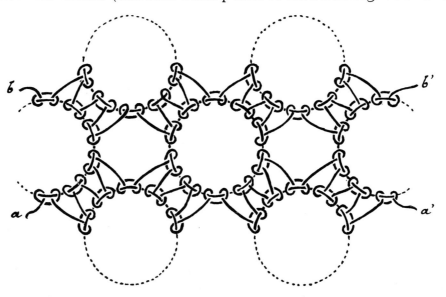

Figure 86. Schematic diagram of a network composed of small rings interknotted

114

called the larkshead). The work was accomplished with successive narrow bands joining the lower half of the rings of one row to the upper half of the rings of the row placed below it, or vice versa. In Figure 86 can be seen the passage of yarns *a–a'*, *b–b'*, which join the rings in the manner just explained. Each ring was encircled by ten knots and thus covered by twenty yarns, as the formation of a knot requires two loops around the ring. In order that the work should be regular and that the joining of a ring to its four neighbors should be even, the number of yarns covering one quarter of the ring had to be uneven. A whole ring had to be covered with five times four, or twenty yarns (that is, two and a half knots per quarter-circle times four), as seen in the specimen shown in Plate 75, or seven times four yarns making a total of twenty-eight covering yarns. In this network, the knots are dissymmetric, so that the two faces of the network have a slightly different appearance. In order that the progression of the yarn joining the rings to each other may be more easily followed in Figure 86, the rings have been arranged at a short distance from each other. Actually they are close to each other, and the knots formed by the yarn touch each other and draw the rings closely together.

TWELVE

Felt

J̲ᴜsᴛ a word about felt: its principle was apparently known to the ancient Peruvians, as the specimen shown on Plate 70, A, seems to show. But until an article of more characteristic compressed pile fibers has been found—and personally I do not know of one—it is wise to reserve one's judgment.

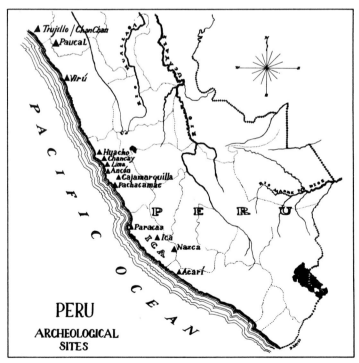

PERU

ARCHEOLOGICAL SITES

PART III

Ornamentation and Trimming of Fabrics

THIRTEEN

Embroideries

Embroideries presuppose the existence of a foundation fabric into which decorative stitches can be incorporated. Among the embroideries I am going to examine are several that, for regularity, continuity, and even in the structure of stitches, are very close to the network studied in the preceding part. They differ from the network, however, in that they are executed on a foundation fabric, from which they cannot be separated and which they sometimes entirely cover.

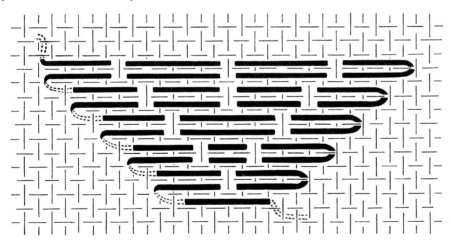

Figure 87.   Embroidery that resembles brocade

SIMPLE EMBROIDERIES RESEMBLING BROCADE OR TAPESTRY

The simplest Peruvian embroidery is similar to weaving with supplementary weft (brocading), which we have already examined (p. 38). In contrast to brocading, however, the decorative yarn is introduced after weaving, by means of a needle, between the two consecutive wefts or two adjacent warp yarns, following the chosen design. This yarn passes successively over varying widths on one face of the fabric or the other, according to the design. It returns to make a second line at the side of the first, then a third at the side of the second, and so on, until the desired surface is covered. The yarns of the embroidery are more or less close to each other, but they remain parallel to either the warp or the weft of the fabric (Fig. 87). It is rare to find Peruvian embroidery in which the yarn crosses the warp or the weft obliquely at will (see, however, the progression of the decorative yarn in Pl. 16, B). Usually the embroidery covers only limited areas, and it generally consists of a scattering of simple motives, such as birds, fish, feathers, and the like, while in weaving with supplementary weft, the design spreads over wide bands, if not over the entire surface of the fabric. However, as the appearance of embroidered fabric and brocade is the same, one can only be sure that the specimen is really embroidery if minute examination of it discloses the incidental overlapping of the decorative yarn from one weft row into another, or the piercing of a yarn by a needle, or the covering of one ornamental yarn by another. Embroidered fabric, like brocade, is different on its two faces (Pl. 80, A, B).

I should also mention one quite rare variant introduced into the method of embroidery just described; it occurs when an ornamental yarn, isolated from its fellows, crosses the surface of the fabric for a long distance without being incorporated into it. It is then fastened at intervals by a perpendicular stitch or by two stitches in the form of a cross, obviously for a decorative purpose (see Pl. 47, B).

Embroidery yarn can be passed twice between each weft of the foundation fabric, picking up on the outward passage the warp yarns of the even rows and on the return passage the warp yarns of the odd rows, or vice versa, as in darning stitch, with the result that the fabric (which as a rule is plain-weave cotton) is quite concealed by the embroidery. This is true tapestry-embroidery, which is sometimes difficult to distinguish from tapestry fabric made by the method described on pages 24–25.

EMBROIDERY WITH FLAT, SMOOTH STITCHES

Embroidery made with flat stitches consists of covering a given surface of a fabric on the right side and on the reverse with parallel yarns placed as close to each other as possible, without regard to the angle at which the embroidery yarns cross the yarns of the fabric. The embroidery is thus the same on both faces of the cloth, but one side is a little more carefully executed than the other. This method was known in Peru, but there the

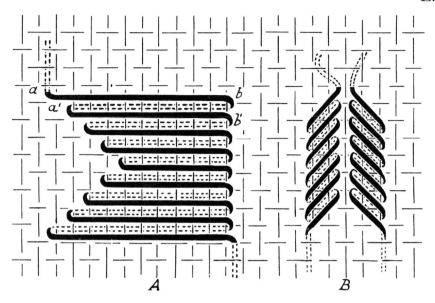

Figure 88. Embroidery in flat stitch. A: in lines parallel to the elements of the fabric;
B: in regular oblique lines forming chevrons

embroidery yarn was usually kept parallel to one of the elements of the fabric, as in the preceding type. As a rule, embroidery made with flat stitches presupposes the stretching of the fabric on the loom or a frame. The old chroniclers—and particularly Garcilaso de la Vega (1609, I, IX, chap. xiv)—have informed us that the Peruvians were still using this method at the time of the Conquest. Figure 88, A, shows the yarn emerging at point *a* and re-entering at point *b'*, very close to *b*, and so on, forming in this way on the two faces of the fabric a sequence of parallel lines that touch each other. This stitch left the embroideress entirely free to choose the colors to be used and the surface to be covered (see Pls. 80, D, E; 82, A). As a rule she avoided long yarn floats so that the embroidery would not be distorted after it was taken off the frame. This principle was especially observed in Peru. If the surface to be covered was wide, it was divided into smaller adjacent sections, which were embroidered successively.

In some cases small, adjacent, polychrome patterns made with stem stitches cover the entire fabric, which then serves simply as a canvas. The specimens in Plates 84, C, E, and 55, E (upper), are embroidered in this way; in appearance they are like tapestry.

As executed by the Peruvians, embroidery in flat stitch permits of a variant, the appearance of which is quite different although the principle of the stitch may be ad-

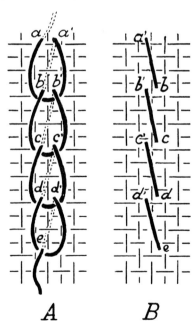

Figure 89. Embroidery in chain stitch. A: right side; B: reverse

121

hered to: the worker covers a given surface of the fabric with narrow adjacent columns of flat stitches that face each other obliquely, thus forming chevrons (Fig. 88, B). The two faces of the embroidery are naturally similar (see Pl. 83, A, B). The embroideress can change the color of the yarn at will.

EMBROIDERY WITH CHAIN STITCH

Chain stitch, as it is executed in our day, consists (Fig. 89, A) of making a loop with the embroidery yarn, which is held to the fabric by a knot at *a*; reinserting the needle at *d'* and drawing it out at *b*; making a second loop with the yarn, reinserting the needle at *b'*, and drawing it out at *c*; and continuing the embroidery in this way. This forms a column of meshes placed one under the other. The column can, of course, change direction and curve to follow the lines of a design; and finally, if the columns are placed close to one another, a given surface of the foundation fabric can be covered. The Peruvians certainly knew chain stitch (see Pl. 84, D), but, contrary to the conclusion to which a superficial examination might lead, they used it very sparingly, preferring the vertical loop stitch, as we shall see. Chain stitch can be made in the reverse direction of that just described, that is, by inserting the needle at *e* and drawing it out at *d'*, and so forth (Fig. 89, A); there is no obstacle to this method, although it is less practical than the first. It is possible that the Peruvians continued using it because of its similarity to loop stitch.

By examining the reverse of the embroidered fabric, one can differentiate at a glance between embroidery done with chain stitch and that done with loop stitch, although they closely resemble each other. In the first case, the column forms a series of small, vertical floats placed one under the other (Fig. 89, B); in the second case, the column forms a series of small, horizontal, parallel floats (Fig. 90, D). This difference in the fastening of the meshes to the fabric was used judiciously by the embroideress, whether it was a question of joining the yarns on the edge of a fabric to each other by a column perpendicular to them (chain stitch) or by a column parallel to them (loop stitch).

EMBROIDERY WITH LOOP STITCH

Horizontal direction

This is a stitch similar to that already described under this name (see p. 104), and like the latter it was most commonly made in horizontal rows; but, instead of the network formed being independent, the yarn is incorporated into the fabric between each loop (see Fig. 90, A). The embroidery thus produces columns of meshes on one face of the fabric and a series of small horizontal lines on the other. The columns may touch each other and cover the fabric with a complete mesh, or they may be more widely spaced and leave the foundation fabric visible (see Pl. 81, A, B, or C, D). In some cases the yarn is incorporated into the fabric only every three or four columns; because the embroideress was using a netting stitch, she was able to dispense, even completely, with a foundation fabric.

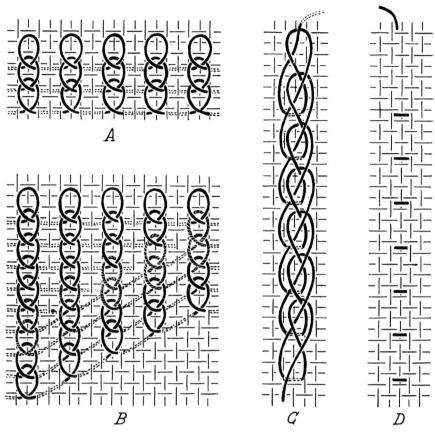

Figure 90.   Loop-stitch embroidery executed, A: in horizontal lines; B: in oblique lines; C and D: in vertical lines (right side and reverse)

Oblique direction

The presence of a foundation fabric permits the making of loops not only in horizontal rows, but also in oblique rows. In this case the yarn, after having made a loop, forms the next one in the neighboring column but in the row above, no longer at its own level (Fig. 90, B). The oblique progression of the yarn does not cause any change in the appearance of the embroidery, but on the reverse the little floats are slanted instead of horizontal. The making of a design is facilitated by this method, which gives the embroideress the opportunity of passing from one level to another with the same yarn.

Vertical direction on an edge or border

Loop stitch can also be made in vertical rows, as I have indicated above. From this fact arises a modification in its form, explained in Figure 90, C. The yarn forms a series of figure-eight stitches passing into one another, the base of each necessarily being fastened into the fabric. After the loop stitch is tightened it looks like chain stitch, but it is thicker. The reverse of the fabric shows little horizontal lines arranged one under the other (Fig. 90, D). The Peruvians made a variety of embroideries with vertical loop stitch, of which the specimens shown in Plate 85 are good examples (see the detached columns on the sides resulting from the destruction of the foundation fabric). In addition, they often used this method for borders of garments, pouch bags with straps, and many other articles. The column of meshes is placed on the very edge of the fabric; the yarn crosses it at each stitch, as in the border made in scallop stitch (see Pl. 17, A, B). See page 135 for descriptions of such borders.

Network embroidery with loop stitch, covering a fabric

Loop stitch was used, particularly in the Paracas region, as network embroidery for covering a fabric on its two faces and sometimes even in a third dimension, on its rounded edges. If the foundation fabric is in the form of a modeled figure, the embroidery follows

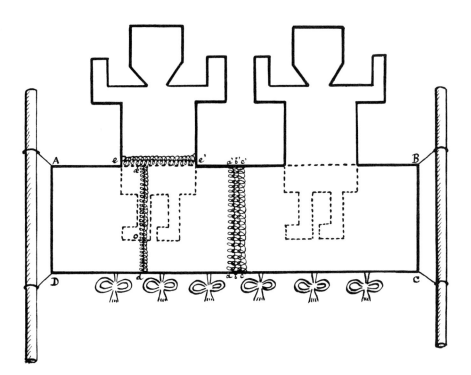

Figure 91. Diagram of embroidered network covering the border of the textile shown in Plate 88

its basic contours and may even complete it with details. Such is the case with the specimens reproduced in Plates 86, B, and 87, and also in the astonishing friezelike border that surrounds the textile shown in Plate 88 and of which Plates 89 to 104 represent the small

124

figures in actual size. These specimens usually have a base made with a tape upon which the small figures are grafted. The covering was done in the following manner. Let us assume that a portion *A B C D* of the tape foundation was stretched between the two bars of a frame (Fig. 91). The worker, starting from *a*, formed a first row of loops from *a* to *a'*. She continued the row *a* to *a'* without interruption around the edge of the tape and then back on the other face; returning on the first face, she crossed her yarn through the tape at point *b*, located next to *a*, and proceeded with the making of the second row of meshes, joining them to the first. She continued her work in this way for as long as the network was of the same color. When the meshes were to be made in another color, the worker discarded her original yarn and made the required number of meshes with a second yarn of a new color. If the design was to be symmetrical on the two faces she submerged this yarn under the meshes of the first yarn in the tape foundation, where it remained as a float until required again. The worker next resumed her first yarn and continued her row. On the other face of the tape she worked in the same way.

We have been considering a simple case in which two colors alternated. Embroidered designs could, in fact, be made in more than two colors, and changes of color made in such manner were frequent. The task of the embroideress was thereby rendered more difficult and intricate, but the method was the same. I had the good fortune to find a partially completed specimen (Pl. 87, B) that revealed the method of construction; it proved my assumption correct. By this method the symmetry of the design on both faces of the fabric was assured; this is disclosed by a careful examination of the friezelike compositions shown in Plates 87 and following.

Loop stitch is not limited to covering the band proper. It covers and completes the small figures, whose forms, roughly set up in simple looping (see p. 101), were attached to the edge of the tape (Fig. 91, *e–e'*). This embroidery (or covering) was pursued in a direction perpendicular to that of the tape foundation, but the regularity of the network embroidery was not affected because the meshes presented reasonably equal dimensions in gauge and compactness and they were linked to each other by equal loops whether in columns or in rows.

The complex forms of the figures make the development very difficult, necessitating frequent widening or narrowing, with changes of direction of the stitches. The work is further complicated by the fact that the figures are carrying all kinds of accessories, such as utensils, arms, plants, and so forth, and are themselves in modeled form—nose, arms, hairdress. It is in these specimens that the manual skill of the workers can be appreciated in its entirety. The accessories are grafted on to the principal figures in the same way in which the latter are attached to the tape; because of their minuteness, their development by loop stitch requires scrupulous care. I point out especially some tubular network around a single yarn whose rows consist of only four meshes, the last interlocked to the first—

125

stems of plants, rays extending from the head, tongues of the figures—and those tubular pieces are often of two colors, one mesh of yellow alternating with one of violet. Some of the accessories are covered with loose rows of excess meshes that have the appearance of small, unattached loops, such as appear in the paws and tails of the animals carried in the mouths of figures 6, 13, 21, etc. of the Paracas mantle. Finally, certain surfaces covered with loop stitch have open spaces obtained by the intentional omission of certain meshes.

The direction of the loop stitch in the network covering a foundation is generally horizontal. To this there is one remarkable exception. With regard to the covering of the tape, I have said that the yarn, having reached the end of each row of meshes on the opposite face to that of its starting point, crosses the tape close to the edge in order to make a new row. This procedure leaves the tape visible on one of its edges. To remedy this defect, the workers covered the surface of the foundation that was still visible with a column of loop stitches made in a vertical direction. The meshes of this column and of the remainder of the network are so similar and so meticulously arranged opposite each other that only a fortuitous examination of an unraveled section of the tape enabled me to isolate the column of edging from the yarn of the foundation that it covered, and thus to understand the method used.

STEM-STITCH EMBROIDERY

This embroidery belongs chiefly to the southern region. It is usually applied with wool yarn to a plain-weave cotton, which is used as a canvas. This fabric is sometimes replaced by simple gauze. Stem-stitch embroidery covers the foundation cloth as tapestry-like stitches executed by needle would, either the whole surface or given parts (bands, squares, figures of persons or idols). The principal types of this stitch are shown in Figure 92. The needle with the embroidery yarn usually picks up two yarns of the canvas at the same time. It can, however, pick up only one. At each stitch it passes over one, two, or three yarns of the canvas, as required, but when a worker adopted a method of surface embroidery for a piece of work she generally continued using it. If the design so requires, the embroidery will follow the direction of the warp yarns or those of the weft yarns of the canvas, or it may cut across them in an oblique direction. The appearance of the two faces of the embroidery differs completely (see Pl. 110, A, D). It is sufficient, in order to understand this, to refer to the horizontal cross section of the stitches shown in Figure 92, B. The fineness of the embroidery is commensurate with that of the canvas and with the number of yarns picked up or passed over at a time.

The direction of the covering by the wool yarn around the yarns of the canvas is usually consistent in the same piece of work. Thus the yarn may go from right to left or from left to right. In some specimens the direction of the embroidery is regularly reversed from stitch to stitch and contrasted from column to column. As a result of this change of direction, the embroidery presents a special appearance with a design of small cells, arranged (in Fig. 92, C) in ranks of five.

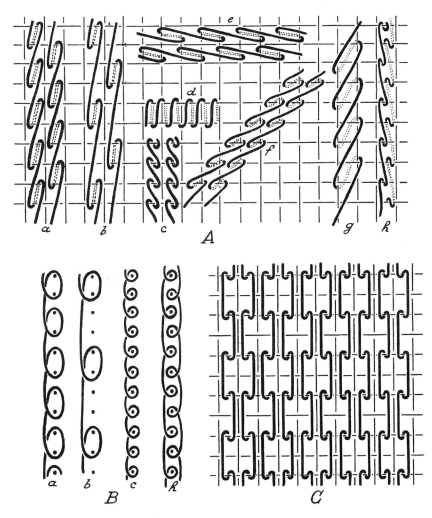

Figure 92. Stem-stitch embroidery. A: various covering stitches that follow the structure of the fabric, *a, b, c, d, e* and *g;* in an oblique direction, *f; h* permits decoration of the fabric on both faces; B: embroidery stitches *a, b, c,* and *h* seen in cross section; C: the direction of the stitch is reversed with each stitch to form facing columns

The canvas may be embroidered on both sides. The specimens of double embroidery that I have been able to examine have identical designs on their two faces, and I am convinced that the worker, as in loop stitch on foundation fabric, executed her embroidery on both sides at the same time, line after line. On the return passage, she picked up the yarns of the fabric that had been crossed by the embroidery yarn on the outward passage, making use of them as a covering. For this reason it was necessary, in double embroidery, to pick up and pass over the same number of yarns of the fabric on each face (Fig. 92, A, h, B, h).

Wrapping of cords with stem stitch

It is appropriate to show the relationship of stem-stitch embroidery to the decorative wrapping used to cover certain cords, especially slings, which may have been used as real weapons or as turban headdresses.

After the central part of the sling was made by means of cords placed side by side like a warp of fabric and interwoven with a fine weft of different colored wool yarns, in the same fashion as a rep, it was necessary to cover the two lateral cords, at least for a certain length. Each cord, therefore, was encircled by a coarse agave or cotton yarn, which formed around it spiral loops that were tightened against each other (these yarns can be seen on sling B in Pl. 61, where wool was used). After completion of this preliminary work, the

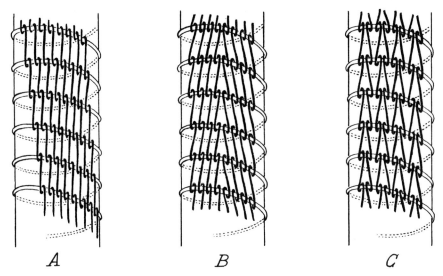

Figure 93. Stem stitch used as a cord covering (soumak). A: columns of stitches executed in the same direction; B: in opposite directions; C: in regularly alternating directions, resembling chain stitch

worker embroidered the foundation loops with wool yarn in accordance with the method described above. In this case the spiraling loops replace the canvas that in the preceding case was used as a base for the embroidery. In short, this is a kind of *soumak* stitch. Figure 93 will make clear the methods of covering formerly in use. Sometimes the direction of the embroidery was uniform, sometimes it was reversed. In the latter case, the meeting of two lines from opposite directions gives the impression of a column of small chain stitches (see Pl. 61, A, B, C, D).

In view of the stiffness of the central cord, it may well be asked how the needle could pass under the coarse spiral yarn that encircled it. I assume that the workers used curved needles. There exist archeological specimens that might have been used as curved needles, but this is not certain. The embroidery stitch permitted changes of yarn, and by means of different colored wools a variety of designs could be obtained. When the sling was not intended for throwing projectiles, but for ornamenting the brow of a chieftain or warrior, its central portion could be replaced by a more supple section, such as a tapestry band. Usually in ornamental slings the central core of the lateral cords was withdrawn after the embroidered cover was completed. The method of fashioning this tubular covering would have been quite mysterious if actual slings, with their cords complete, had not been available for inspection (see Pl. 63).

Little cords covered in the above manner with stem stitch were also used as ornamental borders for certain garments, and in addition to join two fabrics at their edges, as for the sides of pouch bags with straps, and so forth. For this purpose, a small cord, placed lengthwise along the edge, was overcast, as I have shown above, with a coarse yarn—most frequently of cotton—which at each stitch took up in addition the thickness or thicknesses of the fabric. When this preliminary work was completed, all that remained to be done was to join the overcasting stitches to one another by the usual embroidery in stem stitch (see Pl. 20; Harcourt, 1924, Pl. 34).

In addition to its use for decorative cords and pads placed on fabrics as borders, the principle of covering horizontal and parallel yarns with embroidery executed perpendicularly in stem stitch was extended to such objects as dress accessories. An interesting example of this is seen in Plate 83, C. The embroidery is closely related to weaving: rather coarse cotton yarns are warped on two adjacent, parallel surfaces, as in double-cloth weaving; they are joined and covered in stem stitch by vertical wool yarns, some of which alternate among themselves in passing from one face to the other, as in double weaving. This technique produces a thick and stiff fabric with ornamental motives the same on the two sides, but with reversed color values.

EMBROIDERY ON FABRIC WITH SQUARE OPEN SPACES AND ON NETWORK

Embroidery on fabric with square open spaces (see p. 58) is executed in the same manner as modern embroidery on filet. The Peruvians developed this technique but little, or, to be more precise, they contented themselves with forming simple lines, such as diagonals, crosses, lozenges, and other geometric figures, in the open squares (Fig. 94) and grouping them to form a design. We should also mention double diagonals made with rather coarse yarn and joined by a knot at their point of crossing, giving the figure the appearance of a floral motive with four petals (Fig. 94, a; Pls. 40, 41, 42).

Embroidery on network has another appearance altogether, as can be seen by examination of a specimen from Nazca (Pl. 113). The embroidery that fills the meshes completely hides the network and substitutes a design in its place. A decorative wool yarn of suitable color is embroidered in spirals around each knot. This yarn passes successively above and then below each of the four yarns of the mesh that radiate from the knot, adding to these four yarns its own yarn, which is crossed as are the others (Fig. 95). The uneven number of the inactive yarns is necessary in order to reverse regularly the order of the passage of the decorative yarn above and below and to bring about the concealing, after compacting, of all of the yarns of the net, in the same way that one of the two elements of a fabric, warp or weft, disappears in rep. Only the knot remains visible. Changing the color of the wool yarn permits a variety of designs to be made.

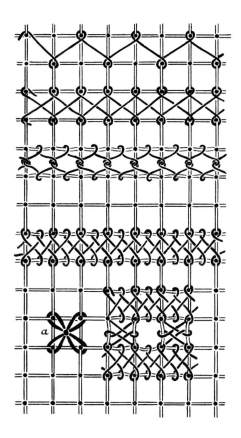

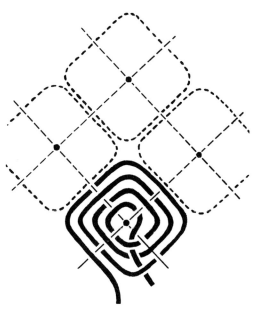

Figure 94 (left). Embroidery stitches on a fabric with square open spaces; *a*, decorative flower executed with a coarse yarn

Figure 95 (above). Embroidery on network

FOURTEEN

Trimmings

HAVING studied embroideries, we cannot pass over in silence ornaments of another variety, which are frequently applied to a fabric to adorn it or at least to give it a "finished" appearance. These ornaments vary in form and in substance, but they may be grouped under four distinct headings: applied objects, fringes, borders, and tassels or pompons.

APPLIED OBJECTS

In this type of ornamentation, objects are attached to a fabric and cover it wholly or in part. The principal objects attached are feathers and small lamellae cut out of metal. These metal leaves, plain or stamped, are usually of silver or gold (actually an alloy of copper and gold which has been annealed until the copper on the surface has oxidized and subsequently been removed with an acid pickle—the process of gilding known as *mise en couleur*). They are perforated near the edges, placed side by side, and sewed to the fabric (Pl. 114, A). Instead of metal, carved pieces of bone or of dull or polished shell may be used (Pl. 114, B). In some cases, flat perforated disks of shell are mounted like modern sequins and completely cover the surface of the fabric to which they are sewed (Pl. 115, B).

Other round pieces of shell, also pierced in the center, but smaller and thicker and resembling beads, were sometimes used by the weavers to outline the decorative motives used in tapestry. For this purpose, the shells were carefully distributed and threaded on the warp yarns before the passage of the sectional wefts forming the tapestry. Special care

131

was necessary in preparing the warp for such purposes before weaving, as in the techniques of *ikat* and of decorative wrapping of warp yarns (see pp. 70 and 60). The Museum of Archaeology and Ethnology at Cambridge has a Nazca tapestry in which the characteristic design is outlined with shell beads (Pl. 117, A). The weaver, having previously threaded the beads on the warp yarns, in order to avoid cutting the terminal loops of the warp, crossed the adjacent warp yarns, thus securing the beads in the position desired. The slits in the tapestry were corrected by the usual methods, that is, either by sewing or by supplementary weft yarns, which completely crossed the fabric at intervals and were then concealed in the wool weft yarns.

The application of feathers to fabrics requires special techniques. Here is the one most generally used. The feathers, selected for their size, form, and color, are first folded in the quill section over a cord, side by side; the fold in each quill is then secured below the initial cord by a fastening yarn, knotted in accordance with one of the methods shown in Figure 96, A. In Paracas, the preliminary cord was dispensed with, and there was only a fastening yarn, which secured the folded quill by a simple knot (see Yacovleff, 1933a, Fig. 2, p. 145). Fringes of feathers were obtained in this way. There remained the matter of attaching these fringes in more or less close parallel lines by means of stitches taken in the cord and in the fastening yarn. The feathers are overlapped, placed one on the other in successive rows, but they can be raised since they are attached to the fabric only near the folded quill (Pl. 115, A).

When the feathers selected are coarse, the method of mounting them for fringes differs. Each feather is provided with a small terminal loop made of a coarse yarn which is fastened to the tapered quill end by a wrapping of fine yarn. The loops are all threaded by a common cord (Fig. 96, B), and the feathers are maintained at equal distance from one another by a second cord, close to the first, which forms a simple knot around each loop. If the regularity of the fringe requires it, a third cord is used in the same manner as the second, but one or two centimeters [⅜ or ¾ inch] below it.

Feather ornamentation often takes the form of monochrome horizontal bands of varying widths, but occasionally the feathers form a polychrome design which may be complex and comparable to a mosaic. Although excavations have furnished very beautiful

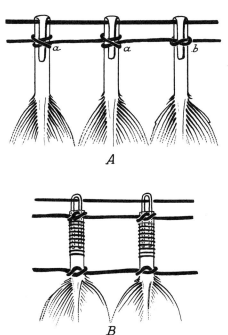

Figure 96. Methods of fastening feathers for imbricating on cloth in overlapping rows. A: fine feathers with folded quills; *a*, knot with two loops; *b*, simple knot; B: coarse feathers with tapered quills provided with a small terminal loop; two small cords fasten the quills and keep them separate

specimens, we probably do not possess feathered articles as fine and as varied as those which amazed the early chroniclers, and for which the tiny, glittering feathers of hummingbirds were used. Aside from their use in fabrics and cords, feathers were used principally to decorate headdresses and to make feather ornaments. For the latter, tufts of feathers or single feathers were mounted at the ends of small braids or split reeds by a delicately wrapped yarn (Pl. 116, A, D). Mention may be made of the discovery at Paracas of beautiful feather fans, which Yacovleff has described in an interesting article (1933a).

FRINGES

There are many varieties of fringes. In general, they may be grouped as follows: (1) fringes that are an integral part of the fabric; (2) fringes of independent construction, sewed to the fabric; (3) fringes incorporated into the fabric in the course of their construction.

1. When the fringe is an integral part of the fabric, it is usually made by the ends of the warp yarns. These ends, which are in the form of loops, because of the great twisting of the yarns naturally form tendrils like strands of cordage. An example of this can be seen in Plate 6, A. Sometimes the yarn of the loops is cut in the center, and the two ends of the yarn thus become free. In practice, the length of the fringe varies from barely one centimeter [⅜ inch] to twenty-five or thirty centimeters [10 to 11¾ inches].

Fringes can also be made with wefts which extend beyond the warp yarns at the selvages, forming loops, which may be cut in the center, if desired, as in the preceding case. To prevent the last warp yarn from separating from its neighbor and thus causing the disintegration of the fabric at the selvage, not every weft is extended to form a loop; certain wefts insure the cohesion of the fabric by weaving the warp normally. In fact, these lateral fringes are chiefly found in the form of little tufts of yarns, particularly in tapestries (Pl. 47, B; see also Harcourt, 1924, Pl. 27, upper specimen).

Instead of being made up of single yarns (loops) or twisted loops, fringes are sometimes formed by special weaving using as a basis the extended warp or weft elements, in groups of three, four, or five yarns. In this way, small pendant tabs are formed (see Pl. 44). They may be woven in tapestry or by the method of two-colored warp with concealed weft, of varied construction, and may vary from one piece to another in length and width, according to the worker's taste (Harcourt, 1924, Pl. 25). Sometimes fringes are found in which the small adjacent tabs of tapestry still have their ends joined to the little cord which originally fastened the warp yarns to the loom bar. In this case there is no doubt as to the method used.

2. The fringe can be an independent piece sewed to the main fabric. In this case it is similar to the pieces just described, but the woven part is reduced to the passage of a few wefts across short, stretched warps, or to the crossing of a few warp yarns by the weft. The

sole purpose of the woven part is to keep in position the warp or weft loops that, strictly speaking, compose the fringe (Harcourt, 1924, Pls. 12, 20).

3. A fringe in the course of its construction can be incorporated into a fabric with a needle after the weaving has been completed. The elements of the fringe made in this way may look like fine cords. This technique, which is close to embroidery, is used especially on the embroidered fabrics of the south coast of Peru (see Pl. 86, A, C). The fringe can also be made up of a series of small repeated forms constructed with a needle in loop stitches. These forms, usually rectangular, are either solid (Pl. 84, B) or have a square open space in the center (Pl. 107, A).

BORDERS AND EDGE FINISHES

Borders, like fringes, were probably created to satisfy a desire to enhance the beauty of the work, to hide a selvage in a decorative way, or to join two superimposed pieces. Several methods were used in Peru.

The simplest edge finish consists of a regular overcasting in which all of the stitches touch the ones next to them. It is often found executed in scallop stitch; on the other hand, an edge finish made with buttonhole stitch is rare.

Borders and edge finishes can also be made by minute weaving in which the warp consists of four or five yarns laid parallel to the edge of the fabric to be decorated. The weft is a yarn which, after each stitch through the fabric edge, passes between the yarns of the small warp, as in actual weaving, taking up the odd and even yarns alternately; then again penetrating the fabric, it passes once more between the yarns, and so on.

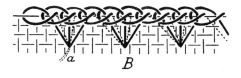

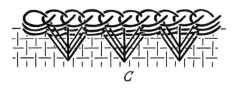

Figure 97. Loop stitch embroidery on the edge of fabric. A: common arrangement; B: more elegant arrangement; C: superimposition of three successive rows of loops

The Peruvians made use of at least three techniques in order to join two fabrics.

The first, very solid and elegant, is similar to what is now termed "long-legged cross-stitch." In order to form the first stitch, the needle penetrates, quite far from their edges, the two fabrics, which are held as if they were to be joined by overcasting. Then the needle passes through them again in order to form the second stitch, not at the side of the first (as in regular overcasting), but four or five millimeters [approximately ⅛ inch] ahead of it and very close to the edge. The third stitch is placed behind the second, but ahead and at the same depth as the first; the fourth stitch is placed in front and at the same depth as the second, and so on. By this means the yarn forms crosses along the edges of the fabrics, which are partly covered, giving the seam a braided appearance when it is finished and opened. In the stitches on the odd rows the needle penetrates the fabrics farther from the edges than in the stitches on the even rows, permitting the concealment of the second by the first if the stitches are placed close together.

The second method consists of making the border in loop stitch in vertical columns, with a yarn whose color may change as desired. The column of loops, comparable to a small chain, is embroidered on the edge of the fabric (Fig. 97, A); see page 123. Many *chuspas* and other small bags have borders of this kind (Harcourt, 1924, Pl. 11, 24). Instead of having only a single column of loops, the border often has three or four adjacent columns if the thickness of the fabric so requires (Pl. 55, A). The technique is similar to that already studied. In some specimens the needle does not penetrate the fabric regularly at the level of each loop stitch; it penetrates three times in the same spot, while continuing its regular column of loops on the edge fabric. Instead of forming small parallel lines (Fig. 97, A), the yarn thus forms on the fabric groups of three diverging lines, that is, a series of **V**'s with a vertical line in the center (Fig. 97, B). This decorative method is sometimes complicated by placing two or three columns of loop stitches on the thickness of the fabric in close position; the base of the **V** corresponds in each row, remaining fixed on the same vertical (Fig. 97, C).

In the third method the border has a supplementary padding yarn, which consists of a small cord, placed at the edges of the two fabrics to be joined, and a heavy yarn, which attaches the cord to the edges by an overcasting stitch in close spirals. The spiral loops are themselves covered in stem stitch with wool yarns of various colors (see p. 129 and Pl. 20).

Round padded borders are also obtained by another technique. I have already discussed loops made by the ends of warp yarns. When in the ordinary weaving of a fabric these loops have been reduced to the length of a centimeter [3/8 inch], or even to half a centimeter [3/16 inch] (see Fig. 98, A), the weft suddenly abandons its plain weave

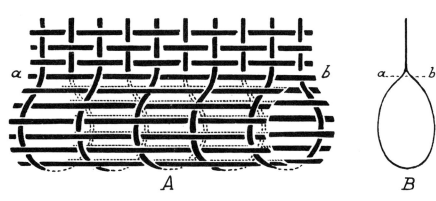

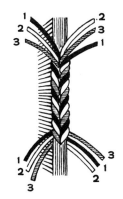

Figure 98.   Thickened edge made by the weaving of terminal loops of warp yarns. A: front view; B: side view

Figure 99.   Method of edging the soles of sandals in Plate 60, A, B

(lines *a–b* of Fig. 98). Here the warp loops are opened into a tube, and the weft continues its passage either in plain weave (as shown in the figure) or in weave of varied construction, according to the desire of the worker, but using only half of the original warps. Successive wefts continue around the curve of the tube and finally meet the main fabric again at *a–b*, where the ordinary weaving had stopped. The work is, of necessity, done with a needle, for the passage of the wefts becomes increasingly difficult as the end of the operation approaches. In this way a very elegant round border may be formed, which is often ornamented with decorative motives woven by complex techniques (see Harcourt, 1924, Pls. 26, 30, 37, upper).

Workers did not always take the trouble to weave the terminal loops of warp yarn in their round form even in fine pieces of tapestry. Toward the end of the weaving they merely used the technique of three or four weft colors with construction subordinated to the design. This technique, because of the numerous floats on the reverse of the fabric, results in a thickening that is used for a special purpose. The part thus made was rolled and then sewed like a hem, forming a little padding resembling the one described above, less perfect, perhaps, but obtained by a simpler technique.

Whatever method of construction was followed, the sandal soles discussed on pages 65 and 99 were finished with a needle-made edge that had the double role of esthetic finish and reinforcement. The edge consisted of three adjacent yarns (1, 2, 3 of Fig. 99), crossed obliquely, which took up only half of the thickness of the sole. Three other yarns (2, 3, 1 of Fig. 99, right) crossed in the same manner but in an opposite oblique direction, taking up the other half of the thickness. It is impossible to see with the naked eye that this regular and tight edge, resembling a small chain, was done with a needle and that it is separate from the plaiting to which it was applied.

TUFTS AND TASSELS

The ornament commonly called a tuft and sometimes a tassel is made of a sheaf of yarns of the same length, doubled at the center over a single yarn and kept in this position by another yarn that holds them together near the fold. The ancient Peruvians at times made immoderate use of such tassels, which were attached singly, in groups, or one below the other on the same yarn. Certain very open network had a tassel applied to each mesh. Reference may be made to Plates 14, A, B; 16, E; 67, B; 68, A, C; and so forth, which show quite different aspects of these tassels.

There are also tassels composed of a light cylindrical construction, either of wood or reed, covered with polychrome yarns or with small glued feathers, from which extended a tuft of feathers or a group of cut yarns.

The simple manufacture of these tufts and tassels makes no further comment necessary.

136

Summary

Having finished the examination of the technical methods employed by the ancient Peruvians in textile art, we may find it of interest to summarize the principles they applied, whether these principles were invented by them or whether they were acquired.

It may be objected, and with reason, that future discoveries may furnish proof of the use of other techniques not known at the present time. It should, however, be remarked that the amount of textile material already excavated from the graves is enormous, and that explorations have been made in many places on the coast. Without prejudice to any later discoveries that may be made, it seems logical to assume, therefore, that future archeological research will but add further details to the types of techniques already known, rather than disclose wholly different ones. It must also be recognized that, owing to the great ingenuity of the Peruvians, the lacunae in their knowledge of weaving techniques (apart from all questions of mechanization) are not very numerous. It is for this reason that it now seems permissible to set up a recapitulation of their inventions in textile matters.

I should point out once more the principle of interchangeability of the role of the warp and weft in the textile techniques mentioned in this study, a principle arising from the rectangular shape and relatively small size of the woven pieces. Everything that is obtained by means of one element could have been obtained by means of the other. We have seen the application of this principle in many techniques: in reps, such as in tapestry; in fabrics woven with varied construction and with two alternating colors of the warp and weft yarns; in weaving with decorative, supplementary yarns; in double weaving; and in weaving with wrapped warp yarns. The only exception to this rule is gauze, since it is practically impossible to reverse the role of the two elements in this fabric.

In weaving the Peruvians knew and applied the following principles: rep; discontinuous and interlocked warp or weft yarns; varied construction of warp or weft pattern; brocading, supplemental element in the warp or weft; double cloth, two supplemental elements (one weft and one warp); gauze, the crossing of one warp yarn over another; the twisting or twining of weft yarns or warp yarns around each other; and open-work fabric obtained by leaving spaces or by grouping of exposed warp or weft yarns, never by drawn threads.

Looped pile fabrics, although known, were not general, and the Peruvians did not develop from this technique the principle of velour (loops opened after weaving).

The Peruvians seem not to have used perforated cards or their equivalent for weaving (see p. 62) although they have produced narrow fabrics that are quite similar in technique and effect to those produced by "card weaving."

In matters of painting and dyeing, the Peruvians painted fabrics in a positive or negative manner, so to speak (in the latter case the reserved portions formed the design). They dyed fabrics with reserves, either after weaving (*planghi*) or after warping and before weaving (*ikat*). These methods remained in a somewhat rudimentary stage, and their products cannot rival in beauty the *ikat*, *planghi*, and *batik* of the Indies.

It has been noted that the Peruvians knew two types of flat plaiting: one with the ends of yarn remaining loose, and the other with the yarns fastened like a warp at their two extremities. In addition to the possibilities innate in plaiting, such as the interlocking of two yarns intended to cross each other, the Peruvians applied to plaiting most of the principles of weaving, particularly those of rep; varied construction, warp or weft pattern; double weaving; and twisted warp and weft yarns.

Except for the last of these techniques, which might have been introduced into weaving from plaiting, these methods were applied in plaiting only as an extension of weaving. It is this consideration which justifies placing plaiting second in this book although it was very probably developed earlier.

We should not neglect to mention plaited cords with round, square, or rectangular sections, sometimes using fifty or more strands, in which the rules of crossing in order to form a design may be very complex.

With respect to network, I have succeeded in distinguishing thirteen different types. We probably know at this time the chief types among them, but the future may reveal others.

The networks that have been studied must all have been made with the aid of a netting needle (netting shuttle). The most important of these networks are: network with interlocked loops, network with simple looping, network with loop stitch (needleknitting), network with simple overhand knot, and network with square knot. The last of these permitted the introduction of a strand of cut wool into the ordinary knot, making "*simili-velours*," or, if the knot was made in a more intricate form, it was capable of holding fast an element as slippery as hair (peruke stitch).

No true knitting has been found; crochet hooks and knitting needles do not seem to have been known.

As for embroideries, of the six stitches analyzed, two of them, loop stitch and stem stitch, have had an important development, especially in the southern coastal region, and have permitted the production of veritable works of art.

Here, then, summarized in a few lines, are the discoveries made in textile art, in the course of centuries, by the ancient Peruvians. They seem to me to form a sufficiently imposing total to justify the admiring appreciation which, at the beginning of this study, I expressed for the inventive genius of their originators.

Bibliography

ANON.
> 1923   "Tecnología indígena." *Inca*, Nos. 2 and 3, Lima. Anonymous work on Indian dyes written at the beginning of the eighteenth century.

ATIENZA, LOPE DE
> 1931   "Compendio historial del estado de los Indios del Perú," in *La religión de los Incas*, by Jijón y Caamaño, Appendices, Vol. I, chap. v, Quito.

BARNETT, ANNA
> 1909   "Étude technologique d'un tissu péruvien antique." *Journal de la Société des Américanistes de Paris*, Vol. VI, N.S., Paris.
>
> 1910   "Étude sur le mode de fabrication des frondes péruviennes antiques." *Journal de la Société des Américanistes de Paris*, Vol. VII, N.S., Paris.

BEL, A., AND P. RICARD
> 1913   *Le travail de la laine à Tlemcen*. Algiers.

BENNERS, ETHEL ELLIS
> 1920   "Ancient Peruvian Textiles." *The Museum Journal*, University of Pennsylvania, Vol. XI, No. 3, Philadelphia.

BERTHON, PAUL
> 1911   "Étude sur le Précolombien du Bas-Pérou." *Nouvelles Archives des Missions scientifiques et littéraires*, N.S., Fasc. 4, Paris.

BIRD, JUNIUS
> 1947   "A Pre-Spanish Peruvian Ikat." *Bulletin of the Needle and Bobbin Club*, Vol. XXXI, Nos. 1 and 2, New York.

BIRD, JUNIUS, AND LOUISA BELLINGER
> 1954   *Paracas Fabrics and Nazca Needlework, 3rd Century B.C.–3rd Century A.D.* The Textile Museum, Washington, D.C.

BRAULIK, AUG.
> 1900   *Altägyptische Gewebe*. Stuttgart.

CARRIÓN-CACHOT, REBECA
> 1931   "La indumentaria en la antigua cultura de Paracas." *Wirakocha*, Vol. I, No. 1, Lima.

Bibliography

CLAUDE-JOSEPH, FRÈRE R.-H.
 1929 "Los tejidos araucanos." *Revista universitaria*, Vol. XIII, No. 10, Santiago de Chile.

COBO, F. BERNABÉ
 1890–5 *Historia del Nuevo Mundo.* Sociedad de Bibliofilos Andaluces, Seville.

CRAWFORD, M. D. C.
 1915 "Peruvian Textiles." *Anthropological Papers of the American Museum of Natural History*, Vol. XII, Part III, New York.
 1916a "The Loom in the New World." *The American Museum Journal*, Vol. XVI, No. 6, New York.
 1916b "Design and Color in Ancient Fabrics." *The American Museum Journal*, Vol. XVI, No. 7, New York.
 1916c "Peruvian Fabrics." *Anthropological Papers of the American Museum of Natural History*, Vol. XII, Part IV, New York.

DIGUET, LÉON
 1909 "Histoire de la cochenille au Mexique." *Journal de la Société des Américanistes de Paris*, Vol. VI, N.S., Paris

DILLMONT, THÉRÈSE DE
 n.d. *Encyclopédie des ouvrages de dames.* Mulhouse.

DRIESSEN, P. AUG.
 1930 "Een Inka- of zelfs Pre-Inka Ikat." *Nederlandsch-Indie, Oud en Nieuw*, The Hague.

ENGEL, FREDERIC
 1957 "Sites et établissements sans céramique de la côte péruvienne." *Journal de la Société des Américanistes*, Vol. XLVI, pp. 67–155, Paris.

EPHRAIM, HUGO
 1905 "Ueber die Entwicklung der Webetechnik und ihre Verbreitung ausserhalb Europas." *Mitteilungen aus dem Städtischen Museum für Völkerkunde zu Leipzig*, Leipzig

ESPADA, JIMÉNEZ DE LA
 1923 "El cumpi-uncu hallado en Pachacamac." *Inca*, No. 4, Lima.

FISCHER, HEINRICH
 1933 *Die altperuanischen Sammlungen des Museums für Länder und Völkerkunde, Linden Museum. Part I: Die Webekunst der alten Peruaner*, Stuttgart.

FLINT, SARAH G.
 1916 "Peruvian Textiles." *Museum of Fine Arts Bulletin*, Boston.

GARCILASO DE LA VEGA
 1609 *Primera parte de los commentarios reales*, Lisbon.

GENNEP, ARNOLD VAN
 1914 "Études d'ethnographie sud-américaine (métiers à rubans, tissage aux cartons)," *Journal de la Société des Américanistes de Paris*, Vol. XI, N.S., Fasc. 1, Paris.

HARCOURT, RAOUL D'
 1924 *Les tissus indiens du Vieux Pérou.* Paris.
 1930 "Technique du point de tricot à Nazca." *Journal de la Société des Américanistes*, Vol. XXII, N.S., Fasc. 1, Paris.
 1932 "Note sur la technique d'un tissu ancien du Chaco argentin." *Journal de la Société des Américanistes*, Vol. XXIV, N.S., Fasc. 1, Paris.
 1933 "Un bonnet péruvien en simili-velours." *Bulletin du Musée d'Ethnographie du Trocadéro*, No. 4, Paris.
 1935 "Note technologique sur un passement de Nazca." *Journal de la Société des Américanistes*, Vol. XXVII, Paris.
 1936 "Technique des tissus péruviens à fils de chaîne et de trame discontinus. Le nœud de

142

filet moderne au Pérou." *Journal de la Société des Américanistes,* Vol. XXVIII, Paris.

1940a   "Note sur un réseau ancien á l'aiguille, Chili-Bolivie." *Journal de la Société des Américanistes,* Vol. XXXII, Paris.

1940b   "Tressage de frondes au Pérou et en Bolivie et les textiles chez les Uro-Chipaya." *Journal de la Société des Américanistes,* Vol. XXXII, Paris.

1948a   "Un tapis brodé de Paracas." *Journal de la Société des Américanistes,* Vol. XXXVII, Paris.

1948b   "Technique de tressage des sandales chez les tribus indiennes de la côte du Pérou." *Actes du XXVIIIᵉ Congrès international des Américanistes,* pp. 615–19, Paris.

1949   "Tressage de frondes à Nazca, Pérou." *Journal de la Société des Américanistes,* Vol. XXXVIII, Paris.

1952   "Un réseau à bouclettes décoratives de Nazca, note technologique." *Journal de la Société des Américanistes,* Vol. XLI, Paris.

1954   "Une broderie sur filet dans l'ancien Pérou." *Bulletin de la Société suisse des Américanistes,* Geneva.

1958   "Représentation de textiles dans la statuaire maya." *Thirty-second International Congress of Americanists,* pp. 415–31, Copenhagen.

HOLMES, WILLIAM H.

1885   "A Study of the Textile Art in Its Relationship to the Development of Form and Ornament." *Sixth Annual Report of the Bureau of American Ethnology,* Washington, D.C.

1889   "Textile Fabrics of Ancient Peru." *Bureau of American Ethnology, Bulletin 7,* Washington, D.C.

HOWARD, LUCILE

1920   "The Relation of the Museum to Modern Design." *The Museum Journal,* University of Pennsylvania, Vol. XI, No. 3, Philadelphia.

HUAMAN POMA DE AYALA, FELIPE

1936   *Nueva corónica y buen gobierno.* Université de Paris, *Travaux et Mémoires de l'Institut d'Ethnologie,* Vol. XXIII, Paris.

IKLÉ, FRITZ

1928   "Ueber Flammentücher." *Festschrift für Maria Andreae Eysen. Beiträge zur Volks- und Völkerkunde,* Munich.

1930   "Ueber altperuanische Stickereien des Trocadero, Paris, St. Gallen." *Mitteilungen der ostschweizerischen geographisch-commerceillen, Gesellschaft in St. Gallen.*

IZIKOWITZ, KARL GUSTAV

1932   "Une coiffure d'apparat d'Ica (Pérou)." *Revista del Instituto de Etnología de la Universidad Nacional de Tucuman,* Vol. II, No. 2ª, Tucuman.

1933   "L'origine probable de la technique du simili-velours péruvien." *Journal de la Société des Américanistes,* Vol. XXV, Paris.

JOHNSON, IRMGARD WEITLANER

1954   "Chiptic cave textiles from Chiapas, Mexico." *Journal de la Société des Américanistes,* Vol. XLIII, Paris.

1957   "Survival of feather ornamented Huipiles in Chiapas, Mexico." *Journal de la Société des Américanistes,* Vol. XLVI, pp. 189–196, Paris.

JOYCE, THOMAS

1913   "A Peruvian Tapestry, Probably of the XVIIth Century." *Burlington Magazine,* Vol. XXIII, London.

1921   "The Peruvian Loom in the Proto-Chimu Period." *Man,* Vol. XXI, London.

Bibliography

1922   "Note on a Peruvian Loom of the Chimu Period." *Man*, Vol. XXII, London.

KIDDER, A. V.

1926   "A Sandal from Northeastern Arizona." *American Anthropologist*, Vol. XXVIII, No. 4, Washington, D.C.

KINGSBOROUGH, (VISCOUNT) EDWARD KING

1831–48   *Antiquities of Mexico*. Vol. I, Manuscript I, London.

KRAUSE, FRITZ

1922   "Schleiergewebe aus Alt-Peru." *Sonderdruck aus Jahrbuch des Städt-Museum für Völkerkunde zu Leipzig*, Vol. VIII, Leipzig.

LEHMANN, JOHANNES

1907   "Systematik und geographische Verbreitung der Geflechtsarten." *Zoologisch und Anthropologisch-Ethnographischen Museums zu Dresden*, Vol. XI, Leipzig.

1920   "Ein seltenes Gewebe aus Alt Peru. Zugleich eine Einführung in die Technik des Webens." *Erläuterungschaft zu den Sammelung No. 3 Städtisches Völkermuseum*, Frankfort-am-Main.

LEHMANN, WALTER, AND HEINRICH DOERING

1924   *The Art of Old Peru*. London.

LEVILLIER, JEAN

1928   *Paracas. Contribution to the Study of Pre-Incaic Textiles in Ancient Peru*. Paris.

LOTHROP, SAMUEL K.

1930   "Notes on Indian Textiles of Central Chile." *Indian Notes*, Vol. VII, No. 3, Museum of the American Indian, Heye Foundation, New York.

LUQUET, G. H.

1930   "Décor de ceintures boliviennes." *Ipek*, pp. 93–108, Berlin.

MEAD, C. W.

1907   "Technique of Some South American Feather Work." *Anthropological Papers of the American Museum of Natural History*, Vol. I, New York.

1916   "Ancient Peruvian Cloths." *The American Museum Journal*, Vol. XVI, No. 6, New York.

1920   "A Prehistoric Poncho from Nazca, Peru." *Natural History*, Vol. XX, New York.

MEANS, PHILIP AINSWORTH

1925   "A Series of Ancient Andean Textiles." *Bulletin of the Needle and Bobbin Club*, Vol. IX, No. 1, New York.

1927   "A Group of Ancient Peruvian Fabrics." *Bulletin of the Needle and Bobbin Club*, Vol. XI, No. 1, New York.

1930a   "The Origin of Tapestry Technique in Pre-Spanish Peru." *Metropolitan Museum Studies*, III, Part I, New York.

1930b   *Peruvian Textiles*. Metropolitan Museum of Art, New York.

1932   *A Study of Peruvian Textiles*. Museum of Fine Arts, Boston.

METRAUX, A.

1932   "À propos de deux objets tupinamba." *Bulletin de Musée d'Ethnographie du Trocadéro*, No. 3, Paris.

MONTELL, GÖSTA

1925   "Le vrai poncho, son origine post-colombienne." *Journal de la Société des Américanistes de Paris*, Vol. XVII, N.S., Paris.

1929   *Dress and Ornaments in Ancient Peru*. Göteborg.

NORDENSKIÖLD, ERLAND

1919–24   *Comparative Ethnographical Studies*. Series I, II, III. Göteborg.

1930   "The Ancient Peruvian System of Weights." *Man*, Vol. XXX, No. 12, London.

OLSON, RONALD L.
1929   "The Possible Middle-American Origin of Northwest Coast Weaving." *American Anthropologist*, Vol. XXXI, No. 1, Washington, D.C.

O'NEALE, LILA M.
1932   "Tecnología de los textiles (una exploración en Cerro Colorado)." *Revista del Museo Nacional*, Vol. I, No. 2, Lima.
1933   "A Peruvian Multicolored Patchwork." *American Anthropologist*, Vol. XXXV, Menasha, Wis.
1942   "Textile Periods in Ancient Peru: II, Paracas Cavernas and the Grand Necropolis." *University of California Publications in American Archaeology and Ethnology*, Vol. XXXIX, No. 2, Berkeley.
1945   *Textiles of Highland Guatemala*. Carnegie Institution of Washington, Publication 567. Washington, D.C.
1946   "Mochica (Early Chimu) and Other Peruvian Twill Fabrics." *Southwestern Journal of Anthropology*, Vol. II, No. 3, Albuquerque, N.M.

O'NEALE, LILA M., AND BONNIE JEAN CLARK
1948   "Textile Periods in Ancient Peru: III, The Gauze Weaves." *University of California Publications in American Archaeology and Ethnology*, Vol. XL, No. 4, Berkeley.

O'NEALE, LILA M., AND A. L. KROEBER
1930   "Textile Periods in Ancient Peru." *University of California Publications in American Archaeology and Ethnology*, Vol. XXVIII, No. 2, Berkeley.

ORCHARD, WILLIAM C.
1929   "Mohawk Burden Straps." *Indian Notes*, Museum of the American Indian, Heye Foundation, Vol. VI, No. 4, New York.

OYARZUN, AURELIANO
1931   "Tejidos de Calama." *Revista chilena de Historia y Geografía*, Vol. LXIX, No. 73, Santiago de Chile.

PEÑAFIEL, ANTONIO
1885   *Nombres geográficas de México*. Mexico.

REESEMA, ELISABETH SIEWERTSZ VAN
1926   "Contribution to the Early History of Textile Technics." *Verhandelingen der Könenklijke Akademie van Wettenschappen te Amsterdam*, Vol. XXVI, No. 2, Amsterdam.

SCHMIDT, MAX
1907   "Besondere Geflechtsart der Indianer im Ucayaligebiet." *Archiv für Anthropologie*, Vol. VI, N.S., No. 4, Braunschweig.
1910   "Szenenhaften Darstellungen auf alt-peruanischen Gewebe." *Zeitschrift für Ethnologie*, Vol. XLII, Berlin.
1911   "Ueber alteperuanische Gewebe mit szenenhaften Darstellungen." *Baessler Archiv*, Vol. I, Leipzig.

SELER, EDUARD
1923   "Die buntbemalten Gefässe von Nazca im südlichen Peru und Hauptelemente ihrer Versierung." *Gesammelte Abhandlungen zur amerikanischen Sprach und Alterthumskunde*, Vol. IV, Berlin.

SINGER, ERNESTINE WIEDER
1936   "The Technique of Certain Peruvian Hairnets." *Revista del Museo Nacional*, Vol. V, No. 1, Lima.

SMITH, HOWELL
1926   *Brief Guide to the Peruvian Textiles* (Victoria and Albert Museum). London.

Bibliography

SNETHLAGE, E. HEINRICH

1930   "Form und Ornamentik alteperuanischer Spindeln." *Baessler Archiv*, Vol. XIV, Berlin.

1931   "Ein figurliches Ikat-Gewebe aus Peru." *Der Weltkreis Zeitschrift für Völkerkunde, Kulturgeschichte und Volkskunde*, Vol. II, Nos. 3–4, Berlin.

TELLO, JULIO C.

1923   "Wira-Kocha." *Inca*, Vol. I, No. 1, Lima.

1931   "Un modela de escenografía plástica en el arte antiguo peruano." *Wirakocha*, Vol. I, No. 1, Lima.

TORRES-LUNA, A.

1923   "El vestuario en la época incáica." *Revista de Arqueología*, Vol. I, pp. 50–64, Lima.

UHLE, MAX

1919   "La arqueología de Arica y Tacna." *Boletin de la Sociedad equatoriana de Estudios históricos americanos*, Vol. III, Quito.

VALETTE, M.

1913   "Note sur le teinture de tissus précolombiens du Bas-Pérou." *Journal de la Société des Américanistes de Paris*, Vol. X, N.S., Paris.

VANSTAN, INA

1957   "A Peruvian Ikat from Pachacamac." *American Antiquity*, Vol. XXIII, No. 2, pp. 150–59, Salt Lake City, Utah.

VERNEUIL, M. P.

1926   "L'ikat et les tissus ikatés des Indes orientales." *Revue des Arts asiatiques*, Vol. III, No. 3, Paris.

VILLAR-CÓRDOVA, PEDRO E.

1923   "La textilaría y el arte decorativo en la provincia de Canta." *Revista de Arqueología*, Vol. I, pp. 5–10, Lima.

WARDLE, H. NEWELL

1936   "Belts and Girdles of the Inca's Sacrificed Women." *Revista del Museo Nacional*, Vol. V, No. 1, Lima.

WIENER, CHARLES

1880   *Pérou et Bolivie*. Paris.

YACOVLEFF, E.

1933a   "La jiquima, raíz comestíble, extinguida en el Perú." *Revista del Museo Nacional*, Vol. II, No. 1, Lima.

1933b   "Arte plumaria entre los antiguos peruanos." *Revista del Museo Nacional*, Vol. II, No. 2, Lima.

PLATES

Description of Plates

The arrows on the plates indicate the direction of the warp; in network the arrow indicates direction in which the knotting proceeded. Metric system measurements are followed by measurements in inches, in brackets. Warp measurement (length) precedes weft measurement (width). The term wool has been used, for the sake of brevity, throughout the description of plates to refer to the fibers of the llama, alpaca, and vicuña.

No special plates have been used for plain-weave cloth, fine or coarse, of the muslin or rep families because of their simplicity and because examples of them will be found combined with other techniques in several places in this work.

Plate 1, A. Cotton cloth, plain weave, with crossed stripes. Colors: white, sky blue, light brown, dark brown. Size of the specimen, four selvages 93 x 67 cm. [36½ x 26½ in.]. Natural size. Provenience: Pachacamac. Collection of R. d'Harcourt, Paris.

B. Cotton cloth, plain weave in natural white and dark brown. The pattern is formed by the special arrangement of brown and white yarns in the warp and in the weft (see Fig. 6). The modification of the pattern to be seen in the left part of the fabric arises solely from the congestion of the warp yarns, which at this point transforms the fabric into rep. Fabrics of precisely this description are still made in Bolivia. Natural size. Provenience: central coast of Peru. Musée de l'Homme, No. 32–22–2.

Plate 2, A. Cotton cloth, plain weave, in squares of dark brown and natural white. The white and brown warp yarns are interlocked at the top and bottom of each square. The same is true of the wefts on the sides of the squares (see p. 17 and Fig. 7). Forty-eight to fifty-three warp yarns and thirty-three to thirty-eight weft yarns to the square. Natural size. Provenience: central coast of Peru. Collection of Fritz Iklé, Saint-Gall.

B. Cotton cloth, plain weave, formed of small squares woven separately (selvages on four sides) and sewed together. Colors: tobacco, dark blue, light blue, yellow beige, white; around the white square four squares have been destroyed, undoubtedly through the action of the dye. Natural size. Provenience: central coast of Peru. Collection of Fritz Iklé, No. 6996.

Plate 3, A. Fabric entirely of wool, rep family, with discontinuous warp and weft yarns interlocked respectively (see pp. 20–21). The warp alone is visible; its yarns are carmine, pale yellow, and brown black. The weft is light brown and pale yellow. Selvages are visible on the sides and the upper part. Twenty warp yarns and four weft yarns to the centimeter [51 x 10 to the inch]. Actual length: 50 cm. [19½ in.]; total width: 52 cm. [20½ in.]. Provenience: Pachacamac. Collection of R. d'Harcourt.

149

B. Fragment of wool cloth of the rep family, made with discontinuous interlocked warp and weft. Generally only the warp is visible. Square or rectangular spaces were left in the course of weaving and were later filled with darning stitch; in these the two elements are equally visible (see Fig. 9). There are two small empty squares that do not seem to have been finished; they may, however, represent a section in which the yarn has been destroyed by the action of the dye. Colors: carmine, rather light blue, yellow brown, golden yellow, natural white; border of decorative motives, dark brown. Selvages on the two sides and on the lower part. Actual length (on the right): 14.5 cm. [5¾ in.]; total width: 38.5 cm. [15¼ in.]. Provenience: Nazca. Collection of Fritz Iklé, No. 7330.

PLATE 4. Loosely made wool cloth, plain weave, with discontinuous interlocked warp and weft yarns (see p. 19). Colors: red, yellow, natural white. The pattern represents two extremely stylized zoomorphic forms with head and extremities alternating. Complete specimen. Size: 235 x 107 cm. [99½ x 42 in.]. Provenience: Nazca. Collection of Heinrich Hardt, Berlin, No. 1076.

PLATE 5. Part of an unfinished specimen showing the warping of a fabric in which the yarns, according to the requirements of the design, were of varying length and interlocked. The provisional transverse yarns, intended to keep the terminal loops of these warp yarns in place, should be noted. Natural size, slightly reduced. Provenience: Ica. American Museum of Natural History, New York, No. 41-0-1561. Photograph courtesy of Junius Bird, American Museum of Natural History.

PLATE 6, A. Wool cloth of the rep family with discontinuous, interlocked warp and weft yarns (see p. 20). Only the warp is visible. When the warp was set up, four bands without warps were reserved; the section photographed shows only two. The weft crossed the empty spaces; these weft yarns then served as local warp for a tapestry that filled the space. Colors of the warp: carmine, natural white, yellow, yellow brown, violet; of the weft: brown or natural white. In the lower part of the photograph can be seen a short fringe; it is formed of groups of six warp yarns twisted together to make a loop around a first (or a last) weft. This special method, which is common to many fabrics made with discontinuous warp yarns, helps, in the absence of other proof, to establish the direction of the weaving. Twenty warp yarns and six weft yarns to the centimeter [51 x 16 to the inch]. Actual length: 43 cm. [17 in.]; total width: 49.5 cm. [19½ in.]. Section photographed: 26 x 38 cm. [10 x 15 in.]. Provenience: Pachacamac. Collection of R. d'Harcourt.

B. Tapestry, cotton warp, wool weft. All sectional wefts are meticulously interlocked (see p. 25). At intervals the warp can be seen between the wefts. Colors: yellow, light brown, red, dark blue, light blue. Natural size. Provenience: Ica. Collection of Fritz Iklé, No. 7101.

PLATE 7. Tapestry band, cotton warp, wool weft, surrounding an almost square piece of cotton cloth in plain weave, half carmine red and half violet red; the two parts are joined by sewing. Size: 332 x 317 cm. [131 x 125 in.]. Width of the tapestry band: 24 cm. [9½ in.]; length photographed: 55 cm. [21½ in.]. Colors of the tapestry: red, rather dark violet, rather dark blue, green, yellow, white, dark brown (this color used exclusively on the borders of the motives). The design consists of highly stylized anthropomorphic figures. Provenience: Nazca. Collection of Hein, Paris.

PLATE 8. Tapestry, cotton warp, wool weft, with an additional weft of white cotton that crosses regularly from selvage to selvage (see p. 24). There are two rows of wool weft to one of cotton. The wool yarns of the tapestry pass over and under two warp yarns at a time; in the border at the bottom, four at a time. Colors: dark blue, light blue, red, violet, green, yellow. Actual size: 40 x 45 cm. [15¾ x 17¾ in.]. Pattern: bird motives (male condor); so-called Tiahuanaco style. Provenience: Nazca. Collection of Schmidt, Paris.

PLATE 9. Tapestry, cotton warp, wool weft, the sectional wefts generally interlocked or turned around a common yarn (see p. 25). In addition, some wefts cross the warp in an oblique direction, chiefly around flowers in the design. Colors: white, dark violet, carmine, almond green, dark ocher (yellow), golden yellow. Design: geometric motives and flowers. Actual size: 17 x 25 cm. [6½ x 10 in.]. Provenience: Nazca. Collection of Schmidt, Paris.

PLATE 10, A. Tapestry, cotton warp, wool weft, sewed to a rep at the left. Design: series of crested sea birds. In one part of the tapestry the weft joins together only two warp yarns and then at intervals four warp yarns, sometimes on the right, sometimes on the left, thus producing ornamental slits. Colors: dull yellow with border of brown black. Natural size. Provenience: Chancay-Huacho. Collection of Fritz Iklé, No. 7116.

B. Tapestry fragment, very coarse cotton warp, wool weft. At intervals single warp yarns are isolated and wrapped by the weft. Design: geometric motives. Colors: dark green, faded yellow, red, violet, white. Natural size. Provenience: coastal region of Peru. Collection of Fritz Iklé, No. 7136.

PLATE 11, A. Fabric with interlocked warp yarns (?), warp and weft of wool. The direction of the weaving is very difficult to establish: it appears from a fragment of selvage that has been preserved, and from the character of the concealed element, which is of wool with the yarns rather widely spread, that this fabric belongs to the group shown in Plates 4 and 6, A; in this case the visible element is the warp. The method of crossing the yarns of the visible element where color changes occur should be noted; these yarns turn by groups of three around a single yarn of the concealed element (see Fig. 12, D). Colors: red, white, violet brown, dark yellow, light yellow. Natural size. Provenience: central coastal region. Musée de l'Homme, No. X, 33–271–23.

B. Tapestry fragment, cotton warp, wool weft. There is a lack of parallelism of the sectional wefts, and their unequal tension leads to a deformity of the warp. Colors: red and yellow predominating, with some touches of green and brown. Natural size. Provenience: coastal region of Peru. Collection of Fritz Iklé, No. 7235.

C. Decorative disk seen from the reverse (see Pl. 14, B), white cotton warp, red wool weft, rep family. The warp is composed of eight concentric rings, joined by a weft yarn passing from the center of the ring to the periphery and back again. In order to close the rings, the two ends are overlapped and woven simultaneously for a short distance by the weft. This illustration shows the overlapped warps. Natural size. Musée de l'Homme, No. X, 33–271–19.

D. Simple gauze in yellowish white cotton decorated with woven sections of two-toned wool tapestry, dark brown and lighter brown. Natural size. Provenience: coastal region of Peru. Göteborgs Museum, No. 28–26–144b.

PLATE 12, A. Tapestry combined with gauze. The brown cotton warp is sometimes crossed by sectional wefts of wool, forming the tapestry, and sometimes by a whole weft row in cotton, likewise brown, following the technique of simple gauze. The sectional wefts of the tapestry pass over and under two warp yarns at a time. It is possible that this specimen may be tapestry embroidered on the gauze. Design: geometric motives. Colors: light yellow, dark yellow, red, rather light blue, white. Natural size. Provenience: coastal region of Peru. Collection of Fritz Iklé, No. 7132.

B. Cotton fabric, warp and weft, consisting of rep surfaces alternated with bands of tapestry combined with gauze. The tapestry weft yarn is coarser than the weft yarn that maintains the gauze crossing of the warp yarns. Color: natural white. Design: small triangular surfaces and heads of facing pelicans. Natural size. Provenience: central coast of Peru. Collection of Fritz Iklé.

PLATE 13. Brown cotton warp divided into groups of eight yarns that alternately join their neighbors on the right and then on the left, thus forming open-space lozenges. Where the two groups are united, these yarns serve as a foundation for a wool weft that connects them as in a tapestry (see Fig. 13). The decorative motive formed represents a stylized pelican. Colors of the tapestry motives: carmine, old rose, pale yellow, white, light brown. Slightly less than natural size. Provenience: central coast of Peru. Collection of Schmidt, Paris.

PLATE 14, A. Tapestry, cotton warp, wool weft. Groups of five warps are separated by open spaces which are crossed periodically by a series of wefts, as shown in Figure 33, B. The tapestry is covered with groups of small wool polychrome pompons which are sewed on. The section photographed was reduced to half size. Provenience: central coast of Peru. Musée de l'Homme, No. X, 33–271–319.

151

B. Tapestry, cotton warp, wool weft. The weft leaves the warp exposed on the rectangular surfaces arranged in groups of five. The warp yarns are joined by a cotton yarn that knots them in pairs; in the center of the open rectangles, a small white tapestry section serves as a base for a decorative disk (see Pl. 11, C) from the center of which emerges a group of pompons made up of three small branches with two pompons and two larger branches subdivided into six subbranches. Colors of pompons: red and violet with yellow, blue, and white ties. Colors of the tapestry: red, yellow, white, brown violet. Design: simple geometric lines. Size of the specimen: 64 x 45 cm. [25¼ x 17¾ in.]. One quarter of the specimen photographed. Provenience: central coastal region. Musée de l'Homme, No. X, 33–271–19.

PLATE 15. Tapestry, cotton warp, wool weft. In certain areas the weft forms rows of loops (see p. 28). In a tapestry with designs of birds, small quadrupeds, plants, and headless large animals (jaguars or pumas), the fur coat of the latter animals and the wings of the birds are represented by small, closely spaced loops. Perhaps formerly each animal possessed a head in relief (separate pieces?). Size of the tapestry: 41 x 88 cm. [16 x 34¾ in.]. In the plate the width is reduced to 23 cm. [9 in.]. Provenience: central coast of Peru. Textile Museum of the District of Columbia, Washington, No. T, 936.

PLATE 16, A. Detail of the tapestry with loops shown in Plate 15. Natural size.

B. Fragment of cotton cloth of the rep family, ornamented with rectangles of tapestry (wool weft) each having nine groups of small loops; in addition, decorative wool yarns are laid over the tapestry rectangles between the groups of loops; they are fastened at intervals by perpendicular stitches. Another embroidery thread forms sequences of lozenges upon the rep part of the fabric. Colors: red, yellow, beige, green. Natural size. Provenience: central coast of Peru. Collection of Fritz Iklé.

C and D. Tapestry band seen on both faces; cotton warp, wool weft. Where changes of color occur in the weft there are rows of small loops. At intervals, in the center of the band, a very long loop can be seen. Colors: red, yellow, brown (this color for the most part destroyed, leaving the warp exposed). Natural size. Provenience: Nazca. Collection of Fritz Iklé.

E. Ornamental motive woven partially in tapestry with loops. The upper part is surrounded by a semicircle of added fringe, the strands of which emerge from a woven band embroidered in cross-stitch. Groups of pompons complete the specimen. Colors: brown, red, yellow, blue. Length: 22 cm. [8¾ in.]. Provenience: coastal region of Peru. Collection of Fritz Iklé, No. 7013.

PLATE 17, A. Part of a pouch bag (*chuspa*) with strap entirely of wool (see the complete specimen in Harcourt, 1924, Pl. 34). The fabric is of varied construction, with two colors of warp and with concealed weft (see Fig. 17). Colors: yellow, brown black, and a somewhat lighter brown (on the sides). Twenty-six warp yarns to the centimeter [66 to the inch]. The upper border is in loop stitch (see p. 124). The design is formed of geometric motives. Natural size. Size of the specimen: 16.5 x 21 cm. [6¼ x 8¼ in.]. Provenience: Pachacamac. Collection of R. d'Harcourt.

B. The same section of the pouch bag with strap seen on the other face.

C. Fragment of cloth, cotton warp, wool weft, of varied construction and multicolored weft, with concealed warp. Every other weft is discontinuous and interlocks with its neighbors on either side (see Fig. 18). Constant color: red; changing colors: white, yellow, violet. The design is composed of stylized heads. Thirty-six wefts to the centimeter [91 to the inch]. Natural size. Provenience: central coast of Peru. Collection of Fritz Iklé, No. 7012.

PLATE 18, A. Double-face cloth, cotton warp, wool weft, of varied construction and with three colors of weft (concealed warp). Two colors are constant: red and dark blue on one side, red and beige (cotton) on the other; the third color changes in each element of the decorative surface corresponding to the part photographed; it includes light blue, yellow, and white, on one face, and green, yellow, and light brown, on the other. Only the red weft yarn passes from one face to the other according to the requirements of the design (see Fig. 25, C, D). The warps in pairs bordering the decorative motives are woven together like rep by the red weft. The specimen in its present state measures 15.5 x 38 cm. [6¼ x 15 in.]. It consists of two equal parts sewed together, the sewing being hidden on one face by a decorative loop stitch; this can be seen on the right side of the photograph. Design: a very stylized animal, surrounded by small hexagonals. Natural size. Provenience: central coastal region. Musée de l'Homme, No. X, 33–271–10.

B. The same part of the fabric seen on the other face.

C. Fabric, cotton warp, wool weft, of varied construction and with two-colored weft, concealed warp. One color of the weft, the red, is constant; the other colors (yellow, white, blue, violet) change. Every other weft passage is discontinuous and interlocks with its neighbors on either side (see Fig. 18). The specimen consists of a long band about 9 cm. [3½ in.] in width. Natural size. Provenience: central coastal region. Musée de l'Homme, No. X, 33–271–11.

D. The same part of the fabric seen on the other face. The lines of interlocking of the wefts with each other can be seen (see Fig. 18).

PLATE 19, A. Band of wool fabric with rep border, woven in the central part with varied construction and several colors of warp yarns, some of which, when they are not used, form floats on the reverse (see Fig. 19, C). Colors of the warp yarns: carmine, blue, light yellow, dark violet, white (the last, which is of cotton and very fine, was perhaps formerly wrapped); weft of light brown. Twenty-seven warp yarns to the centimeter [68 to the inch]. Design: bird forms (stylized pelicans). Natural size. Provenience: Huacho. See Harcourt, 1924, Plate 34. Collection of R. d'Harcourt.

B. The same part of the fabric seen on the other face. The floats formed by the unused part of the yarns can be seen.

C. Band of fabric, cotton warp and wool weft, rep borders; woven in the central part with varied construction and with several weft yarns, concealed warp. Fret design formed of small adjacent squares. On the borders, yellow and red rep; in the center the pattern is formed of one constant color, black, and of one of the following colors: yellow, rose, red, natural white. Where the color changes occur, the wefts are interlocked. Natural size. Provenience: central coastal region. Musée de l'Homme, No. X, 33–271–12.

PLATE 20. Pouch bag with strap (*chuspa*) in wool fabric of varied construction and several warp colors (concealed weft), alternating with bands of rep. Colors: carmine, yellow, black, mauve. Design: series of stylized pelicans and geometric motives. Length: 22 cm. [8½ in.]; width 35.5 cm. [14 in.]. The lateral border is made with a cord covered with stem stitch (see Fig. 93). Carrying strap of tubular fabric, varied construction (see p. 47). Colors: red, yellow, mauve. Width: 3 cm. [1¼ in.]. Design: fret and stylized pelicans. Provenience: Cajamarquilla. Collection of R. d'Harcourt.

PLATE 21, A. Wool fabric with concealed weft and with two colored warp yarns, which cover each other alternately, following the technique described on page 36 and in Figure 20. Colors: red and yellow in one half of the fabric, light green and brown black in the other; joined on the sides by saddler's stitch. Design: heads and stylized animals. Natural size. Provenience: central coastal region. Musée de l'Homme, No. 30–19–1684.

B. Fabric made of brown cotton warp and a weft formed of red and yellow wool yarns, used at the same time. A design is formed on one face of the fabric by floats of the colored wefts, while their counterparts of the other color cross the warp yarns forming a plain weave on the other face (see Fig. 24). Design: stylized pelicans. Natural size. Provenience: central coastal region. Musée de l'Homme, No. X, 33–271–5.

C. The same fabric seen on the other face.

PLATE 22, A. Yellowish white cotton fabric, plain-weave construction with supplementary decorative brown cotton weft passing over a maximum of four warp yarns on the right side and twenty on the reverse (see Fig. 22). Natural size. Size of the entire specimen (four selvages): 48 x 50 cm. [19 x 19¾ in.]. The design depicts sequences of small rodents (*viscaches*?). Provenience: central coastal region. Collection of R. d'Harcourt.

B. The same part of the fabric seen on the other face.

PLATE 23. Part of a fabric made with supplementary decorative weft. The fabric is of natural white; the basic weft crosses the warp two yarns at a time. The decorative weft is of wool in a series of colors: black, light red, dark red. The design is geometric. In the lower 3.5 cm. [1½ in.] of the fabric, the specimen is woven first of rep, then according to the technique of varied construction with two colored wefts and concealed warp. In the rep, the wool weft covers the warp yarns in groups of eight at a time. Color of the weft: yellow, black, white. Natural size. Provenience: central coastal region. Collection of R. d'Harcourt.

PLATE 24, A. Corner of a piece of white cotton fabric, with supplementary weft yarn of blue black wool. The decorative wefts extend over only one part of the width of the fabric. Allover design of lozenges, each containing the stylized representation of a bird. The lower part is woven either in rep or according to the varied-construction technique and with several colors of weft yarn. Bird motives. Colors: black, Vandyke brown, earth yellow, dark green, dark blue, lighter blue. Total size of the specimen: 142 x 117 cm. [56 x 46 in.]. Length photographed: 67 cm. [26½ in.]. Provenience: central coastal region. Museum of the American Indian, Heye Foundation, New York, No. 17/8920.

B. Another corner of the same specimen, the surface lozenges of which contain geometric and anthropomorphic decorative motives.

PLATE 25, A. White cotton fabric, muslin family, with supplementary wool weft. The brocading weft passes over six warp yarns, then under two warp yarns, and so forth. Cotton wefts are alternated with wool wefts. Two consecutive wool wefts follow the same passage, the following two overlap half of the preceding, and so on. The decorative wefts are interlocked when color changes occur. Colors: red, black, rose, yellow, brown. Design: fret motives. Natural size. Provenience: central coastal region. Musée de l'Homme, X, 33–271–15.

B. The same fabric seen on the other face.

C. Natural white cotton fabric, rep family, concealed weft, ornamented with a decorative weft in old rose forming lozenges. On the reverse face the decorative weft floats are divided by the passage of the decorative weft under the warp yarns; this passage is not visible on the right side because of the texture of the rep (concealed weft). Natural size. Provenience: central coastal region. Musée de l'Homme, No. X, 33–271–14.

D. The same fabric seen on the other face.

E. Cotton rep with blue and white stripes. The regular weft is concealed and covered by a decorative weft of carmine wool, which is visible only on one face of the fabric because of the texture of the rep. At intervals the decorative yarn passes under the warp yarn, thus forming a lozenge design. Natural size. Provenience: central coastal region. Musée de l'Homme, No. X, 33–271–8.

F. The same fabric seen on the other face.

PLATE 26, A. Fabric of navy blue wool, plain weave, enhanced by decorative white cotton yarns (in warp and weft), which cross each other and form fret motives (see p. 42). Natural size. Provenience: central coast of Peru. Collection of Fritz Iklé, No. 7096.

B. Cotton fabric, warp of alternate brown and white yarns, then white only (on the side); weft brown (white in the lower part). The design is formed by alternately incorporating the white yarns into the fabric and then leaving them on the reverse side to form floats. When the white yarns are incorporated in this way the plain weave becomes a rep. Natural size. Provenience: central coastal region. Musée de l'Homme, No. X, 33–271–28.

C. The same fabric seen on the other face.

PLATE 27, A. Blue cotton fabric, plain weave, ornamented in both warp and weft with supplementary white and beige yarns that cross each other in pairs, with a construction distinct from that of the underlying plain weave. The decorative warp yarns are continuous; the decorative weft yarns extend over only a given width of the fabric and on the return passage cover the same area (see p. 42). Design: anthropomorphized animals holding in their hands some sort of weapon or baton. Length of the part photographed: 19 cm. [7½ in.]. Provenience: Pachacamac. Musée de l'Homme, No. X, 33–271–4.

B. The same fabric seen on the other face.

PLATE 28, A. Cotton rep with concealed weft. The fabric is made of light blue and light brown bands on which stand out blue and white cotton warp yarns, forming, by lateral displacement, series of lozenges that alternate from one face to the other. Natural size. Provenience: central coastal region. Collection of Fritz Iklé, No. 7253.

B. Cotton fabric, plain weave, in beige and blue. On one face are lozenges formed of four beige warp yarns, which, in pairs, incline alternately to the right, then left (or to the left, then right), and are secured by the weft every fourth passage. When these yarns are not used, they pass to the other face, where they form floats. Natural size. Provenience: central coastal region. Musée de l'Homme, No. X, 33–271–7.

C. The same fabric seen on the other face.

PLATE 29, A. Double cloth of beige and brown cotton, plain weave. Design: step and scroll motives on which two felines are depicted. Total length: 60 cm. [23½ in.]; width: 15.5 cm. [6 in.]. Provenience: central coastal region. Collection of Fritz Iklé, No. 13026.

B. The same fabric seen on the other face.

PLATE 30, A. Part of a wool girth made in tubular weaving, rep family, with double-cloth weaving in the central section. Colors: on the sides, carmine; in the center, blue, yellow, dark brown. Length of the entire specimen: 168 cm. [66 in.]; width: 10 cm. [4 in.]. Provenience: Nazca. Collection of R. d'Harcourt.

B. Complete fabric of cotton made of white and tobacco brown, double weave. One of the faces is enhanced by dots resembling peas embroidered in variously colored wools. According to some Peruvianists, this specimen was an almanac or calendar. The design consists of fifty-six squares, that is, seven horizontal bands of eight squares each. The decorative lines inside the squares vary from one band to another, except in the case of the sixth, which repeats the fourth with the exception of one detail (the little square in the lower left corner and to the left of the fourth band is missing in the sixth). In a single band the arrangement, the color, and the number of the dots vary from one square to another. Size: 55 x 53 cm. [21½ x 21 in.]. Provenience: central coastal region. Musée de l'Homme, No. 30–49–21.

PLATE 31, A. Wool band of double weave, irregular construction, with multicolored warp. Its ends are made of intercrossed yarns, according to the technique of double plaiting, and terminate in a fringe. Colors: bright blue, carmine, golden yellow, violet brown, white. Length: 54 cm. [21¼ in.]. Provenience: Nazca. Collection of Fritz Iklé.

B. Small bag of wool and cotton of double weave, rep family. Design: procession of llamas. Colors: carmine wool and white cotton. Twenty warp yarns to the centimeter [51 to the inch]. The upper edge is embroidered, and the sides are joined with loop stitch (see p. 135). Colors: red, light yellow, dark brown, green, white, beige. The flat braid is plaited in yarns of yellowish brown and carmine red. The cord is plaited in yarns of natural white, red, almond green, and dark blue. Total length of the braid: 53 cm. [21 in.]; width of the lower end of the bag: 18 cm. [7 in.]. Provenience: Nazca. Schmidt Collection, Paris.

PLATE 32, A, B, C. Central portions of slings. The technique of the woven parts of these three specimens has been discussed on pages 47 and 96. Lateral cords were affixed to the ends.

A. Double band of agave fiber. Double warp, natural white and brown black, with red and yellow brown wool yarns superimposed. Weft natural white and brown black, the latter almost completely destroyed. Actual length of the central woven portion: 29 cm. [11½ in.]; width: 22 mm. [¾ in.]; thickness: 3 mm. Provenience: central coastal region. Collection of Fritz Iklé.

B. Four double bands of quite stiff agave fiber. Double warp, natural white and brown black, the latter almost completely destroyed. Weft, natural white. Pattern in red wool. Length: 24.5 cm. [9¾ in.] not including the terminal yarns; width: 10 cm. [4 in.]; thickness: 4 mm. Provenience: central coastal region. Musée de l'Homme, No. 30–19–1683.

C. Two double bands of agave fiber (there were formerly more). Double warp of natural white and brown black. Pattern in red wool. Total length: 34 cm. [13½ in.]; width: 3.5 cm. [1¼ in.]; thickness: 2 mm. Provenience: central coastal region. Collection of Fritz Iklé.

D. Small wool ornament, probably representing a trophy head, placed at the end of a tapestry band. Colors: red mask surrounded by two blue circles made of loop stitch; eyes and mouth in white, beard in red and pale yellow, hair in pale yellow and greenish color; green, yellow, and red band. Length: 8 cm. [3¼ in.]. Provenience: central coastal region. Musée de l'Homme, No. X, 33–271–24.

Plate 33, A. Light brown cotton fabric, consisting of alternating bands of plain weave and simple two-yarn gauze; the latter is intersected every twelve warps by a column of six warps, which cross each other by threes. Natural size. Provenience: central coastal region. Collection of Fritz Iklé, No. 13015.

B. White cotton fabric consisting of narrow plain-weave bands, alternating with wide bands of gauze (see p. 52). Design: simple geometric lines, developed in open-work, three-yarn gauze. Natural size. Provenience: central coastal region. Collection of R. d'Harcourt.

Plate 34, A. White cotton fabric of two-yarn and three-yarn gauze, the two techniques alternating regularly every four wefts and every six or eight warp yarns (see p. 52). Natural size. Provenience: central coastal region. Musée de l'Homme, No. 31–33–3.

B. White cotton fabric in three-yarn gauze, with open spaces for a length of seven to eleven wefts. In the upper part, a band of cotton rep, concealed warp, and the terminal selvage. Natural size. Provenience: central coastal region. Collection of Fritz Iklé, No. 7173.

Plate 35. White cotton fabric in three-yarn gauze with open spaces. The decorative motives, which are difficult to interpret, are outlined in a coarse, knotted cotton yarn. Actual size of the specimen: 71 x 21 cm. [23 x 8¼ in.], three selvages. Length photographed: 38 cm. [15 in.]. Provenience: central coastal region. Musée de l'Homme, No. 31–33–4.

Plate 36, A. White cotton fabric in two- or three-yarn gauze, with irregular open spaces. Design: geometric with stylized feline heads. Size of the part photographed: 25 x 19 cm. [10 x 7½ in.]. Provenience: central coastal region. Musée de l'Homme, No. 31–33–16.

B. White cotton fabric, plain weave with open spaces produced by gauze weave (see p. 53). A coarse cotton yarn, knotted to the fabric, outlines the decorative motives: at the right, stylized slings; at the left, zoomorphic motives. Natural size. Provenience: central coastal region. Collection of Fritz Iklé, No. 7146.

Plate 37, A. White cotton fabric in three-yarn gauze, with open spaces. The open spaces are arranged to form lozenges in the center of which is an unidentified stylized motive. Length of the specimen: 100 cm. [39¼ in.]; width at the base: 50 cm. [19¾ in.]. One terminal selvage and one lateral selvage. Length photographed: 26 cm. [10¼ in.]. Provenience: central coastal region. Musée de l'Homme, No. 31–33–8.

B. White cotton fabric, plain-weave cloth, with lines of gauze weave that cross each other diagonally, forming lozenges (see p. 53). A decorative motive (stylized bird) is woven into the center of each lozenge, also in gauze weave. Size of the entire specimen: 73 x 48 cm. [28¾ x 19 in.], four selvages. Length photographed: 36 cm. [14 in.]. Provenience: central coastal region. Musée de l'Homme, No. 31–33–7.

Plate 38. White cotton fabric in three-yarn gauze with open spaces. The decorative motives (stylized sea birds, either complete or heads only) are outlined with a coarse knotted cotton yarn. Size of the specimen: 61 x 36 cm. [24 x 14 in.]. Length photographed: 41 cm. [16 in.]. Provenience: central coastal region. Musée de l'Homme, No. 31–33–6.

Plate 39, A. Cotton fabric consisting of plain-weave bands alternating with open-space bands made in accordance with the principle of gauze, by the crossing of warp yarns: a group of four warp yarns crosses a corresponding group of four warp yarns and is secured by one heavy weft yarn of dark color. Size of the entire specimen: 79 x 71 cm. [31 x 28 in.]. Provenience: Peru. American Museum of Natural History, New York, No. B 8598.

B. White cotton fabric with alternate bands of plain weave and three-yarn gauze, with regular open spaces (see p. 53). Natural size. Provenience: central coastal region. Collection of Fritz Iklé.

C. Small white and rose carmine cotton bag, the construction of which (gauze family) is explained on page 52. The two faces of the fabric are the same with reversed colors. Natural size. Provenience: Nazca. Collection of Fritz Iklé.

D. White cotton fabric of three-yarn gauze, with regular open spaces intersected in both the warp and the weft by yarns of dark blue cotton which form stripes perpendicular to each other, in plain weave. In the vertical stripes every fourth white weft crosses the surface of the blue warp yarns without being incorporated into them, and moves back between the odd and even yarns; it then resumes its original direction on the surface on the other side before commencing the gauze again. Natural size. Provenience: central coastal region. Collection of R. d'Harcourt.

PLATE 40. White cotton fabric with square open spaces obtained by the technique described on page 58. It is embroidered with a white cotton yarn, which forms a lozenge in each open square. The design represents series of felines and stylized pelicans. Part photographed: 54 x 63 cm. [21¼ x 24¾ in.]. Provenience: central coastal region. Musée de l'Homme, No. 31–33–2.

PLATE 41. Blue cotton fabric with open spaces obtained by the technique described on page 58. It is embroidered in blue cotton in a design of two-headed felines. Terminal selvage at the bottom of the photograph; the warp ends are secured by fourteen compacted wefts. The embroidery stitches filling the open spaces are varied (see Fig. 94). A heavy yarn forms the eyes of the felines. Size of the specimen: 27 x 34 cm. [10½ x 13¼ in.]. The sides of the open spaces measure 4 to 5 mm. Provenience: central coastal region. Musée de l'Homme, No. 31–33–9.

PLATE 42. White cotton fabric with square open spaces obtained by the technique described on page 58. The fabric is embroidered in a design of pelicans, either in repose or in flight, and the motives are outlined in a white cotton yarn. Size of the specimen: 151 x 28 cm. [59½ x 11 in.]. Length photographed: 54 cm. [21¼ in.]. The sides of the open spaces measure 8 mm. Selvage on the left side. The arrow on this plate indicates the direction of the weft. Provenience: central coastal region. Musée de l'Homme, No. 31–33–12.

PLATE 43. White cotton fabric with square and triangular open spaces obtained by the technique described on page 58. The square mesh fabric is embroidered with a motive of a pelican with a fish in its beak. The groups of pelicans are separated by a curving band of triangular mesh fabric embroidered with a small reptile design. The decorative motives and the band are outlined with a white cotton knotted yarn. Selvages on two sides, at the base and on the right. Size of the part photographed: 48 x 57 cm. [19 x 22½ in.]. Sides of the open spaces measure 4 to 5 mm. Provenience: central coastal region. Musée de l'Homme, No. 31–33–5.

PLATE 44. White cotton fabric with square open spaces obtained by the technique described on page 58 and embroidered. The heavy border woven between every twelve warps and every twelve wefts divides the fabric into rectangles of 144 open spaces. Alternate blocks contain embroidery. Size of the photographed part of the open-work fabric: 22 x 43 cm. [8¾ x 17 in.]. A tapestry band with human figures is attached by overcasting to the lower edge of the open-work fabric. Colors: red background; brown, yellow, rose, and white figures. Between the figures the tapestry band is crossed by a narrow band of weaving with varied construction in which the two-colored weft extends beyond the tapestry band and forms the warp, which assumes the dominant role in accordance with the technique described on pages 44–45. Colors: rose and red, or yellow and brown black. Width of the band, including the tabs: 9.5 cm. [3¾ in.]. Provenience: central coastal region. Hein Collection, Paris.

PLATE 45, A. White cotton fabric, very yellowed, consisting of plain-weave bands and sections in which the warp is exposed. A yarn added after weaving knots the warp yarns together in groups of fifteen, and the wefts in groups of eight or ten, which gives the fabric a very special character. Natural size. Provenience: central coastal region. Collection of Fritz Iklé, No. 7050.

B. White cotton fabric consisting of narrow bands in plain weave separating sections of two-yarn gauze and open-space sections obtained by omitting weft yarns at intervals. An independent yarn knots the unwoven warp and weft yarns together in groups of four in such a way as to divide the woven band into small squares. Natural size. Provenience: central coastal region. Collection of Fritz Iklé, No. 13020.

PLATE 46, A. Fabric in wool and cotton, showing plain sections and sections in open-work lozenges, according to the technique described on page 55. The warp is formed of groups of four yarns of yellow wool, alternating with four yarns of white cotton. The weft is of cotton. Where the lozenges join, the wefts unite and cross as a pair, as in Figure 34, *a*. In the lower part, the fabric becomes solid in a weaving of varied construction; the yellow wool yarn produces a pattern with geometric lines, which stands out on the white cotton foundation. Slightly less than natural size. Provenience: central coastal region. Musée de l'Homme, No. X, 33–271–16.

B. Natural white cotton fabric with one section in plain weave and one band of open-work lozenges produced by the technique described on page 55. In the band the warp is divided into groups of twelve yarns, which separate into two groups of six yarns to form the lozenges. Slightly less than natural size. Provenience: central coastal region. Collection of Fritz Iklé, No. 7057.

PLATE 47, A. Specimen of white cotton and colored wool with interlocked warp yarns and a weft knotted in accordance with the technique described on page 59. The specimen consists of alternate bands of yellow and red violet wool, developed by interlocking with the white cotton yarns, which have the appearance of a background; the design shows motives of stylized pelicans or sequences of crosses, arranged obliquely. The specimen was originally at least 130 cm. [51¼ in.] in length and 130 cm. [51¼ in.] wide. It is in very poor condition. To facilitate examination of the design, the photograph was taken with the elements of the fabric shown diagonally. Length photographed: 33 cm. [13 in.]. Provenience: central coastal region. Musée de l'Homme, No. X, 33–271–6.

B. Rectangular piece comprising:

1. A central part of white cotton yarn, plain weave, with large open spaces formed by omitting warp and weft yarns. Yarns composed of twisted white cotton and red wool cross the open spaces both vertically and horizontally and knot together the unwoven sections of the warp and weft yarns.

2. A framework consisting of an initial band woven in fairly thick white cotton, of the rep family, embroidered on one face by securing an azure blue wool yarn with red wool crosses and two yarns of yellow wool (couching). A second band, placed on the outside of the rep band, consists of tapestry (cotton warp, yellow wool weft) crossed by two rows of loops at a distance of 1.5 cm. [½ in.] from each other. In addition, the outside edge of the braid is ornamented with groups of three small cords (weft extensions), which emerge from the tapestry and form a kind of fringe.

Slightly less than natural size. Full size of the specimen: 70 x 120 cm. [27½ x 47¼ in.]. Provenience: central coastal region. Musée de l'Homme, No. X, 33–271–5.

PLATE 48, A. One half of what is probably a small bag or *chuspa*, woven in accordance with the method described on page 64. The warp yarns of alternating colors of yellow and brown are twisted around each other in pairs and are held in place at each twisting by a hidden weft yarn. In general, the direction of the twisting reverses from one pair to another; its simultaneous reversal in two adjacent pairs, and its return, produce a design of small lozenges in the fabric. But there are other reversals of direction in the twisting of the yarns that seem to result from simple negligence. If the specimen were complete, there would undoubtedly be proof that the work had been accomplished according to the schematic drawing shown in Figure 39. Any other technique would require the warp yarns to be free in their lower part, and this would make the weaving very difficult. Slightly less than natural size. Provenience: Nazca. Museum für Völkerkunde, Munich.

B. Fragment of fabric made of vegetable fiber, in which the warp yarns are secured about every 15 mm. [½ in.] by two weft yarns, which are twisted around each other (twining). Size: about 18 x 27 cm. [7 x 10½ in.]. Provenience: Rio Culebras (325 km. north of Lima). Preceramic culture. Collection of Frederic Engel, Lima.

C. Fragment of cotton fabric in which the weft yarns are twisted in pairs around warps (twining), forming a series of open spaces arranged in oblique lines. Preceramic culture. Collection of Frederic Engel, Lima.

PLATE 49, A and B. Two fragments of the same wool braid, woven according to the method shown on page 64 (see Fig. 40). In the center of the first fragment can be seen the irregularity due to the reversal of the direction of twisting of the warp yarns, a reversal necessitated by the technique. The specimen is complete (the yarns at the two ends form warp loops); it consists of four twists of eight yarns of four colors, bordered on each side by a twist of four yarns of the same color, giving a total of

158

forty yarns. Length: 148 cm. [58¼ in.]; width: 17 mm. [¾ in.]. Natural size. Colors: dark blue, red, yellow, white (cotton). Provenience: central coastal region. Musée de l'Homme, No. 30–19–1681.

C. Cotton fabric, rep family, resist-dyed (*planghi*). The section photographed consists of two parts woven separately and joined together on the lateral edges by a thread that passes through the two looped ends of the warp yarns of the two parts. The perpendicular woven edges are sewed. The dark part was dyed twice. First the design was prepared by tying certain portions and dyeing the fabric blue. After it was untied, the fabric was overdyed yellow, so that it was yellow and green. The other, lighter part was dyed red after the design was tied and was, therefore, red and white. Two other parts, of which only a few yarns remain, were dyed: one was dyed blue with reserved white; the other was dyed blue with reserved sections, then overdyed red without reserve, so that it was red and violet. Natural size. Provenience: central coastal region. Collection of Fritz Iklé, No. 3727.

D. Band with twisted warp yarns, concealed weft, constructed according to the technique described on page 63. Colors: warp, yellow and black; weft, old red. Natural size. Provenience: Peru. Collection of Fritz Iklé, No. 4052.

E. Another band with twisted warp yarns. Colors: warp, yellow and light blue at the right and left, red and blue in the center; weft, old red. Natural size. Provenience: Peru. Collection of Fritz Iklé, No. 4052.

PLATE 50, A. White cotton fabric, rep family, painted. The colors are pale red and four browns of graduating intensity. The specimen contains two breadths sewed together; the total dimensions are 166 x 142 cm. [65¼ x 56 in.]. The panel shown in the plate is one of nine similar ones arranged in two lateral bands. Size of the panel depicted: 24.5 x 25.5 cm. [9¾ x 10 in.]. Provenience: Ancón: Musée de l'Homme, No. 84–91–65.

B. White cotton fabric, rep family, painted on one surface with a light brown color (café au lait). Design: sawtooth surfaces of a solid light brown color, alternating at intervals with white bands ornamented with Maltese cross, bird, and fret motives. Part photographed: 25 x 34 cm. [10 x 13½ in.]. Provenience: Ancón. Musée de l'Homme, No. X, 33–271–27.

PLATE 51, A. Natural white fabric, rep family, painted on one face with a reddish brown color. The pattern in white (reserve) consists of regular zigzag lines and a repeated ornithomorphic motive (negative image). Natural size. Provenience: central coastal region. Collection of Fritz Iklé.

B. Natural white cotton fabric, plain weave, painted on one face. Design: divinities arranged head to foot, with plants in their hands (some with wings). The subjects are painted with uniform yellow and reddish dyes and are outlined in black. Natural size. Provenience: Nazca. Ratton Collection, Paris.

PLATE 52, A. Fabric of three-yarn cotton gauze, resist-dyed (*planghi*); see page 69. The light parts are yellow, the dark parts brown. Natural size. Provenience: central coastal region. Musée de l'Homme, No. 31–33–1.

B. White cotton plain weave dyed brown red with reserve (*planghi*). Length photographed: 30 cm. [11¾ in.]. Provenience: Pachacamac. Göteborgs Museum, No. 21–6–196.

PLATE 53, A. Cotton fabric, plain weave, with warp yarns tied in preparation for the design and dyed before weaving (*ikat*). The warps, between the warping and the weaving, were tied and dyed twice, blue and brown. The specimen has, therefore, with the white foundation fabric, three colors. Design: simple step motives. The weft, beige in color, passes over two warp yarns at a time. The specimen consists of three breadths, only two of which were dyed with the *ikat* technique. Length: 123 cm. [48½ in.]; width of each breadth: 50 cm. [19¾ in.]. Width of the photographed part: 42 cm. [16½ in.]. Provenience: central coastal region. Musée de l'Homme, No. X, 33–271–3.

B. Cotton fabric, plain weave, muslin family, consisting of striped pieces between which is sewed a section dyed by the *ikat* method. Color of the warp yarns of the striped pieces: yellow, beige, brown, red brown, blue green, darker blue (in the yellow stripe, white decorative yarns are woven in irregular construction); uniformly brown weft. In the *ikat* section, the warp is white, dyed brown in places; the weft is white or brown (eight wefts white, two brown, two white, eight brown, two white, two brown, eight white, and so forth). Design: simple step motives. Fifteen warp yarns and ten weft yarns to the centimeter [38 x 25 to the inch]. Provenience: Barranca, near Pacasmayo. Total size: 300 x 220 cm. [118 x 86½ in.]. Collection of I. G. Farbenindustrie A. G., at Ludwigshafen am Rhein.

PLATE 54, A. Small bag of wool yarn plaited by the method described on page 80. In the middle of the bag itself can be seen a line in which the yarns are slacker and the direction of the crossing is reversed. Colors: white, yellow, red, green, blue. On the lower edge, red fringes on the sides, yellow in the center. A narrow wool braid, made with a square cross section (colors: green, red, yellow, violet), is used to close the bag, which still contains some coca leaves. Total length: 27 cm. [10½ in.]; width: 17 cm. [6¾ in.]. Provenience: Nazca. Musée de l'Homme, No. 30–19–445.

B. Specimen plaited in accordance with the method shown in Figure 45. The wool yarns, which are brown, are twisted in pairs. In the upper left-hand corner can be seen the turning of the yarns upon reaching the selvage. Natural size. Provenience: central coastal region. Collection of Fritz Iklé, No. 7113.

PLATE 55, A. Band of wool plaited according to the technique described on page 77. Colors: dark blue, dark brown, yellow. The yarns are twisted together in pairs of the same color. The direction of the twisting changes with each pair of yarns (the one from right to left, the other from left to right), giving the appearance of small adjacent chains. The yarns are arranged in the following order: two pairs of blue, one pair of brown, one pair of yellow, two pairs of blue, and so forth. The borders of the band are made in loop stitch of yellow, blue, green, and red wool. Natural size. Provenience: central coast of Peru. Collection of Fritz Iklé.

B. Band of wool plaited in accordance with the technique described on page 76, Figure 46. Colors: yellow, red, plum violet, dark green, dark blue. The band consists of nine groups of twenty-four monochrome yarns, each group being divided into two subgroups in the part that is covered. Natural size. Provenience: central coast of Peru. Collection of Fritz Iklé.

C. Band of wool plaited in accordance with the technique described on page 77, Figure 47. Colors: red, rose, olive green, Prussian blue, very dark blue. Each colored band forming the pattern is composed of fifty-six monochrome yarns, dividing into seven subgroups of eight yarns each in the part that is covered. Total length: 129 cm. [50¾ in.]. Length photographed: 34 cm. [13½ in.]. Provenience: Nazca. Museum of the American Indian, Heye Foundation, New York, No. 17/8929.

D. Band of plaited wool terminating in a fringe consisting of five small braids. It is made of twenty yarns: eight red, eight blue, and four yellow. The red and blue yarns are covered in pairs during one half of the passage, and during the other half they themselves form the covering element. The yellow yarns, which remain in the central part of the band where they form a series of X's, always constitute the covering element in pairs. Natural size. Provenience: Arica. Musée de l'Homme, No. 87–115–169.

E. A woven and embroidered band, extended at its two ends by a braided part that terminates in a fringe. It may be compared to specimen A of Plate 31. The part photographed, in natural size, includes a portion of embroidered fabric, the plaiting, and the beginning of the fringe. The fabric is of light brown cotton plain weave, entirely covered by embroidery resembling tapestry, in red, yellow, blue, and dark brown wool, which covers four weft yarns at a time and forms a design of geometric lines. The plaiting is partially double: thus, the arms of the crosses, which are blue on one side and red on the other, are made of double plaiting, while the rest of the plaiting in colors of brown and yellow is simple. The fringe is made of four-strand braids. Length of the entire specimen: 80 cm. [31½ in.]. Provenience: south coast of Peru. Collection of Fritz Iklé, No. 7329.

PLATE 56, A. Plaiting with rectangular cross section, in the course of construction. The plaiting utilizes at least forty-two dark brown wool yarns. The unused portion of each of these yarns remains in the form of a small roll at the lower end of the plaited part. The beginning of the plaiting in the form of a loop, where the elements are folded back, is covered with a vegetal fiber that is itself finely plaited. Length: 18 cm. [7 in.]. Provenience: central coastal region. Musée de l'Homme, No. 78–2–554.

160

B. Specimen plaited of brown wool in accordance with the technique by which the yarns are fastened at their two ends and twisted together. This plaiting produces open spaces (see Fig. 53), the arrangement of which permits the making of a design (birds, fish, stylized serpents). The column of loops on the left part of the photograph shows the method of terminating the interlocking of the yarns in the center of the plaiting (see Fig. 52, C). Size of the entire specimen: 130 x 60 cm. [51¼ x 23½ in.]. Provenience: Cerro Colorado (Paracas). Museo Nacional de Lima, No. 8430.

PLATE 57. Wool neck covering obtained by the method of double plaiting described on page 81. In one system the two leases are red, and in the other system the two leases are yellow. At first the two systems of plaiting are independent, so that the lower edges of the piece of work are made up of two bands of simple plaiting—the upper one red, the lower one yellow—superimposed upon, but not joined to, each other. The two systems of plaiting exchange their positions as required by the design, using irregular techniques (crossing and interlocking). In the upper part of the neck covering, near the section covered by loop stitch, the two systems again become independent as in the beginning. The top of the specimen is made up of nonplaited yarns, which occupy the center of the warp during the plaiting. The plaited fabric was folded after construction, and loop-stitch embroidery unites the unplaited yarns in a single thickness. Colors of the embroidery: yellow, red, rose, pale blue, and white on a brown background. Length of the neck covering: 29 cm. [11½ in.]; width at its base: 24 cm. [9½ in.]. Provenience: Nazca. Collection of Fritz Iklé, No. 13024.

PLATE 58. Neck covering of two similar sections joined by a small cord. The specimen is formed of two double plaitings which intercross in accordance with the method described on page 82. One of the systems is green and blue, the other is red and yellow. The unplaited yarns at the top of each of the two sections are covered with a kind of blue wool fabric of the rep family, made locally by needle; this fabric is decorated with a motive of S's in a prone position, embroidered in loop stitch with red and yellow yarns. Length: 21.5 cm. [8½ in.]; width at the base: 13 cm. [5 in.]. The little cord that joins the two sections is woven with wool yarns of different colors following the technique of tubular weaving (see p. 47). Provenience: Nazca. Musée de l'Homme, No. 34–145–2.

PLATE 59, A. Part of a lateral cord from a sling plaited with sixteen strands of wool (eight dark brown, eight pale yellow) according to the method described on page 86. Chevron design. Natural size. Provenience: central coast of Peru. Musée de l'Homme, No. X, 33–271–29.

B. Part of a lateral cord from a sling plaited with sixteen wool strands (eight dark brown, eight pale yellow) according to the method described on page 86. Lozenge design. Natural size. Provenience: central coast of Peru. Musée de l'Homme, No. 30–19–460.

C. Part of a lateral cord from a sling with square cross section, plaited with thirty-eight strands in wool of four colors (white, red, yellow, yellow brown) and of different thicknesses, according to the method described on page 94. Provenience: Nazca. Musée de l'Homme, No. 48–76–280.

D. Part of a lateral cord from a sling, plaited with twenty-four strands of wool in three colors (yellow, gray, red) and of three different thicknesses, giving the cord heavy embossing that is symmetrically arranged. The plaiting is done according to the method described on page 89. Provenience: Nazca. Musée de l'Homme, No. X, 47–5–786.

E. Part of a lateral cord of a ceremonial sling with round cross section, plaited with thirty-two strands in wool of four colors (brown, yellow, white, and black), according to the method described on page 92. A number of wool yarns, untwisted and fastened with a needle, are used as ornaments. Ethnographic specimen from the Peruvian Highlands. Musée de l'Homme, No. 38–147–33.

F. Fragment of passementerie made of two plaited braids arranged one at the side of the other. These join and edge on the outside a small ornament in zigzag design, which is also plaited. The yarns of the braids, which are of vegetable fiber, are wrapped locally with wool yarns of different colors. This wrapping increases their bulkiness. The plaiting is done according to the method described on page 78 (Fig. 49). The yarns of the ornament are also plaited (Fig. 50). Colors: red, blue, yellow, brown, plum

Description of Plates

violet, sage green. The plaiting of the ornament was done in position, the yarn, at the tips of the zigzags, passing across the braids in order to be secured there. Length of the entire specimen: 258 cm. [101½ in.]; width: 5 cm. [2 in.]. Provenience: Nazca. British Museum, London, No. 1933-12-16-5.

PLATE 60, A. Sandal made of *cabuya* fiber plaited according to the method described on page 65. Length: 20 cm. [8 in.]. Provenience: Ancón. Musée de l'Homme, No. X, 47-5-62.

B. Sandal made of *cabuya* fiber, consisting of two long flat braids with three strands superimposed and joined in accordance with the method described on page 99. Length: 19.4 cm. [7¾ in.]. Provenience: Ancón. Musée de l'Homme, No. X, 47-5-61.

C. Portion of a kind of belt plaited in light yellow wool yarn. The specimen consists of about forty sections regularly alternated, one in which the yarns cross each other in twos and the other in which the yarns, grouped by fours, form twenty small adjacent independent plaitings. Length: 210 cm. [82¾ in.]; width 7 cm. [2¾ in.]. Provenience: Nazca. Museum für Völkerkunde, Munich.

D. Part of a band plaited with wool yarns of four colors: brown (two tones), reddish yellow, and yellow green. The colors have deteriorated. The method of plaiting is a combination of the second and third types described on pages 77 and 78. The principle applied is that of yarns alternately covering-separated and covered-joined, according to the requirements of the design and the principle of yarns twisted in pairs. Thus, when they are covered, the yarns of one single color are joined in groups of four; when they have the covering role, these four yarns twist around each other in pairs, taking up in each spiral the grouped yarns of the opposite color. The direction of the twisting of the yarns is reversed from one pair to the other. Actual length of the braid: 57 cm. [22½ in.]; width: 3.8 cm. [1½ in.]. Provenience: central coast of Peru. Musée de l'Homme, No. X, 33-271-30.

PLATE 61, A. Ceremonial sling with "furred" center of dark brown wool, made in accordance with the method described on page 111. At each end of the "furred" center are short sections covered with red, yellow, and dark brown wool yarn in stem stitch, which terminate in small braided cords of vegetable fiber (agave?). Length of the part photographed: 24 cm. [9½ in.]. Provenience: Nazca. Collection of R. d'Harcourt.

B. Sling made with a center of vegetable fiber cords, joined and covered by a wool yarn woven in the manner of a weft in rep. The edges of this central part and the flat parts that continue it are spirally wrapped with a heavy yarn, the adjacent turns of which are themselves joined and covered with wool embroidery executed in stem stitch in a perpendicular direction. The embroidery forms a series of decorative motives resembling hooked X's. On the flat section at the right, the threadbare embroidery reveals the wrapping of the underlying heavy yarn. At the lower ends, the extensions of the two cords are covered with a plaiting of red wool. Colors of the embroidery: red, yellow, white, black. Lengths: cords, 74 cm. [29 in.]; flat parts, 14.5 cm. [5¾ in.]; center, 20 cm. [8 in.]. Provenience: Nazca. Musée de l'Homme, No. 30-19-457.

C. Sling consisting of a center formed in the same manner as B, above. The edges of this central part are wrapped with a heavy yarn in adjacent spirals that are themselves joined and covered with a wool embroidery executed in stem stitch in a perpendicular direction. At the lower ends the extensions of the two cords originate in a plaiting of twenty-four strands, in accordance with the method described on page 89; they are then reduced to a plaiting with eight strands. Colors of the embroidery: red, dark green, moss green, natural white, yellow. Length of the cords as far as the central part: 91 cm. [36 in.]; length of the center: 13.5 cm. [5½ in.]. Provenience: Nazca. Musée de l'Homme, No. 30-19-459.

D. Sling consisting of a center formed like that of B, above. The edges of this central part and the cylindrical parts that continue it are wrapped with a heavy yarn of twisted cotton in adjacent spirals that are themselves joined and covered with wool embroidery executed in a perpendicular direction in stem stitch. Colors: red, yellow green, white, black. The two cords are plaited of white wool and terminate, one in a tassel of red wool and the other in a tassel of yellow wool. Lengths: cords, 68 cm. [26¾ in.]; tassels, 20 cm. [8 in.]; round sections, 9.5 cm. [3¾ in.]; center, 18.5 cm. [7¼ in.]. Provenience: Nazca. Schmidt Collection, Paris.

PLATE 62. Sling consisting of a center similar to that shown in Plate 61, B. The edges of this central

162

part and the flat parts that continue it are wrapped with a heavy twisted cotton yarn in adjacent spirals that are themselves joined and wrapped with a wool embroidery executed in stem stitch in a perpendicular direction. Colors: carmine, yellow, white, brown, black. The cords are plaited in brown black and white wool in accordance with the technique described on page 99. Near their extremities they have a short section in which the yarns of these two colors alternate without being plaited; successive fastenings at intervals encircle the yarns of the concealed color and cover the yarns of the visible color. The cords terminate in fine ropes. Total length of the cords: 132 cm. [51¾ in.]; length of the center and flat sections: 44.5 cm. [17½ in.]; width in the center: 6 cm. [2¼ in.]. Provenience: Nazca. Collection of Fritz Iklé, No. 7254.

PLATE 63. Ceremonial sling, the central part made of polychrome wool tapestry. In this case the sling cords are represented only by their tubular wrapping made of a heavy cotton yarn whose adjacent spirals are joined and covered with wool embroidery in stem stitch. Colors in the center: white, yellow, violet, green, red, dark brown. Colors of the embroidery: white, yellow, red, dark brown, and violet in the first part, and then plain carmine red, including the terminal fringe, from which the wrappings are separated by a violet-colored tassel head. Total length of the specimen: 245 cm. [96¾ in.]. Provenience: Ica. See Harcourt, 1924, Plate 16. Collection of R. d'Harcourt.

PLATE 64. Sling made of natural white and dark brown wool, the central part of which is similar to that shown in Plate 61, B, but without borders embroidered in stem stitch. The lateral portions are made by the plaiting-weaving method (see p. 97) and are later transformed into round cords braided with four strands that terminate in small ropes. Lengths: central part, 16.5 cm. [6½ in.]; flat parts, 55 cm. [21¾ in.]; round parts, 173 cm. [68 in.]; fringe, 15 cm. [6 in.]. Provenience: Nazca. Musée de l'Homme, No. 30-19-458.

PLATE 65, A. Small bag of agave fiber, made with complex looping (see p. 102). In the network of the bag, the yarn, after having threaded the mesh of the upper row, makes a complete turn around its own loop. In the upper border the yarn turns twice, and in the band forming the handle it turns three times, around itself. Length: 15.5 cm. [6 in.]; length of band: 22 cm. [8¾ in.]; width at center: 16 cm. [6¼ in.]. Provenience: central coast of Peru. Musée de l'Homme, No. 30-19-494.

B. Small cotton bag made of simple loops joined to one another (see p. 101). The lower part of the bag is decorated with two pompons. It contains hair. Natural size. Provenience: coastal region of Peru. Riksmuseum, Stockholm, No. 10-19-22.

C. Fragment of beige cotton network made of loop stitch (see p. 101). This network forms the foundation of a bonnet. Natural size. Provenience: central coast of Peru. Musée de l'Homme, No. 29-14-667.

D. Small wool bag made of rows of simple loops joined to one another (see p. 100). Colors: dark brown and pale yellow, with the upper border and the bottom in lighter brown. The wool band attached to the bag is made in plain weave (rep family) with alternating brown and yellow warps; the pale yellow weft is invisible. Length of bag: 19 cm. [7½ in.]; length of band: 41 cm. [16¼ in.]. Provenience: Pachacamac. Collection of R. d'Harcourt.

PLATE 66, A. Regular network of agave fiber, made in square knotting (see p. 106). Slightly less than natural size. Provenience: Ancón. Collection of R. d'Harcourt.

B. Network of agave fiber, made in square knotting. At times the knots touch one another to form solid blocks, while at other times they leave a mesh between them (see Fig. 77). Slightly less than natural size. Provenience: central coast of Peru. Collection of Fritz Iklé, No. 13025.

C. Network of agave fiber, with regular meshes made with a simple knot. This network is partially painted in blackish and red brown colors forming step motives. Slightly less than natural size. Provenience: coastal region of Peru. Collection of Fritz Iklé.

D. Network of regular meshes made in square knotting in gray beige and brown wool (two rows in each color). Slightly less than natural size. Provenience: Pachacamac. Collection of Fritz Iklé, No. 7148.

PLATE 67, A. Wool network of meshes made in filet stitch with simple knots (see Fig. 75) and

Description of Plates

with the following alternations: in the first row the yarn forms meshes; in the second row the knots touch each other. Colors: red, yellow, light blue, green, yellow brown. The design consists of overlapping lozenges. Slightly less than natural size. Provenience: Paracas. Schmidt Collection, Paris.

B. Specimen made of wool network with simple adjacent knots (see p. 106). This open-work fabric, which is very decorative (no doubt a costume accessory), is finished at one of its ends with a tassel. The upper part of the tassel has a surface decoration made of the same network; the other end is incomplete. Colors: red, blue, brown (dominant colors); small motives: light yellow, dark yellow, dark brown, violet, light green. Actual length of the large oval piece: 18 cm. [7 in.]. Length of the tassel: 12 cm. [4¾ in.]. Provenience: Paracas. Musée de l'Homme, No. 33–59–4.

C. Wool network made of simple adjacent knots. It shows the special features described on page 106. Colors: dark brown, forming the background; light yellow, dark yellow, red, dark green, light green. Slightly less than natural size. Provenience: Paracas. Collection of Walter Lehmann, Berlin.

Plate 68, A. Cotton network with regular mesh, made in square knotting. A small tuft of red wool is caught in each knot. Size 200 x 17 cm. [78¾ x 6¾ in.]. Natural size. Provenience: central coast of Peru. Musée de l'Homme, No. X, 33–27–25.

B. Specimen covered by a network of wool, apparently of simple looping. It represents a marine bird. Colors: breast and throat, light brown; back, head, and beak, black speckled with yellow. Natural size. Provenience: Peru. Museum für Völkerkunde, Munich, No. G, 2685.

C. The network shown in A of this plate, seen on the reverse.

Plate 69, A. Wool netting made by superimposed rows of small chains in accordance with the technique described on page 103. Colors: brown and pale yellow. Design: llamas. Natural size. Provenience: Poroma. University of California, Museum of Anthropology, Berkeley, No. 171363 d.

B. The same specimen seen on the other face.

C. Wool braid in three colors: green on one edge, red on the other, with a barely visible brown yarn in the central part (see the progression of the yarns in Fig. 42). Actual width, 3 mm. Provenience: Nazca. Collection of R. Wegner, Frankfort.

D. Small bag made of wool network, the technique of which is described on page 103, Fig. 71. Colors: pale yellow bands alternating with dark brown or lighter brown bands. The network is made spirally, each color making only two complete turns. The photograph was taken in such a way as to show the displacement of the bands where the color changes occur. Length: 17 cm. [6¾ in.]. Provenience: Peru. Museum für Völkerkunde, Munich, No. G, 2520.

Plate 70, A. Cap (or bag) of tangled human hair, compressed as in a felt. Diameter 34 cm. [13½ in.]. Provenience: Nazca. Museum of the American Indian, Heye Foundation, New York, No. 17/8928.

B. Cotton cap (with a slight layer of clay adhering to the fiber) made of network of square knotting, with meshes of unequal size (see Fig. 78). The two lateral parts of the cap are mounted symmetrically. In order to show the knotting of the network clearly, a white screen was placed in the interior of the cap to conceal the opposite side (see a similar cap, Montell, 1929, p. 147, Fig. 73). Length: 14 cm. [5½ in.]; diameter: 20 cm. [8 in.]. Provenience: central coast of Peru. Collection of Fritz Iklé, No. 7149.

Plate 71, A. Part of a very thick cap in the shape of a truncated cone made in loop stitch with a heavy yarn of beige wool consisting of several strands 6 mm. in diameter. The surface photographed shows the actual size of the specimen. Length of the piece: 15 cm. [6 in.]. At the right and left, the cap has a cylindrical ornament, 7 cm. [2¾ in.], made in the same stitch. The beginning of the network, shown at the top of the photograph (crown of the cap), is actually open. Diameter at the base: 24 cm. [9½ in.]. Provenience: Ancón. Musée de l'Homme, No. 78–8–70.

B. Yellow and brown wool cap made in loop stitch (see pp. 104–5). The cap has a flap on each side, terminating in yarns to be tied under the chin. Diameter: 16 cm. [6¼ in.]. Length (including the flap): 19 cm. [7½ in.]. Provenience: Ancón. Musée de l'Homme, No. 78–8–71.

Plate 72, A. Polychrome wool cap made in square knotting, shaped with upright points at each of

164

its four corners. Colors: natural white, light yellow, dark brown, azure blue, carmine red, old rose. The specimen consists of separately knotted sections joined to each other by fine stitches. In the lower part of the cap, in the center of each of its four faces, there is a double fold in the form of a pleat. The design is generally of geometric forms, having in addition an ornithomorphic motive arranged under the upright points. Tiahuanaco style. Circumference at the base (around the head): 50 cm. [19¾ in.]. Height (including the points): 14 cm. [5½ in.]. Provenience: Nazca? Riksmuseum, Stockholm, No. 10–4–73.

B. Fragment of a wool cap, of which only the bandeau is well preserved. It is made in square knotting in alternate directions (see Fig. 79). Colors completely spoiled; however, some stitches in Prussian blue can still be discerned at the top of the cap. Circumference: 50 cm. [19¾ in.]; height of the bandeau: 8 cm. [3¼ in.]. Natural size. Provenience: Ollachea. Göteborgs Museum, No. 06.1.528.

Plate 73, A. Cap of polychrome wool made in square knotting with cut pile ("*simili-velours,*" see p. 109). The upper part and the four upright points were knotted without the pile. Design generally of geometric forms. Height, not including points: 10 cm. [4 in.]. Provenience: Nazca. Collection of Heinrich Hardt, Berlin, No. 1058.

B. Cap made of network, entirely of wool, in square knotting, with cut pile introduced into every other row of knots ("*simili-velours,*" see p. 110) except in the upper part where the network is exposed. The ornaments of the cap are also made in square knotting with cut pile introduced into each knot. The spiral construction results in a small central cavity. The cap was constructed in four equal rectangular sections, 12 cm. [4¾ in.] wide and 8.5 cm. [3¼ in.] high, joined to each other. Gathers made at the four upper edges of the side panels give the cap its shape of a pyramid base and reduce the top to a square of 6 cm. [2¼ in.] on each side. The four faces are ornamented with the same design of geometric lines. Colors: dark blue, light blue, red, yellow, white, olive green, violet. Provenience: Nazca. Schmidt Collection, Paris.

Plate 74, A and D. Circular bandeau entirely of wool, made with square knotting, with cut pile introduced into every other row of knots ("*simili-velours,*" see p. 110). The two ends of the bandeau are joined with fine stitching. The specimen is lined inside with a very yellowed cotton fabric of the rep family, woven circularly and joined to the edges of the bandeau by stitches of red wool. Between the "*simili-velours*" and the lining, wads of human hair were introduced and formed a stuffing. Color of the cut pile: carmine, plum violet, dark blue, light blue, moss green, Indian yellow, natural white. The yarn of the foundation mesh is of beige yellow wool. Circumference of the bandeau: 44 cm. [17¼ in.]; height, 4 cm. [1½ in.]; length of the pile, 5 mm. Natural size. Provenience: Nazca. Ratton Collection, Paris (formerly Capitan Collection). See Berthon, 1911, Plate VII.

B. Fragment of the above-mentioned bandeau seen on the reverse, with the lining open. Natural size.

C. "Furred" cord made by wrapping a short wool fringe around a central cord. The fringe was constructed by the method described on page 111 and in Figure 83, B. Colors: dark brown, yellow, old red. Natural size. Provenience: central coast of Peru. Musée de l'Homme, No. X, 33–271–26.

Plate 75, A. Small headband seen from the right side. It consists of a network of white cotton, in square knotting, which holds in each of its knots an ornamental wool yarn, forming a loop between two consecutive knots and giving the specimen the appearance of fleece on one of its faces. The ornamental yarn changes color as required by the design. Colors: dark indigo blue, lighter indigo blue, dark green, lighter green, very pale yellow, darker yellow, garnet red, brighter red, rose, natural white. The design consists of small triangular sections and of motives resembling human features, stylized after the patterns of local ceramics. Length: 18 cm. [7 in.]; width: 6.3 cm. [2½ in.]. In each of the four corners is a small tying cord, 5 to 8 cm. [2 to 3¼ in.] long, terminating in a knot. Provenience: Nazca. Collection of Henry Reichlen, Paris.

B. The same specimen seen on the reverse.

C. Fragment of network made by needle with a double wool yarn in natural white and brown color. It was used as the wrapping for a corpse. It is made with a series of small rings in wool yarn, joined together and covered by knotting made with another yarn, in accordance with the technique described on page 114. Natural size. Provenience: desert of Atacama, Chile. Musée de l'Homme, No. 08–23–2500.

PLATE 76, A. Case of cotton network with pile in wool, made in peruke stitch (see p. 113). Colors: upper part, yellow, black, red; lower part, carmine red. Length: 31 cm. [12¼ in.]. The case contains coarse wooden needles. Provenience: Nazca. Collection of Fritz Iklé.

B. Shell with worn spines to which is attached a "furred" cord, made in square knotting, with cut pile introduced into each knot. The spiral construction results in a small central cavity. The network is of natural white cotton, and the pile of wool. Colors: brown, white, red, yellow, blue, pale green. Design is of overlapping lozenges. The "furred" cord is introduced into the canal of the shell, is glued with a gray material, and in addition is tied by the dark brown wool yarn. Height of the shell: 18.5 cm. [7¼ in.]. Length of the entire cord: 81 cm. [32 in.]. Provenience: Nazca. Schmidt Collection, Paris.

C. Fragment of "furred" cord made around three small central cotton cords according to the method described on page 111 and in Figure 82. Colors: red, yellow, violet brown. Natural size. Provenience: central coastal region. Musée de l'Homme, No. 30–19–1682.

D. Fragment of a case similar to A of this plate, having the same technique and the same colors. Natural size. The form of the knots of the network from which the cut pile is missing is clearly shown. Provenience: Nazca. Collection of R. d'Harcourt.

PLATE 77. Wig consisting of a cylindrical bandeau made spirally in peruke stitch (see p. 113), from which emerge locks and strands of pale golden blond or sand-colored wool. Interior circumference: 49 cm. [19¼ in.]; height: 7.5 cm. [3 in.]; length of the longest locks: 55 cm. [21¾ in.]. Provenience: Ica. Göteborgs Museum, No. 30–28–17.

PLATE 78, A. Wig made of coarse circular plaiting, through which small adjacent braids of hair pass. These braids hang down and, after being fastened with a tie, also made of hair, terminate in an unplaited section. The two ends of the coarse bands are joined together behind the head. The braids on the sides are about 33 cm. [13 in.] long. In the center they are hardly a third of this length. Photograph taken full face. Provenience: coast of Peru. Museum für Völkerkunde, Berlin.

B. Bonnet wig of network made in peruke stitch (see p. 113), from which emerge locks of white, ocher, brown, black, and red wool. Diameter: 29.5 cm. [11½ in.]; total height: 24 cm. [9½ in.]; length of the cord: 60 cm. [23¾ in.]. Provenience: Ica. Göteborgs Museum, No. 30–28–49.

C. Wig consisting of a hemispherical skullcap of coarse cotton, made in simple loop stitch (see p. 104) by turning in spirals around a central point. Through the skullcap are passed tufts of black hair, which cover it and which, on the lower edges and at the sides and back, join other tufts of hair and extend in long, thin braids to the number of about 220. The braids of hair are fastened by a knot or merely passed through to the middle of their length (see p. 113). Four of them on each side are braided together to form a chin strap. The specimen is seen in profile. Total length: 80 cm. [31½ in.]. Provenience: central coastal region. Musée de l'Homme, No. X, 33–271–1.

PLATE 79, A. Part of a strong carrying bag made of coarse vegetable fiber. The especially solid network was made as indicated in Figure 85. Enlarged: actual width of the specimen photographed: 7.5 cm. [3 in.]. Provenience: burial grottoes, Chanta, Cordillera de Contumaza, Department of Cajamarca. Collection of Henry Reichlen, Paris.

B. Lower part of the same bag, showing the beginning of the network turning around a central point.

C. Part of a network of vegetable fiber made as shown in Figure 71. Enlarged: actual width of the specimen photographed: 7.5 cm. [3 in.]. Provenience: burial grottoes, Chanta, Cordillera de Contumaza, Department of Cajamarca. Collection of Henry Reichlen, Paris.

PLATE 80, A. Fragment of brown cotton fabric, plain weave, sprinkled with embroidered motives (stylized feathers) in white cotton, with a small area in old red. The embroidery gives the fabric an appearance similar to that of brocade. It is actually embroidery, however, for there is superimposition of threads in the stitching of the design of the quill of the feather. Distance between one motive and another: 5.5 cm. [2¼ in.]. Natural size. Provenience: coastal region of Peru. Collection of Fritz Iklé.

B. The same fragment seen on the other face.

C. Head of a small figure in wool (see Harcourt, 1924, Plate 17, b). The center is composed of network in Venice stitch (see p. 102), surrounded by a circular zone of loop stitch (p. 104) and bordered by loops of yarn forming a kind of fringe. Colors: red, yellow, brown, black, white. Natural size. Length of the entire specimen: 22 cm. [8¾ in.]. Provenience: Cajamarquilla. Collection of R. d'Harcourt.

D. Fragment of beige cotton fabric, half plain weave, half simple gauze. It is sprinkled with small zoomorphic motives in yellow, red, and dark brown wool, embroidered in flat stitch on the plain-weave bands (see p. 121). Natural size. Provenience: central coast of Peru. Musée de l'Homme, No. X, 33–271–18.

E. The same fragment seen on the other face.

PLATE 81, A. Cotton fabric of light tobacco color, plain weave sprinkled with motives embroidered in wool in loop stitch (see p. 122). The motive depicts a pelican. Colors: dark brown, natural white, red, yellow, beige. Length of motives: 16.5 cm. [6½ in.]; width: 13.5 cm. [5¼ in.]. Provenience: central coast of Peru. Ratton Collection, Paris.

B. The same fabric seen on the other face.

C. Fabric of yellowed white cotton, plain weave, embroidered in loop stitch with vertical columns two meshes wide, in red and yellow wool. Slightly less than natural size. Provenience: central coast of Peru. Musée de l'Homme, No. X, 33–271–17.

D. The same fabric seen on the other face.

PLATE 82, A. Fabric of yellowed white cotton, plain weave ornamented with a dark blue green stripe near the selvages and embroidered in wool in flat stitch. Design: procession of llamas and step motives. Colors: red, yellow, green, violet, brown. The appearance of the embroidery is similar on both faces. The embroidery thread passes over six warp yarns at a time. There is a red pompon in each of the four corners of the specimen. Size: 34 x 32 cm. [13½ x 12½ in.]. Provenience: Nazca. Musée de l'Homme, No. 30–49–20.

B. Small band of cotton fabric entirely covered with embroidery in stem stitch. Colors: yellow, blue, green, with a red line outlining the motives. Lower border in loop stitch (see pp. 122 and 135). Width: 3.8 cm. [1½ in.]. Provenience: Nazca. Ratton Collection, Paris.

PLATE 83, A. Fabric of brown wool embroidered with wool in flat stitch in small columns. The embroidery yarns, passing in an oblique direction, face each other and appear to form small chains (Fig. 88, B). Colors: brown, light yellow, carmine red, light blue. Natural size: Provenience: Peru. Stuttgart Museum, No. 24.932.

B. The same fabric seen on the other face.

C. Ornament in the shape of an epaulet, terminating in a deep fringe of red wool, bordered with yellow. The flat part of the ornament, which is thick and rigid, is made of coarse cotton yarn stretched in parallel form and in two layers. The yarns of each layer are joined to each other by stem-stitch embroidery, red and blue on one face, and red and yellow on the other; the yellow and blue are substituted for each other, as the design requires, when changing from one face to the other, as in double cloth (see p. 129). The edges are also embroidered in stem stitch in brown and white. Ornaments such as this are attached to the lower edges of small bags. Total length: 26 cm. [10¼ in.]. Provenience: Nazca. Musée de l'Homme, No. 30–19–450.

PLATE 84, A. Cotton double cloth in brown and white, embroidered locally in relief on stretched yarns with yellow or red wool yarn (forming the eyes and mouth of the stylized head). Natural size. Provenience: Barranca de Pacasmayo. Collection of Fritz Iklé.

B. Fragment of red cotton fabric, plain weave, embroidered in wool. On one edge is a needle-made fringe (see p. 134), and on the other a border of small squares made of wool in simple loop stitch (see

p. 134). The design shows the head and part of the body of a bird with a long stylized tongue in light red. Colors of the bird: yellow, dark blue, light blue. Natural size. Provenience: Nazca. Collection of Fritz Iklé.

C. Band of fine brown cotton, plain weave, covered with wool embroidery in flat stitch. The effect produced corresponds to that of tapestry. In the lower section of the photograph can be seen a portion of the fabric which has been left exposed by the destruction of the embroidery. The wool yarn of the embroidery passes over eight warp yarns at a time. Colors: red, light yellow, dark yellow, olive green, plum violet, blue. Natural size. Provenience: Nazca. Collection of Fritz Iklé.

D. Ornamental piece made of red wool fabric, decorated with embroidery in a reversed U design, embroidered in true chain stitch (see p. 122). The lower part has a fringe of red and rose wool. Colors of the embroidery: pale yellow, violet mauve, yellow green, rose. Total length: 16 cm. [6¼ in.]; width at the level of the fringe: 7.5 cm. [3 in.]. Provenience: Chancay. Musée de l'Homme, No. 78–2–555.

E. Band of cotton fabric, rep family, a large part of which is covered with embroidery in flat stitch in light blue, black, white, red, and beige. Natural size. Provenience: central coast of Peru. Musée de l'Homme, No. X, 33–271–13.

PLATE 85, A. Cotton fabric entirely covered with wool embroidery in loop stitch (see pp. 122 ff.), arranged in horizontal oblique and single vertical lines. The foundation fabric is partially destroyed. Colors: brown, red, yellow, white, light violet. The lateral parts are embroidered with yellow fret designs on a red background, terminating in a very stylized head, surrounded by a white and brown fret and a yellow fringe with looped strands. Size of the central part: 26 x 21.5 cm. [10¼ x 8½ in.]. Provenience: Ancón. See also Crawford, 1916c, p. 133, Fig. 16. Musée de l'Homme, No. 78–2–55.

B. Ornamental piece in the form of a fish, covered with a network embroidery in cotton and wool loop stitch. Colors: gray, white, rose, yellow. Slightly less than natural size. Provenience: Nazca. Musée de l'Homme, No. 30–19–486.

PLATE 86, A. Band covered with a network embroidery in wool loop stitch (see pp. 122 ff.), the lower part of which has a wool, needle-made fringe. In the upper part there is a sequence of small adjacent rectangles, which are also covered with embroidery in loop stitch. Colors: rose, red, brown, light yellow, dark yellow, light green, dark green, dark blue, gray blue, white, and yarns resist-dyed blue and red, white and red, rose and red. Design of S-shaped motives. Slightly less than natural size. Provenience: Paracas. Hein Collection, Paris.

B. Necklace constructed on several yarns used as a foundation for small motives (birds and flowers) developed in a network embroidery in loop stitch with polychrome wools. Width of the small motives: 2.5 cm. [1 in.]. Circumference of the necklace: 106 cm. [41¾ in.]. Provenience: Paracas. Musée de l'Homme, No. 30–49–17.

C. Band covered with wool network embroidery in loop stitch, the lower part of which has a wool, needle-made fringe. Design: step motives. Colors: red, light blue, dark blue, light yellow, dark yellow, almond green, dark green, violet, dark brown. Length: 6.25 cm. [2½ in.]. Provenience: Paracas. Schmidt Collection, Paris.

PLATE 87, A. Band covered with network embroidery of wool in loop stitch. On one of its edges are grafted small rectangles also covered with loop stitch, and on the other edge are grafted branched vegetal stems (cactus?) and heads and wings of birds, made by the same method. The bodies of the birds appear in the embroidery on the band. The rectangles are all decorated with a small quadruped, which can be seen clearly in the fifth rectangle at the left. Colors: violet, red, light yellow, dark yellow, light green, dark green, blue, rose, white, brown. Slightly less than natural size. Provenience: Paracas. Hein Collection, Paris.

B. Band of natural white cotton fabric, plain weave covered with a network embroidery of wool in loop stitch. The embroidery, which is similar on both faces of the band, is in the course of being made. Colors: background red; decorative motives violet, dark blue, light blue, dark yellow, light yellow, green, white, brown (some yarns resist-dyed in two tones). Width: 1.5 cm. [½ in.]. Provenience: Paracas. Collection of Fritz Iklé.

C. Band covered with network embroidery of wool in loop stitch. Hummingbirds and flowers covered with network embroidery in loop stitch are grafted onto one edge of the band. The hummingbirds are arranged to the right and left of little flowers, into which their beaks are plunging. Protruding beyond the opposite edge of the band can be seen the three-lobed tails and the ends of the wings of the birds. Colors: three shades of blue, three shades of green, three shades of yellow, carmine, brown red, pale violet. Slightly less than natural size. Provenience: Paracas. Hein Collection, Paris.

PLATE 88. This mantle or ceremonial cloth was found, according to Mme. Jean Levillier, in a pre-Inca tomb on the peninsula of Paracas on the body of a person who was buried with other valuable clothing and golden ornaments. The bodies of five infants surrounded him. It may be assumed that the grave was that of a chieftain or a priest.

The specimen, because of the beauty of its manufacture, its state of preservation, and above all because of the many representations of personages on its border, is of prime interest.[1] It belonged to the late Señor Rafael Larco y Herrera, who placed it in the Musée de l'Homme, in Paris, where I had an opportunity to make a thorough study of it. It is now in the possession of the Brooklyn Museum, New York. The color plate facing p. 30 shows a detail of this specimen.

CONSTRUCTION

The mantle consists of a rectangular central part of natural white cotton, plain-weave construction, in which the warp yarns were locally wrapped, after warping and before weaving, with various colored woolen yarns in accordance with the method described on p. 60; and of a frieze or border around the central part on its four sides. The frieze consists of a band or tape of cotton fabric covered on its two sides with loop stitch in polychrome wool yarns (see pp. 122 ff.; for similar techniques see the band in Plate 87, B). On the outside edge of the band are grafted forms of abstract figures, the lower portions of which (feet, paws, and legs) are depicted in embroidery on the tape on a red background. Each form is made on a network of cotton, sometimes of wool, in simple looping (see p. 101) and is itself covered on both faces, like the tape, with a network embroidery in polychrome wool in loop stitch, forming the outline and the emblems of the figures. The network embroidery that covers the figures is done in a direction perpendicular to that of the tape. The line of demarcation of the two directions is scarcely visible, the meshes being very similar in gauge and tension: fourteen meshes to the centimeter [thirty-five to the inch]. A series of small motives in the form of flowers, also in loop stitch, 1.5 cm. [½ in.] in length, joins the frieze to the central fabric.

The fabric is 124 cm. [49 in.] long and 49 cm. [19¼ in.] wide. It is covered with thirty-two anthropomorphic motives of equal size (4 x 8 cm. [1½ x 3¼ in.]), developed by the method of warp wrapping already mentioned, in one of the following six colors: red, rose, blue, green, yellow, or brown violet. The eyes and the mouth of the mask in the center of each motive are of a color different from the rest of the motive.

The frieze has ninety small figures, which have been given Arabic numerals in the plates and in the text that follows. The length of these figures (over and above the tape, which is 2.5 cm. [1 in.] wide) varies generally from 5 to 7 cm. [2 to 2¾ in.]. The two faces, identical in appearance and construction, are also identical in representation of subjects, except in five matters of detail which are mentioned later (16, 28, 40, 49, 75). The base of each figure on the tape is very much narrower than its body, which is frequently provided with numerous accessories; thus the figures partially overlap one another. In order to secure a complete photograph of each figure, it was necessary to isolate them by means of a screen.

The embroideress used a fine wool yarn, single ply (or double ply of two colors in mottled or variegated sections). The following twelve colors were used: violet brown or dark plum, cobalt blue of medium intensity, rather light cobalt blue, dark emerald green, light olive green, brown green or natural Sienna, dark Indian yellow, light Indian yellow, Naples yellow, light putty yellow, old rose or shrimp, carmine red. To this should probably be added a very dark color, black, with which certain parts were embroidered,

[1] I had the opportunity to examine a second specimen of almost equally great interest, which belongs to the Etnografiska Museet, Göteborg (Harcourt, 1948).

and which today no longer exists. This color is very often missing from Peruvian fabrics taken from graves, its basic fiber having been gradually corroded by the action of the dye.

The figures in Plates 89 to 104 are reproduced in natural size.

GENERAL DESCRIPTION

The figures on the frieze in their form, emblems, and stylization are very closely related to the representations shown on the polychrome pottery of Nazca. The resemblance in many cases reaches actual identity, if one takes into account the differences arising from the techniques used: embroidery on the one hand, painting on the other.

It is extremely difficult to give an exact interpretation of the ninety figures. It is easily seen that the embroideress depicted human beings, animals, and figures—part-human and part-nonhuman—in which the imaginative part certainly greatly prevails over the realistic part. But, as in the case of the Nazca ceramics, any statement identifying the figures as men or divinities should be made with great caution. Furthermore, the frieze has another complicating factor, which is also seen on vases in exceptional cases, but which here is almost constant: the animal and vegetal kingdoms are intimately intermingled. No example giving more convincing proof of the pantheistic concept of the Paracas Indian could be found. From animal to man, from animal or man to imaginary being—god or demon—the transition is imperceptible. For the Indian there is no barrier whatsoever between them; whether one or the other is involved, the symbols and the postures themselves are similar. Furthermore, these subjects participate in the vegetal world. The majority have branches in their hands or on their bodies, and some are united to the plants in a yet more intimate manner: a plant emerges from a sustenance-giving belly into which it is rooted; or it rises from the soil, crosses the body, and terminates in a flowering tongue; or, again, pushing the embryonic head of the subject to one side, the plant replaces the head with a sheaf of leafy and flowering branches; elsewhere, a branch of butterfly plant may have its pods transformed into little rodents, whose tails blend with the stalks of the pods. Thus there is no essential difference from the plant to the superior creature from which man must gain power. Life is one in all of its manifestations. One general concept seems to emerge from the representations on the frieze: they appear to express the exaltation of the vital force; it might be said that they are meant to record the festival of spring. Perhaps the textile was intended to figure in some pastoral ceremony.

The ninety subjects are not all different. Certain of them are repeated several times, identically in form and color, or in form only. The following personages are repeated in the textile shown in Plate 88: 2, 32, 48, 52, and 79; 3 and 77; 4, 11, 35, 54, 76, and 89; 5 and 55; 6, 13, 21, 58, 71, and 84; 7, 47, and 83; 8, 14, and 27; 9 and 20 (in part); 10, 24, and 74; 17, 18, and 49; 19, 51, and 65; 22, 29, and 46; 25, 44, 56, 63, 66, and 78; 26 and 50; 28 and 75; 41 and 85; 42 and 80; 53 and 72; 57, 59, 60, 61, 69, 70, and 86; 67, 73, and 88. There are no repetitions of the following personages in the textile: 1, 12, 15, 16, 23, 38, 39, 40, 43, 45, 62, 64, 68, 81, 82, 87, 90. All of the figures will be described individually in the text that follows.

Did the workers follow a plan? Yes, undoubtedly, but it must have been a plan of esthetic order, rather than a plan explanatory of the arrangement of the figures. Except for certain corner subjects, and especially the two domesticated llamas (26, 50) and the two jaguars (3, 77) that occupy corresponding places on the long sides of the frieze, the other subjects appear to be arranged according to the whim of the embroideress—some set closely together and thus appearing in great quantity, and others wider and less numerous. The figures bearing the following numbers are to be found on each side of the rectangle, not including the corner subjects: 30, 10, 35, and 11. The arrangement of the figures on the frieze is as follows: from the center of the short sides the rows of figures turn their backs to each other in order that they may face each other in the center of the long sides. There is but one exception to this rule: figure 38 has his feet turned in the direction opposite to those of his neighbors and seems to form with the following two subjects a trinity that is frequently depicted on the pottery of all of coastal Peru.

If the personages in their representative capacity cannot be completely understood, and for this understanding it would be necessary to know myths that today are extinct, at least the emblems and objects they carry can be interpreted. In this respect, the frieze is very instructive. The clothes and ornaments, the arms and instruments, and the plants will be considered separately.

Vestments and ornaments

Thanks to the precision of the embroideress, the frieze gives an excellent picture of the styles of the period.

Footwear. This item is missing. Although sandals (with the large toe exposed) have figured very definitely in the ornamental jars of Chimu, here they are lacking. The feet and hands have no protection at all; these extremities are always embroidered in one color for the flesh and another for the nails. In certain cases and for no apparent reason, the large toe is placed opposite the other toes, thus giving the man or the god a four-handed appearance.

Leg ornament. Nearly all of the personages wear a simple ring (see 17), a kind of double ring, or a wide bracelet around the ankles. Perhaps certain of them wore another below the knee (21 or 84).

Breechcloth and skirt. The breechcloth, which is visible only if the *cushma* or *unku* is short enough for it to show, consists sometimes of a simple band of fabric that passes between the legs and is fastened to the belt (59), and sometimes of a pair of short drawers with decorative motives (16, 60).

The skirt (of a more precise form) consists of a piece of fabric falling about to the knees, rather ample and often having long teeth or deep indentations (14, 47, 61). It resembles in all respects the skirt of the Chimu warriors painted on vases.

Shirt (cushma *or* unku). This principal piece of clothing varies in appearance and especially in length. The shortest falls to the hips over the breechcloth or skirt; it has sleeves that cover the shoulders and the upper part of the arms, and a neck opening in the form of a square or a V (40). It is of a solid color (7), or has a striping on the sides (60), or has lines forming a sawtooth design at sleeve level and below the waist (61). Its center is often decorated with a square of a color different from that of the remainder of the garment (63) or with trophy heads (12). This shirt is similar to those of the Chimu warriors.

A shirt longer than the preceding one does not have sleeves, and the neck opening is square. It is ornamented with two decorative bands at armpit level and on the lower edges (2, 19).

The very long shirt or robe reaches to the feet; it is straight in form, with or without sleeves. Its ornamentation includes a decorative band or trophy heads (24, 64, 67).[2]

Mantle. The form of this garment, as represented, is difficult to see and is not always constant. It can be observed best on the profile figures. The longer and more typical mantle may be identified in 21 and 84, where it appears on the tape foundation between the left leg of the subjects and the serpents; in 18, however, it is reduced to a simple flap, which might have been considered merely an addition to the belt, if the truer types had not been recognized. The figure in 87 shows the flap extended into a centipede tail. In 16, the very beautiful mantle that hangs from the shoulders is also extended into a centipede tail; the same applies to 68, where the mantle first covers the back. In 22 and 29, the mantle floats out behind like a standard. Up to this point the mantle appears to be a garment much more ornamental than useful. In 49, it covers the neck and the upper part of the shoulders; thrown over the right arm, it hangs like a cape on the side. It may also be likened to the feline skin mantle which covers the back of the figures in 28 and 75. In this connection, mention should also be made of the parts of animals hanging from the belts in 19, 51, and 65.

The decoration of the breechcloth, shirt, and mantle generally consists of bands of horizontal S's, series of step motives, or groupings of small multicolored squares. The trophy head is often introduced as an ornament. There can also be found representations of small felines (center of the subjects in 4, 11, 54) and serpents (on the robe in 39).

Face ornaments. The decorative disks, usually three in number, that hang from the ears of figures painted on Nazca ceramics have been interpreted as earplugs. Such ornaments are depicted so clearly on the frieze that all doubt as to identification has been removed. The ornament consists of one, two, or

[2] On the style of Paracas garments see also Tello (1931).

most frequently three small disks joined to each other by a cord like the beads of a rosary. Some of them are star-shaped (49, 57). The earplugs were probably attached to the headband and not to the ears themselves. A similar arrangement existed among the Chimu.

Mustaches are false ornaments. Most frequently each mustache has the form of an open, three-fingered hand with three stitches embroidered to form a triangular, schematic head in the palm. The two pieces are joined together by a cord that passes around the mouth and the chin (8). In the most highly ornamented faces the mustaches on each side are double or triple (16). Their usual form may be changed into serpents (16, 22, 55) or flowers (80, 86). These sham mustaches belong characteristically to the Nazca region.

Hair in the ceramic designs is always black and is invariably stylized in the same fashion, although it can only rarely be seen because of the complicated headdresses. The same is true for the subjects on the frieze, but it is worth noting that three of them (10, 24, 74) are ornamented with wigs of long, flowing hair of yellow beige color, similar to wigs made of llama wool found in graves chiefly at Ica (see Pl. 77).

Headdress. The headdress consists of one essential piece: the headband. This, in its simple form, is a horizontal bandeau placed on the forehead and no doubt fastened by a cord tied behind the head (unless it was attached to a cap, such as the one in 40, in which the two faces are not alike).

The bandeau has a motive in the form of a head (11, 12). The headband may consist of two parallel bandeaux (6, 20); it may have a more elegant form (57). It is not only found on the heads of the personages, but may be held in both hands, like a staff (23); it may ornament a spear (22, 29, 46); it may seem to be the produce of a plant that bears it as if it were a flower or fruit (19, 51, 65). An important ritualistic significance must be connected with this piece of wearing apparel.

The headbands in the frieze correspond in appearance with those seen on painted vases. This does not apply, however, to the upper part of the headdress consisting of vertical rays or rays arranged in a semicircle above the headband. This feature apparently does not exist on the ceramics, but it can be found on the embroidered fabrics. What are these rays? Are they a diadem of feathers, having a purely decorative character? Are they rays emanating from the being and having a mythological significance? Their interpretation is difficult (see Tello, 1923, p. 220).

In addition to the regular headdresses described above, there are unusual ones, more or less fantastic, which are creations of the imagination (22, 46, 89). The skin of an animal may also be used as a headdress (65, 68, 80).

Additional design motives. Certain motives, based principally on the serpent and the centipede, are added to the costume of the figures. These two creatures by successive stages of simplification have reached a point where they differ from each other only in the presence or absence of indented edges that represent feet. They have as important a place on the frieze as on the Nazca ceramics.

The serpent is quite realistically depicted in 4, 11, 13, 21, and so forth. Its curving body, its small head, and its visible tongue cannot be mistaken; sometimes it springs from the back or arm of the figure, and sometimes it dangles from the belt, to which it appears to be attached. It is used, in places, to depict mustaches or a tongue (62); it may also ornament a ceremonial staff (12). In Chimu pottery the serpent likewise appears very often, only its stylization differs from that of Nazca.

The centipede is better defined on the frieze than on the vases. In 20 and 23, for example, it cannot be confused with the serpent. It is used as an accessory for the costumes in 9, 12, 16, 45, and so forth, and it is used as a tongue in 20, 23, 39, 45, and 72. Finally, its body alone is used as a tongue in 10, 24, and 74, where the motive is terminated in a highly stylized bird.

Instruments, arms, and insignia

In addition to objects already known, which the frieze enables us to study more deeply, there are to be seen on it other objects, which have been unidentified up to the present time, or which are of entirely new forms.

Baton or staff. Is it a weapon or an insignia? It seems that the symbolic interpretation is more correct, Short and cylindrical, the baton is usually held calmly, like an article that is being displayed or presented, and in no wise like the threatening club or spear that is consistently found in Chimu art. When

Figure 100. Various forms of ceremonial batons carried by the figures portrayed in the border of the textile reproduced in Plate 88

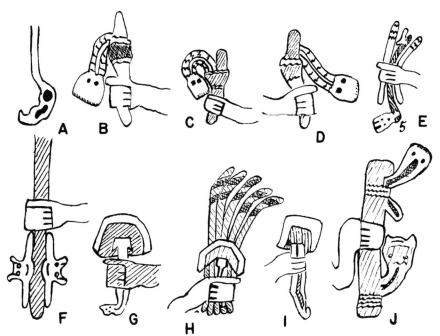

Figure 101. Weapons and implements carried by the figures portrayed in the border of the textile reproduced in Plate 88

the baton is longer, it is so made in order to support more easily the various ornaments with which it is decorated. The following are the principal varieties of batons (Fig. 100). Most frequently the baton is short and thick, decorated with transverse lines, like the vases. In 3, it is in the form of an actual club and is decorated with a mask at its upper end; this is enlarged in 8, 14, and 60. The rather long baton has one or two rings (7, 45, 47, 63), or even three rings from which can be seen emerging an appendage in the form of a corolla of *Convolvulus* (simple in 15, 61, 68, 86; double in 27). Some of these corollas have a red pistil that supports, or used to support, a shrunken trophy head (*tsantsa*) (17, 59). The creatures embroidered on the Nazca fabric reproduced by Crawford (1916a, p. 388) also have a long and knobby staff from which hang two trophy heads. Only the staff carried by each of the little personages in 6, 13, 21, and so forth has one or two crossbars near the summit. The subject of 87 is holding a baton provided with short crossbars placed above and below the hand that carries it; the baton has a fork at the top from which hangs a sort of animal tail. The baton is sometimes decorated with serpents (12 has a veritable caduceus) or with a fantastic animal with tail and wings like a bird, paws like a quadruped, and head and headdress like a man (16). The spears held by the personages in 22, 29, and 46 are provided toward the lower end with two headbands that face each other (Fig. 101, F).

Throwing stick or atlatl. This weapon, which is frequently depicted on ceramics, appears clearly on the frieze (18, 45, 60, 69). Sometimes it is light and delicate and sometimes enormous, but it is always provided with two hooks whose fastening ties are wound several times around the rod of the weapon (Fig. 101, E, J).

Darts. Because of the difficulty of fashioning in loop stitch the point of the weapon in the form of a circumflex accent, darts are represented in the frieze as simple rods (12, 18, 53, 60, and so forth).

Slings. This weapon is shown in 8, 14, and 27 but in rather an inexact manner in the form of a coarse cord whose central part is divided in two (Fig. 102, A).

Figure 102.   Small figures held by the personages portrayed in the border of the textile shown in Plate 88

Semicircular knife (tumi). The cutting knife with a semicircular blade, called a *tumi*, appears on a great number of subjects (12, 19, 22, 29, 46, 51, 65, 67, 73, 88); its distinctive shape could, in certain instances, cause it to be taken for a short-handled spade or a fan.[3] This cutting knife is straight or curved at the end. The large part of the instrument should be rounded and regular; the difficulty in making this curved part in loop stitch is no doubt responsible for the angles and irregularities that can be noticed (Fig. 101, G, H, I).

The miniature figures held in the hands of the principal figures (6, 8, 13, 21, and so forth) have in their hands objects which might be *tumis* or fans; the very small dimensions and the execution of the objects in simple looping must be borne in mind in seeking their interpretation (see also Fig. 102, A, B, C).

[3] The discovery at Paracas of beautiful feather fans (Yacovleff, 1933a) supports this suggestion made by me a long time ago; but, since the object is so often found grasped by the warrior with his weapons, I have not dismissed the possibility of its being a *tumi*.

Club or mace. This agricultural implement or weapon, reminiscent in shape of a cup and ball toy, is carried only by three (19, 51, 65) of the figures (see also Fig. 101, B, C, D). It is composed of a rather short handle to which is attached a double cord that terminates in a large knot or a hard body of stone or metal. It is brandished with upraised arm, like a whip. I have so far been unable to find any description of this object that would identify it.

Implements or objects difficult to interpret. These are two in number. The first is a cord or stem which can be seen extending from the thigh of the figures in 67, 73, and 88 (Fig. 101, A), and which then descends onto the tape, where it widens, curves inward, and terminates in a hook. Is it an agricultural implement, a hook, or a lever?

The second is held in the left hand of the personage in 68, together with a plant having a large tuber, which appears to be split by the tool or implement; this implement seems to consist of a large cord, with a bulge at either end, the center of which is enlarged (Fig. 103, B).

Shrunken heads (tsantsas)

The place held by trophy head designs in the art of Nazca is well known. In the frieze under consideration they occupy an equally important place. The *tsantsa* is used as a decorative motive on the *cushmas* and is seen suspended from the hands of a warrior (49) or of fantastic beings (8, 14, 15; in the last two the cord is destroyed). It is also seen suspended from a headband (68) and from the batons with corolla appendages already described (17, 59).

Miniature figures

These are minute figures which decorate the headbands of certain subjects, or which are suspended from their garments or held in their hands like puppets. Was this an attempt to portray bodies reduced by methods akin to those which were, and still are, used by the Jivaros to obtain shrunken heads, or are they merely figurines? It is very difficult to say. In any event their representation is very rare on ceramics (see, however, Seler, 1923, Fig. 27, c). These miniatures are seen on the subjects in 6, 13, 21, and so forth, holding in their hands either a plant with three roots and a *tumi* or a plant with a large tuber and a baton. They are joined to the headband of the principal subject by their belts. In 8, the figurine is quite convex; see also 22, 39, and 64. In addition to the figurines held in his hand, the figure in 39 has two other small figures attached to his headband, in reverse position, like the head of the principal figure itself. The figurines are wearing long robes that leave only the feet visible. Mention should also be made of the figurines depicted on the bodies of the principal subjects (67, 73, 88). The figurines are generally provided with implements similar to those of the principal subjects (Fig. 102).

Plants

The art of coastal Peru did not generally neglect the vegetal kingdom. In Chimu pottery there are numerous vases in the form of fruits and roots; on the ornamental vases, cactus or other prolific desert plants are frequently found painted in sepia. On the ceramics from the south there are paintings of plants that Seler (1923) has been able to identify in part; but, never before, as I have already stated, has the vegetal world been so well portrayed as on the frieze now under discussion.

Thirty-nine of the ninety subjects possess characteristics or attributes of the vegetal world; nineteen personages hold plants in their hands (2, 5, 6, 10, 13, 21, 24, 42, 48, 58, 64, 68, 71, 74, 79, 80, 82, 84, 90). Plants seem to be an integral part of the personage or to sink their roots into the body of each of the subjects in 1, 3, 19, 26, 41, 50, 51, 65, 77, and 85, and these could with accuracy be designated as plant subjects. Finally, personages in 4, 11, 35, 45, 55, 62, 67, 73, 88, and 89 are furnished with vegetal motives or are transporting tubers or branches.

The types of plants depicted are quite numerous, although certain of them may be reproduced several times in a similar manner. In spite of their obvious stylization, it is tempting to attempt to identify them. Two plants appear persistently under the needle of the embroideress. In all probability they are food plants. One is invariably depicted with three fleshy roots (6, 13, 21, 58, 71, 82, 84, 90). This plant can be identified as the yuca or sweet manioc (see Fig. 103, C), which even in our own times forms an important element in the food of the coastal population. It is often depicted in Chimu art with a realism that leaves no room for doubt as to its identity; here the tubers are reduced to three.

The second plant could be the sweet potato (*camote*). It appears in 2, 5, 13, 21, 42, 48, 55, 58, 68, 71, 73, 79, 80, 82, 88, and 90 (see also Fig. 103, A). Peñafiel illustrates in his *Nombres geograficas de Mexico* (1885, Pl. VI) an almost identical picture of a plant having a large tuber which he identifies as *camotl*. That an ancient Mexican and an ancient Peruvian both conceived one stylization of the same plant is not at all implausible. It must be remembered that the sweet potato was cultivated in great abundance on the Peruvian coast, while the common potato originated in the high Andean valleys.[4]

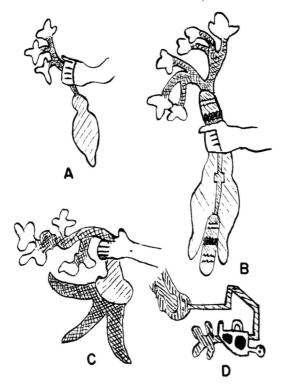

Figure 103 (left). Plants and implements held in the hands of the figures portrayed in the border of the textile shown in Plate 88

Figure 104 (above). Figure modeled in relief on the body of a vase in black pottery of Mochica style. It holds in the right hand a piece of yuca (sweet manioc) and in the left a stalk of maize

The cactus is depicted quite specifically on the subjects in 19 and 51; the representation in 65 is different.

Vegetable pods (beans) appear very clearly in 50 and 62. In 80 the vegetal outgrowth from the animal's tail, which is used as the hair arrangement of the subject, has among the leaves two pods in the form of animals; in addition, in 80 and 42 a sprouting pod that is probably a bean can be seen growing out of the arch formed by vegetal stalks.

Side by side with the vegetables that can probably be identified are others that one would like to be able to name, such as the climbing plant with roots fastened into the back of the llama in 26; the tree rising from the back of the jaguar in 3; and the bushes with red flowers and trilobate fruit in 42 and 85. Perhaps the plant in 65 with its natural white flowers and green fruit represents a cotton plant. There

[4] Yacovleff (1933b) has voiced the opinion that the representations on Nazca ceramics, as well as on Paracas embroideries, of certain tubers in the form of a coarse and elongated turnip might well be those of the *jiquima* or *ajipa* (*Pachyrhizus tuberosus*), a leguminous plant with an edible root, almost unknown in Peru today, but still cultivated in Central America. This possible interpretation should not be overlooked.

176

is one curious lack: nowhere at all is maize clearly depicted, although representations of it abound on Mochica ceramics, and its stylized ears form a frequent decorative theme on Nazca ceramics.

The personages described in the following pages and plates are numbered beginning at the upper left corner of the fabric in Plate 88 and continuing in a clockwise direction.

PLATE 89. 1. Zoophytic subject. The lower part of the body on the tape is embryonic. The paws are detached from the tape, as is also a head, whose powerful tongue gives birth to four branches, continues, and then terminates in two small arms and a head that is itself provided with a tongue.

2. A figure that holds in the left hand a short baton (incomplete), and in the right a plant with a large root; on the head is a headband surmounted by a double ray. Comparable to 52, 79, and 32.

3. Combination of jaguar and plant. The jaguar holds in its left forepaw a ceremonial staff. From the middle of its back rises a bush with leaves, flowers, and fruit. The green line that crosses its body between the forelimbs has its counterpart in 77, where it forms the stalk of the plant; it may be the result of a change of plan on the part of the embroideress in the course of execution.

4. Mythical subject with human legs and a body bent horizontally from the hips. On its back is a large decorative motive composed of a central band on which are depicted two small felines and which is surrounded by five flowers. Two arms form a framework for the principal head, whose tongue terminates in a small head. Four serpents twist their coils above the body, and a fifth (on the tape) is extended by a cord that assumes a vegetal motive (sprouting grain?; Fig. 103, D). For similar figures see 11, 54, and 76; see 89 for the lower part only.

5. A poorly preserved figure, which fortunately the figure in 55 allows us to complete. On the tape is a human body; the lowered right hand holds a plant near its tuber; the uplifted left hand also holds one, but near its branches. A large decorative serpent descends from the shoulders to the ground like a train. The head is crowned with a small animal in reverse whose tongue is transformed into a tuber surmounted by leaves and flowers. See 55.

PLATE 90. 6. The description will be followed more easily in 13 or 21. This important personage, executed six times, has very special features. It consists of human legs (the big toes opposing the other toes) with a slight body and an enormous head. Each of the hands holds one of the forepaws of a beige and brown animal with six paws and a ringed tail; the mouth of the personage and the jaw of the animal are almost in contact through penetration of the tongue. At the right and left of the head is a small red puppet, fastened to the headband by its belt. Each of the puppets has its own special paraphernalia. The one on the left holds in his left hand a plant with three fleshy roots (sweet manioc) and in his right hand a fan-shaped object (stylized *tumi*?). The small red figure on the right (not illustrated in this plate) bears in his left hand a plant with a single tuber and in his right a small baton. In order to make the two puppets identical and complete, the lower one has a pair of legs on each face of the frieze. Three serpents, of which two are on the tape and the third in the air, complete the accessories of the principal figure (see 13, 21, 58, 71, 84).

7. Personage holding in his left hand a baton decorated with two knobs. On each side of his face hang three earplugs; seven vertical rays surmount the headband (see 47, 83).

8. Figure with the legs and body of a man. The body is bent forward from the hips. The much-decorated head has a mustache and decorative chin piece in addition to the headband and numerous fanlike rays. The right hand holds a mace and a trophy head, which is visible on the tape, and the left hand holds a stylized sling, to which is fastened above the hand a small puppet with a curved body holding a baton and a stylized *tumi* or fan.

9. Figure in which the lower part is that of a man. One foot is turned to the right and the other to the left; the big toes oppose the other toes. The head, with a voluminous handband in reverse, is rather formless. The arms are raised. The figure is flanked by four serpents, two above and two below on the tape. The figure partially resembles that of 20.

Description of Plates

10. The figure consists of a human body clothed in a narrow robe that extends to the feet and is embroidered with trophy heads. The outstretched arms hold in their hands on one side a plant and on the other a small puppet. On the head is a wig of long, light-colored hair. From one side of the mouth emerges a long centipede tongue, which curves to one side and rises, terminating in a bird or a very stylized insect, seen from above, and on the other side a combination bird-man, seen in profile. See 24 and 74.

PLATE 91. 11. Subject similar to 4, except in the following respects: the serpent in 4 is replaced by a small feline in reverse; the tongue of the subject is longer; one of the serpents in the air is replaced by a larger animal. See 4, 54, 76; see 89 for the lower part only.

12. Richly attired personage. On his head, above the headband, is a halo consisting of six motives of branched rays resembling decorative mustaches. In his right hand he holds a scepterlike object ornamented with four serpents, each of which has a head at its two extremities; in his left hand are five darts and a *tumi*.

13. Subject similar to 6 (see description of 6). See also 21, 58, 71, and 84.

14. Subject similar to 8 (see description of 8). The small figure attached to the end of the sling in 8 is missing here. See also 27.

15. Humanized jaguar. The legs and arms are those of a man. The garment covering the back of the figure is spotted like the fur of a jaguar. On the tape is an appendage in the form of a tail. The head has the ears of a feline; it is surmounted by rays, partly red (the only exception on the frieze; all the other subjects have yellow rays). The small trophy head embroidered on the border of the tape must have been fastened to the hands by a light cord.

PLATE 92. 16. Richly attired personage. His left hand holds a baton on which appears a man-bird combination, like that already described in 10. His mouth is decorated with enormous mustaches and with a two-headed serpent. His headdress is different on each of the two faces, and consists of five flowers similar to those which join the frieze to the central fabric. From his mantle emerges a decorative centipede, which terminates in a quadruped with a macelike tongue.

Note: the following subjects face in the direction opposite to that of the subjects just described.

17. Personage with a double tongue; the body is partially destroyed. The right hand holds a dart and a three-ringed baton with corollas from which hang trophy heads, only one of which is still in existence. See 18 and 49.

18. Personage with a double tongue, similar to 17. In his right hand he holds two darts and a throwing stick. See 17.

19. Combination plant and human, whose left hand holds a *tumi*, and whose raised right hand holds an instrument consisting of a handle to which is fastened a double cord terminating in a knot or a hard substance of either stone or metal (see p. 175). An animal skin hangs from the neck. From the side of the inclined head extends a cactus, which has a small headband representing flowers or fruit. See 51 and 65.

20. This subject is seen full face. The lower part of the body is similar to that of a man, with the feet turned outward in opposite directions. The figure has two hands, in one of which he holds a combination headband and baton. A stylized centipede falls from each side of his belt onto the tape, then curves and rises vertically, terminating in two small arms and a feline head. The reversed head of the subject is provided with false mustaches joined under the mouth by a large ring; the tongue terminates in a small head.

21. The subject is similar to 6 (see description of 6). See also 13, 58, 71, and 84.

PLATE 93. 22. Personage with body bent forward from the hips. In his left hand he holds a *tumi* and in his right a long baton decorated in its lower section with two headbands. He has a large mustache in the form of a serpent. A very large centipede mantle falls from his neck, follows his curved spine, and then rises a little as if floating in the wind; it terminates in two arms and a head. The huge headdress consists of a wide band bordered with small motives forming crenelations and terminating in a tongue portrayed as a small figure holding a *tumi* in one hand. See 29 and 46.

23. Personage with the body of a man. The two hands hold by its two ends a headband to which should be fastened the small trophy head placed on the edge of the tape (only a faint section of it can be seen in the photograph). The head of the subject is reversed. Two serpents form the mustaches. The tongue consists of a stylized centipede, as does the large appendage that emerges from the back, descends upon the tape, and then rises again in the form of a U.

24. Personage similar to 10 (see description of 10). The serpent above his head must have been taken from another subject. See also 74.

25. Incomplete personage, poorly preserved. He has large false mustaches. In his right hand he carries a baton. See 44, 56, 63, 66, and 78.

26. Combination of llama and plant. The animal, in spite of its stylization, is easily recognizable; it is domesticated since it wears around its neck a cord, the end of which is on the tape and is held by the little figure who is leading it. It has cloven hoofs. Between its ears it carries a decorative motive in the form of a young shoot. From its neck emerges a plant with spontaneously growing roots that are inserted into the flesh in the dorsal area. The body is ornamented with leaves and vegetal shoots. See 50.

PLATE 94. 27. Personage similar to 8 (see description of 8). The small figure at the end of the sling is missing. See also 14.

28. This personage holds in his right hand a baton with three corollas, two of which have two additional corollas. He is wearing on his back the skin of an animal whose four paws and tail can be recognized (this is a separate piece fastened to the center by a stitch). The head, which is visible in 75, is missing here. In the photograph one can distinguish little except the left forepaw close to the face and the right hindpaw between the bodies of 27 and 28. See 75.

29. Personage very much like 22. The mantle, however, is different. Instead of being raised it falls, and it is the only example on the frieze that continues in the form of a centipede's tail joined to the figure that follows. The large headdress of 22 is lacking here. The head itself is incomplete.

30. Incomplete subject, the upper part missing. The legs, which are very wide and straight, are decorated in the center with superimposed triangular motives. The toes are represented by five small rose dots placed one above the other on the lower part of the tape. In the right hand is an incomplete instrument. Two centipede tails cross the figure: the one on the right comes from 29, the other falls symmetrically upon the tape, where it curves in the form of a U.

31. Of this subject only the legs, which are visible on the tape, now exist.

32. Of this personage only the legs and the lower edge of the robe are visible. The robe is decorated with horizontal S's. It may be compared, without great risk of error, to 79, which also occupies a corner of the frieze. See 79.

33. Personage of which only the legs, on the tape, are visible.

34. Personage of which only the legs and lower part of the body, on the tape, are visible. Between 34 and 35 is a space, followed by a motive of zigzag design. The part above the tape, which is now imperfect, may not belong to the figure.

35. This personage, of which only the legs on the tape are visible, can be compared with 4, 11, or 89 because of the accompanying motive (small feline having in its jaws a cord that terminates in a kind of pod). Note that it occupies a place on the frieze symmetrical with that of 89.

PLATE 95. 36. Personage of a special form, whose proportions were probably larger than those of the other figures. All that remains on the frieze are the large legs and feet on the tape, and a curved body, the center of which is destroyed. Barely visible is a head, the headdress of which is missing; the wide face has a nose in relief, and a serpentine tongue that descends onto the tape and there curves twice. There are faint indications on the tape of an arm and a hand probably holding a *tumi*.

Note: the following subjects face in the direction opposite to that of the subjects just described.

Description of Plates

37. Personage with a particularly outstanding headdress. In each hand he holds an accessory of which only fragments remain.

38. Personage facing in the opposite direction to that of his neighbors (see p. 170).

39. Personage consisting of a body seen full face, with one foot turned outward to the right and the other to the left. The head is reversed. From the mouth emerges a centipede tongue, at the end of which is a small quadruped whose tongue terminates in small bells, which it appears to be shaking. The personage has in his left hand a small figure holding a baton in one hand and a *tumi* in the other. On the right and left of the headband are seen two other small figures, in reverse position like the principal head. Thus, the arm of one of the small figures, which seems to be uplifted, is actually hanging down. On each side of the principal subject can be seen a centipede, which descends below the robe and turns horizontally.

40. Small personage without insignia whose head is covered with a bonnet. This detached headgear can be seen clearly from the other face of the frieze; only the edges can be observed to the right and left of the figure in the photograph.

41. Combination of plant and man, whose head is thrust firmly to one side, permitting a bushy plant bearing leaves, flowers, and fruit to emerge from the neck. At the level of the branches the plant itself has a head, and its central stem terminates in another head. These are not clearly visible on the plate. The body of the personage does not extend beyond the tape. The left hand holds a baton, probably with three corollas, of which only the third one is visible on the tape. See 85.

PLATE 96. 42. This subject is poorly preserved; the description of it will be more easily followed in 80, which differs from 42 in only a few details. The personage, with a tiny body and a huge head, holds in his hands a vegetal arch that, leaving the tape, returns to it after encircling the head of the bearer. The arch consists of three parallel colored bands; the violet, in the center, represents a branch that terminates on the tape, on one side in roots, and on the other side in leaves. Five double-headed motives decorate the arch. These motives, except the top one, are not arranged with their two parts directly opposite to each other. From the uppermost motive on the arch emerges a root still attached to its pod, probably a bean; a young green sprout also emerges from the same bean pod. The personage has an enormous head, still further enlarged by false mustaches in the form of flowers and by his headdress, which is formed of an animal with a seven-rayed head. On one side of the headdress the tongue of the animal is extended as a tuber plant—root, stalk, and leaves; its tail, on the other side, gives birth to another plant, which has among its leaves two small animalistic pods. In the center of the animal used as the headdress of the personage is seen a head in reverse, whose tongue blossoms into large flowers. See 80.

43. Bird subject or insect situated in the corner of the frieze. Its form can be compared with the birds or insects that terminate one of the tongues of 10 and 24, and the two tongues of 74. The stylization of the head, mustaches, and tail is similar, only here the wings are curved instead of being straight.

44. Personage that may be compared with 25 (see description of that number), 56, 63, 66, and 78.

45. Anthropomorphic subject holding in the left hand a large throwing stick, and in the right a baton, which gives a horizontal barred effect to the *cushma*. The end of the baton, seen only in relief, has a ring from which hangs an ornament in the form of an ear pendant. The head, which is without precise form, has double-headed serpentine mustaches and a voluminous centipede tongue. Above the headband can be seen a plant shoot comparable to that which the llama in 26 has between its ears. A centipede tail in the form of a U completes the costume.

46. For a description of this subject, reference can be made to that of 22, noting, however, the following differences: a serpent tail crosses a centipede appendage, which comes from the headdress and takes the place of the mantle that is to be seen in 22; there are no small figures at the extremities of the voluminous headdress.

PLATE 97. 47. Personage closely resembling 7. See also 83.

48. Personage comparable to 2 (see the description of that number), 52, and 79, from which it differs only in the headdress, which is made of two serpents falling on the right and left of the face.

49. Personage with a double tongue (as in 17 and 18). He holds in his left hand a baton and in his right a small trophy head hanging from a short cord. A mantle falls on his right side from the shoulders;

180

a serpent appears to extend this mantle onto the tape. Ear pendants, which are found only on the right, have a special star shape. A yellow bonnet edged in blue and rose covers the head as far as the neck on the reverse side of the frieze; only the edging can be seen in the photograph.

50. Combination of llama and plant, partially destroyed, which must have been similar to 26. In the parts that now lack embroidery, the foundation network in simple looping, which molds the forms, can be clearly discerned. The plant rising from the back of the animal has an appearance different from that of 26. The cord around the llama's neck, instead of being merely indicated by embroidery, actually exists in relief; it forms a loop and finishes with a knot. The other end is held in the hand of the little conductor who can be seen on the tape, as in 26.

51. Combination of man and plant. For description refer to 19.

52. Personage closely resembling 2. For description refer to 2. See also 79.

PLATE 98. 53. Anthropomorphic subject with reversed head, which has a centipede tongue. The hand of the upraised arm no doubt held an accessory of some kind; the other holds two darts. The mantle cuts across the *cushma* diagonally. See 72.

54. Subject corresponding to that of 4, except in the following respects: the serpent on the tape does not terminate in a vegetal motive; to the four serpents is added an animal which differs from that in 11; the tongue of the figure is relatively short. See 4, 11, and 76.

55. Subject corresponding to 5. See 5.

56. Incomplete personage. See 25, and also 44, 63, 66, and 78.

57. Personage comparable to 59, 60, 61, 69, and 70, which present the same characteristics without being entirely similar to each other. The representation is of a man with uplifted arms having in his hands, as the case may be, a staff (such as in 57), darts, or a throwing stick. The man wears a large headdress with rays arranged in a semicircular arch.

58. The subject is similar to 6. For description see 6. One of the small personages is incomplete. See also 13, 21, 71, and 84.

59. Personage comparable to 57. He holds a baton in each hand; the longer of them has two corollas, the pistils of which once supported a small trophy head, as in 17. The headdress is incomplete. See also 60, 61, 69, and 70.

PLATE 99. 60. Personage comparable to 57. He holds in his left hand a mace, and in his right a throwing stick and a dart. See also 59, 61, 69, and 70.

Note: the following subjects face in the direction opposite to that of the subjects just described.

61. Personage comparable to 57. He has a baton in one hand and in the other an additional baton with corollas, as well as two darts. See 59, 69, and 70.

62. The subject consists of a body with two human legs and a huge reversed head, in which the tongue is formed of a serpent flanked at the right and left by a pod with visible grains. The arms are uplifted. Two serpents of unequal size fall from his belt onto the tape.

63. Personage comparable to 25, 44, 56, 66, and 78. In one hand he holds a ringed baton. Because of its facial ornaments, this is the most easily identified subject of the group. It is generally very well preserved.

64. Subject with one foot turned to the right and the other to the left. It wears a long robe flanked by serpentine centipedes. One hand is bearing a leafy branch, while the other holds a small puppet with a baton and a *tumi*. The reversed head of the principal subject is decorated with three serpentine mustaches. The tongue is now imperfect.

65. Personage similar to 19. For description refer to 19 and 51. Here the head is more powerful; the plant that emerges from the headband has the appearance not of a cactus but of leafy branches. Yellow flowers and green fruit are completed with a headband.

PLATE 100. 66. Personage comparable to 25. For description refer to 25. See also 44, 56, 63, and 78.

67. Extremely confused subject, consisting, first, of a principal personage with uplifted arms and a huge reversed head provided with a tongue that is transformed into a quadruped. (The tongue here is vertical, but in 88 the tongue is in horizontal position.) There is also a smaller, secondary personage ap-

pliquéd onto the principal figure. The secondary figure holds a *tumi* in one hand and a baton in the other; its head, which is also reversed, can be seen between the *tumi* and the arm that holds the baton. On the tape is an appendage formed of a stalk that divides in two and forms a terminal hook. At the level of the headbands on one side hangs a large green tuber. See 73 and 88.

68. The subject has legs, body, and arms of a man. A long mantle falls from the shoulders and terminates in a centipede tail, which curves in the form of a U on the tape. The head is reversed, has no visible tongue, and is wearing a headband from which hangs a cord that subsequently turns, forming a right angle and ending in a small trophy head. Below the headband on the figure is an animal comparable to those shown on the headdresses in 42 and 80; from its stomach hang two red flowers, one of which is in relief. One hand is holding a baton with corollas, and the other a plant with a large split tuber on which is clearly delineated an implement difficult to identify. See Figure 103, B.

69. Personage comparable to 57 (for description refer to 57), 59, 60, 61, and 70. In the right hand he holds a throwing stick and two darts, and in his left a baton.

70. Incomplete personage in poor state of preservation; comparable to 57, 59, 60, 61, and 69. He is holding a baton in the left hand.

71. Subject similar to 6 (for description see 6), 13, 21, 58, and 84. The legs of the little personage in the lowest position are missing.

PLATE 101. 72. Subject similar to 53 (for description see 53). Instead of having two darts in his hand, however, he is holding a baton.

73. Subject similar to 67 (for description refer to 67) and 88. The tongue and the animal that originally formed its extension have been destroyed.

74. Subject similar to 10 (for description refer to 10) and 24. The right hand should be holding a small figure, which is no longer in existence.

75. Subject similar to 28. For description refer to 28. He holds in his right hand a simple baton, and the left arm is folded.

76. This subject, which is in very poor condition, is similar to 4. For description refer to 4; see also 11 and 54. The vegetal motive on the tape is missing here. In its place, however, from the lower hand a centipede cord falls onto the tape, curves in the form of a U, and terminates in a small trophy head.

77. Animal similar to 3. For description refer to 3. The plant is different from that of the other jaguar-plant. The meaning of the green line that crosses the body vertically can be explained here: it is the stalk of the plant. This subject is partially destroyed.

PLATE 102. 78. This personage, of which only the legs, trunk, and one arm remain, must have been similar to 44. See also 25, 56, 63, and 66.

79. Personage comparable to 2 (for description refer to 2), 32, and 52.

80. Subject similar to 42. For description refer to 42.

81. Combination of bird and man. On the tape can be seen the feet of a bird and the profile of a wing; the tail is in poor condition but can be conjectured. Above the tape, the body has two arms, one hand of which holds a baton. The huge head has false mustaches, a headdress with semicircular rays, and a tongue that terminates in an animal closely resembling those in 67 and 88, but with ringed paws like those of the animals in 6, 13, and so forth.

82. Unique subject, quite confused, consisting of an embryonic body with two feet, two arms, and in each hand a plant with a tuber. The tongue in the huge reversed head has the same motive as that terminating both the tongues in 74 and one of the tongues in 10 and in 24.

83. Personage comparable to 7 and 47. He has three darts in his right hand and a baton in his left.

PLATE 103. 84. Subject similar to 6 (for description refer to 6), 13, 21, 58, and 71. The small personage placed in the lowest position is now missing.

85. Subject similar to 41. For description refer to 41. Instead of rays on his head the personage is wearing a small animal, shaped somewhat like that in 81.

Note: the following subjects face in the direction opposite to that of the subjects just described.

86. Personage comparable to 57, 59, and so forth, but with more numerous emblems and ornaments. The sham mustaches are stylized into ornamental flowers. Three serpents, the parallel upper sections of which form a square panel on the side of the personage, fall onto the tape.

87. Anthropomorphic subject. The left arm is uplifted. The right hand holds a baton provided with two crossbars (situated above and below the hand) and with a terminal fork from which hangs the ringed tail of an animal. In the original plan of the worker, the head was probably intended to lie in reversed position; for this reason the rays were embroidered upon the body. However, the head is turned only at right angles, and the headdress is completely separated from the top of the head. The head has a centipede tongue. On the tape the mantle is transformed into a centipede and terminates in a small head (seen only in part on the photograph).

88. Subject similar to 67 (for description see 67) and 73.

PLATE 104. 89. Subject whose lower part, embroidered on the tape, is comparable to 11 and 35 and partially to 4. The upper part of the body is not bent forward. The personage holds in one hand a baton and in the other a *tumi*. The head resembles that of a feline; it is decorated with a headdress comparable to that of 22, 29, and 46, and has a mustache in serpent form.

90. Subject in which the anthropomorphic characteristics are limited to the arms and the legs; these, in atrophied form, are placed at one side. A centipede tail takes the place of the body. The head is reversed. Each of the hands holds a plant with a tuber. The centipede tail terminates in a head whose tongue is transformed into four leaves. A serpent falls from the side of the headband, which terminates in a plant with a tuber, stalk, and leaves, on the tape.

Lower part of the plate. Portion of the fabric forming the center of the Paracas textile (Pl. 88). The wrapping of the warp yarns can be seen more clearly in this detailed photograph (see Fig. 37).

PLATE 105, A. Rectangular piece of crimson wool, plain-weave construction, strewn with personages embroidered in polychrome wool in stem stitch. These personages do not differ from each other except in color and in the fact that those on the border are larger. At the waist on either side is a serpent-centipede; each holds in one hand a throwing stick and in the other a *tumi*. Their heads are richly dressed and are turned at right angles to the bodies. They have serpent tongues. Size: 242 x 68 cm. [95¼ x 26¾ in.]. Provenience: Nazca (?). Museum of Fine Arts, Boston, No. 21.2556. At Nazca, wool foundations for embroidery are rare; the majority of pieces are embroidered on cotton cloth.

B. Rectangular piece of black wool, plain-weave construction, strewn with personages embroidered in polychrome wool, in stem stitch. These personages do not differ from each other except in color. The arms are outstretched and hold in each hand a kind of ceremonial baton from which is suspended a shrunken head (*tsantsa*) or an object in the form of a flower. Two serpents fall to their feet. They appear to be wearing rich mantles, spread out in voluminous folds and decorated with shrunken heads. At the left is an unfinished motive, only the outlines of which are embroidered. Size: 245 x 120.5 cm. [96½ x 47½ in.]. Provenience: Pisco. Museum of Fine Arts, Boston, No. 16.34.

PLATE 106, A. Band of dark green cotton, plain-weave construction, which has a creped appearance by reason of the overtwisting of the yarns. Nine to ten yarns to the centimeter [22 to 23 to the inch]. It is, for the most part, covered with a uniform carmine red embroidery in stem stitch, which covers two to five yarns of the fabric in a stitch. Total length: 242 cm. [95¼ in.]; width of the band: 24 cm. [9½ in.]. The design consists of a series of motives, of which only one is shown in the photograph. Provenience: Paracas. Ratton Collection, Paris.

B. Band of polychrome wool embroidery in stem stitch on green cotton plain-weave fabric. The embroidery completely covers the fabric, which is edged on two sides with a fine padding of loop stitch, and with a fringe made by needle. A series of small round motives is placed on the border on the third side. Colors: red foundation fabric; motives yellow, dark green, dark blue, dark red brown, light moss green. Design: series of six different personages of strange form, placed one above the other, armed with darts or stone-pointed knives. Width of the band: 12 cm. [4¾ in.] with the fringe. Length photographed: 52 cm. [20½ in.]. Provenience: Paracas. Collection of R. d'Harcourt.

PLATE 107, A. Fragment of fabric entirely covered on its two faces with a polychrome wool embroidery in stem stitch. It is decorated on one edge with a black needle-made wool fringe, and on the other with a series of small squares open in the center and made on a network of simple looping in wool (see p. 134). Colors: rose, light red, dark red, light green, dark green, blue, brown violet, dark yellowish brown, clear yellow, light yellow. Design formed of extremely complicated personages. Actual dimensions slightly reduced. The embroidery is identical on the two faces (see p. 127). Provenience: Paracas. Schmidt Collection, Paris.

B. Band of polychrome wool embroidery in stem stitch on beige cotton, plain weave (the lower part of a *cushma*). Colors: red foundation; anthropomorphic motives in bright yellow, dark green, dark blue. Border in loop stitch. Length: 300 cm. [118 in.]; width 3.5 cm. [1¼ in.]. Provenience: Nazca. Ratton Collection, Paris.

PLATE 108, A. Band of beige cotton fabric, plain weave, covered with wool embroidery in stem stitch; the border of the band is in loop-stitch embroidery. The embroidered band surrounds a rectangular piece. Colors: red foundation; embroidery in yellow, blue, green. The decorative motives represent a principal personage and stylized felines of different sizes. Size of the section photographed: 32.5 x 14 cm. [12¾ x 5½ in.]. Provenience: Paracas. Ratton Collection, Paris.

B. Part of a band embroidered in wool in stem stitch surrounding a large cotton fabric, plain-weave construction. Length: 240 cm. [94½ in.]; width: 110 cm. [43¼ in.]; width of the band: 10.5 cm. [4 in.]. Length photographed: 60 cm. [23¾ in.]. The decorative motive is repeated over the length of the band; it is formed of two personages who face each other, with the lower part of the body tapering like a tail and having four paws at the side. Small stylized felines complete the design. Colors: red foundation; motives yellow, green, blue. Provenience: Paracas. Ratton Collection, Paris.

PLATE 109, A. Part of a band embroidered in wool in stem stitch on cotton fabric. Sometimes the stem stitch is transformed into a flat stitch (see Fig. 92, A, *d*). The design is formed of a single very complex anthropomorphic motive, which is repeated. Colors: brown foundation; motives, green, red, blue, yellow and brown, dark red. Total length: 250 cm. [98½ in.]; width: 14 cm. [5½ in.]. Length of the section photographed: 39 cm. [15¼ in.]. Provenience: Paracas. Ratton Collection, Paris.

B. Band of solid green cotton, plain-weave construction, partially covered with red wool embroidery in stem stitch. The nonembroidered parts of the fabric form the design consisting of a series of personages placed one above the other, each holding in one hand a trophy head attached to a semicircular knife (*tumi*) and in the other a baton. Actual length: 240 cm. [94½ in.]; width of the embroidered band: 13 cm. [5 in.]. Length of the section photographed: 50 cm. [19¾ in.]. Provenience: Paracas. Ratton Collection, Paris.

PLATE 110, A. Band of light brown cotton fabric, plain-weave construction, covered with wool embroidery in stem stitch. Design: series of personages placed one above the other, each carrying in one hand a trophy head attached to a knife, and in the other a baton. On one side there is a raised border in loop stitch, to which is sewed a narrow fringe of brown cotton; this fringe is fragmentary. Width: 4.33 cm. [1¾ in.]. Colors: dark blue, light almond green, moss green, dark yellow, medium yellow, cream yellow, carmine red. Slightly less than natural size. Provenience: Paracas. Ratton Collection, Paris.

B. Band of cotton fabric, covered with wool embroidery in stem stitch. Design: series of personages leaning backward from the hips, with reversed heads and hanging hair; no doubt in dancing position. Each holds a bell in one hand and a cord or baton in the other. Colors: dark olive green foundation; personages, red, rose, azure blue, dark blue, yellow, yellow brown, dark brown, green. Slightly less than natural size. Provenience: Paracas. Hein Collection, Paris.

C. Detail in natural size of one of the figures appearing on a band embroidered in wool in stem stitch, bordering the small *cushma* shown in Plate 111.

184

D. Reverse of the fabric band illustrated in A of this plate.

PLATE 111. Small *cushma* made of brown cotton fabric, plain-weave construction, decorated in the center and on the sides with a band embroidered in wool in stem stitch with an edging in loop stitch. Design: series of personages having birds' claws and a mantle in the form of a wing, with a baton in each hand; the longer of the batons is decorated with two appendages. Near the corners, facing each other diagonally, are embroidered a small feline and a small personage. Colors: red foundation; design motives, dark yellow, light yellow, dark blue, light blue, dark green, brown. Size: 55 x 40 cm. [21¾ x 15¾ in.]. Length of the slit: 25 cm. [9¾ in.]. Width of the band: 4.5 cm. [1¾ in.]. Provenience: Paracas. Ratton Collection, Paris.

PLATE 112, A. Band of red cotton fabric, plain-weave construction, covered with wool embroidery in stem stitch. Design: series of highly decorative personages, each having a *tumi* in one hand and two long arrows or lances in the other. From the top of the headdress emerges a cord that terminates in a bird; at the side of the headdress is a long and voluminous appendage with serrated edges, probably a centipede. Opposite the bird, on the other side of the headdress and between the main figures, is a puppet with the same insignia and ornaments as the larger personages. Colors: olive green foundation; figures, carmine red, rose, dark Indian yellow, yellow brown, dark blue, light blue, dark green. On the edge is a border in relief in loop stitch, with a needle-made fringe of polychrome wool. Width of the embroidered band: 17 cm. [6¾ in.]. Length of the fringe, 3 cm. [1¼ in.]. Provenience: Paracas. Hein Collection, Paris.

B. Band of cotton fabric covered with wool embroidery in stem stitch, with a lateral border in relief in loop stitch. Design: series of highly decorative personages holding a small trophy head in each hand. The three small trophy heads that decorate the upper and lower parts of the garment should be noted. Colors: red foundation; personages, brown, dark blue, lighter blue, green, rose, yellow, violet, white. Slightly less than natural size. Provenience: Paracas. Hein Collection, Paris.

PLATE 113, A. Belt in the form of a regular band, similar on each of its two faces, becoming narrower toward the two extremities and terminating at each end in a point to which a decorative tassel is attached. Length of tassel: 9 cm. [3½ in.]. The specimen includes a central section and an edge 1 cm. [½ in.] wide, joined together by needle. The central part consists of a band of fourteen-mesh network (simple knot) made with a somewhat coarse wool yarn, of very dark color. The network, with the exception of the knots, is entirely concealed by needle embroidery executed as explained on page 130, with decorative wool yarns in the following colors: cream white, yellow, brown, brown red, moss green, dark green, sky blue, dark blue, rose. The edge consists of a tape of red wool, plain weave, with hidden weft. Length: 146 cm. [57½ in.]; width: 12 cm. [4¾ in.]. Provenience: Copara, southern sector of Nazca. Epoch close to that of the Incaic occupation of the coast. Collection of Henry Reichlen, Paris.

B. Fragment of the same specimen greatly enlarged.

PLATE 114, A. Fabric of light-colored cotton ornamented with small silver disks in fish or shell forms. These disks are pierced at the edges and sewed to the fabric. Their arrangement on the fabric in series forms lines or arrows with the points woven in wool. The specimen, open in the center, is a shirt or *cushma*. Width: 108 cm. [42½ in.]. Provenience: region around Lima. Museum of the American Indian, Heye Foundation, New York, No. 17/8957.

B. Fabric of dark blue cotton decorated with turquoises and carved rose and white shells. Width: 115 cm. [45½ in.]. Provenience: ChanChan, near Trujillo. Museum of the American Indian, Heye Foundation, New York, No. 15/7381.

PLATE 115, A. Corner in natural size of a square piece of white plain-weave cotton, bordered on its four sides with overlapping feathers attached in accordance with the method described on page 132. The feathers form two distinct bands, the outside one of yellow and the inside one of dark turquoise. The center of the fabric is unornamented. A tassel of blue feathers glued to a wooden core and terminating in a sheaf of yellow feathers is suspended from each corner. Size of the specimen: 32 x 32 cm. [12½ x 12½ in.]. Provenience: Trujillo. Musée de l'Homme, No. 87–115–168.

185

Description of Plates

B. Beige cotton fabric with brown stripes, of the rep family and quite heavy. One face is covered with white shell disks sewed on like overlapping sequins, in adjacent columns. Natural size. Length: 80 cm. [31½ in.]; width: 19.5 cm. [7½ in.]. Musée de l'Homme, No. X, 33–271–2.

PLATE 116, A. Sheaf of feather quills joined at the base by yarns. Each quill is wrapped and covered with red wool yarn and is completed at its top with three or four white feathers, which are joined together by the wrapping. Height: 37.5 cm. [14¾ in.]. Provenience: central coastal region. Musée de l'Homme, No. X, 33–271–20.

B and C. Heavy white cotton band, rep family, in the center of which light turquoise overlapping feathers are held by a yarn that forms a lacing. The quill of the feather is not bent. Length: 590 cm. [232 in.]; width: 1.5 cm. [½ in.]. The band is shown on both faces. Natural size. Provenience: central coastal region. Musée de l'Homme, No. 30–19–452.

D. Upper: sheaf of forty-five small braids of agave fiber, each terminating in two or three little red feathers, the bent quills of which are fastened at the commencement of the braid. Length: 12.5 cm. [5 in.]. Provenience: central coastal region. Musée de l'Homme, No. X, 33–271–21.

Lower: ornament made of small cords of agave fiber, which are fastened at one end with a small transverse cord and have at the other end a little tuft of red and gray feathers held by an external tie. Length: 10 cm. [4 in.]. Provenience: central coastal region. Musée de l'Homme, No. X, 33–271–22.

PLATE 117, A. Fragment of tapestry, cotton warp, wool weft, in which the decorative motives are outlined with round shell beads threaded on two yarns of adjacent warps and placed in position during the warping before the passage of the weft (see p. 132). Size: 15 x 22 cm. [6 x 8¾ in.]. Provenience: Nazca. University Museum of Archaeology and Ethnology, Cambridge, England.

B. A kind of ball, slightly oblong, use unknown. It is an independent specimen, like a ball for games or an ornamental ball, perhaps attached to a cord. It consists of a mass of raw brown cotton, well compressed by the regular twisting of brown cotton passing through the poles of the ellipsoid. These yarns are joined perpendicularly to each other by a network of needle embroidery in loop stitch, also in brown cotton. The network forms small regular chains, leaving the bare yarns visible between them. It includes a skullcap covering each of the two poles (eighteen to twenty yarns), a central belt (sixteen yarns), and two narrow intermediate belts (three yarns). Length: about 9 cm. [3½ in.]. Diameter: 7 cm. [2¾ in.]. One of the polar sections is in poor condition. Provenience: central coast of Peru. Musée de l'Homme, No. X, 53–288.

PLATE 1

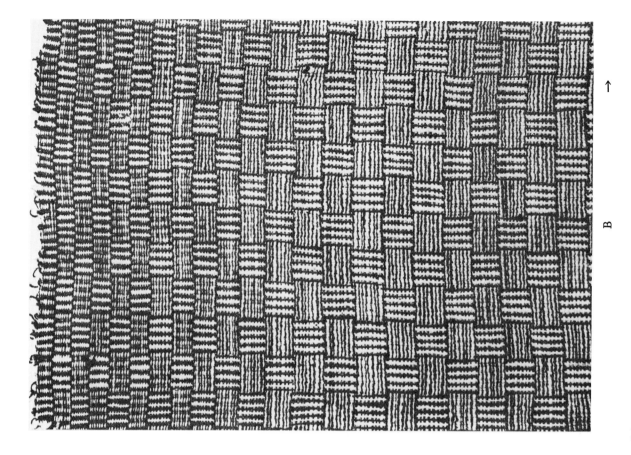

Plaid fabrics, plain weave

A

B →

PLATE 2

A, fabric with interlocked warp and weft yarns;
B, fabric of small squares, woven separately and sewed together

PLATE 3

↑

A

↑

B

Rep fabrics with interlocked warp and weft yarns

PLATE 4

Fabric with interlocked warp and weft yarns (plain weave)

PLATE 5

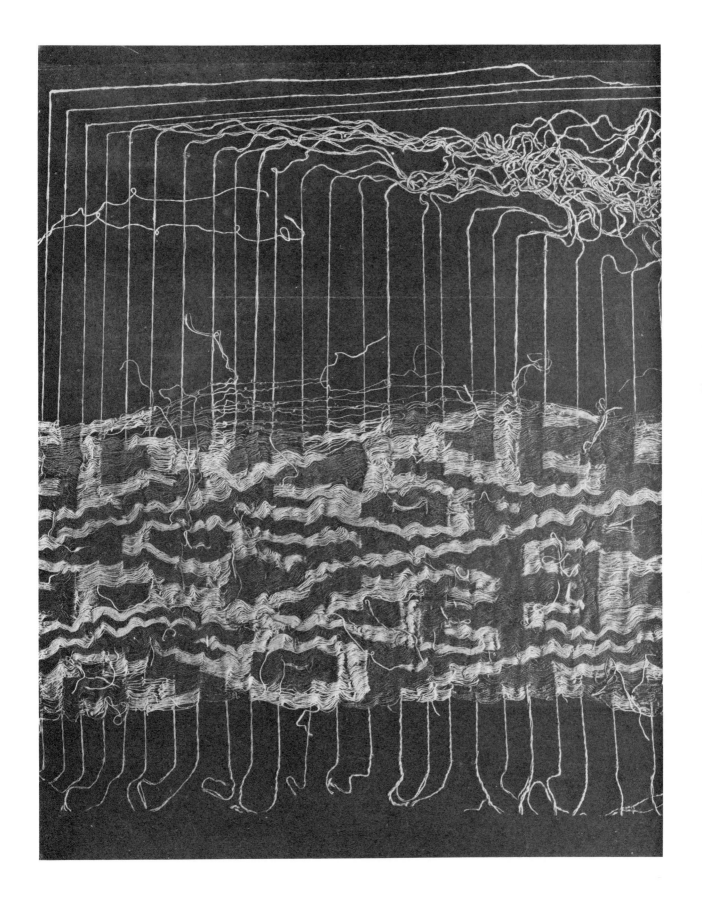

Warp of discontinuous yarns prepared for weaving

PLATE 6

A, rep fabric with interlocked warp yarns; B, tapestry with interlocked wefts

PLATE 7

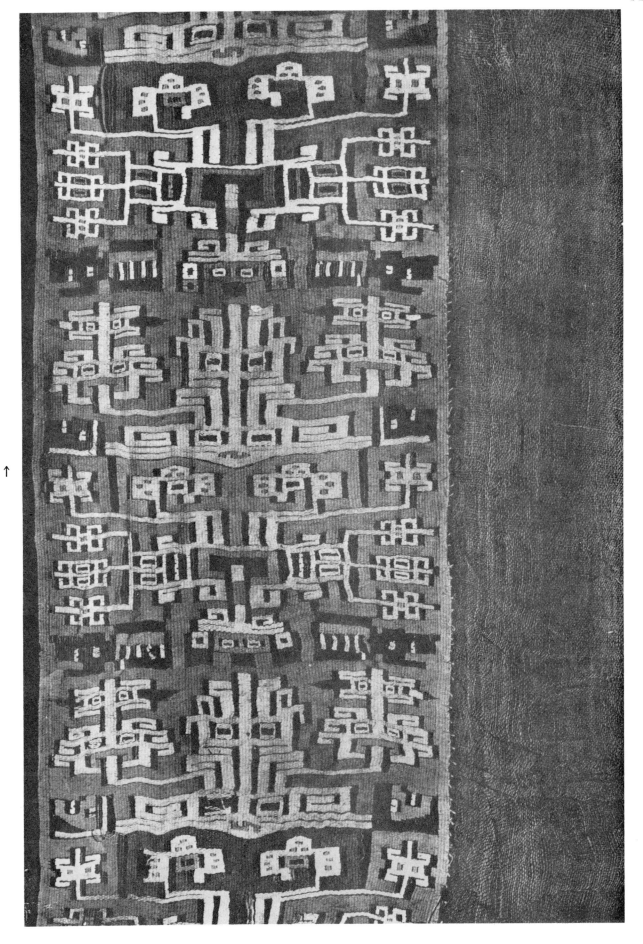

Tapestry

PLATE 8

Tapestry with an added cotton weft

←

PLATE 9

Tapestry

←

PLATE 10

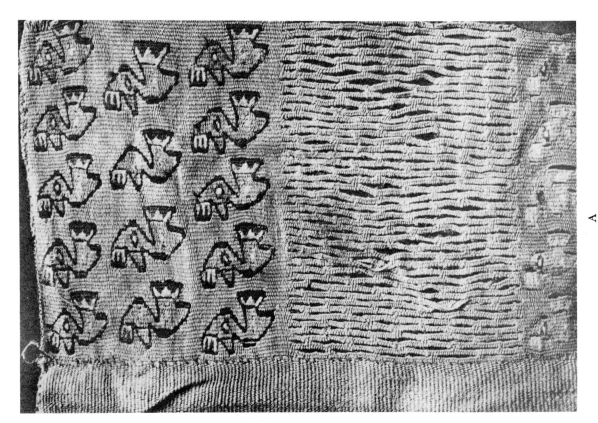

Tapestry with decorative slits

B

A

PLATE 11

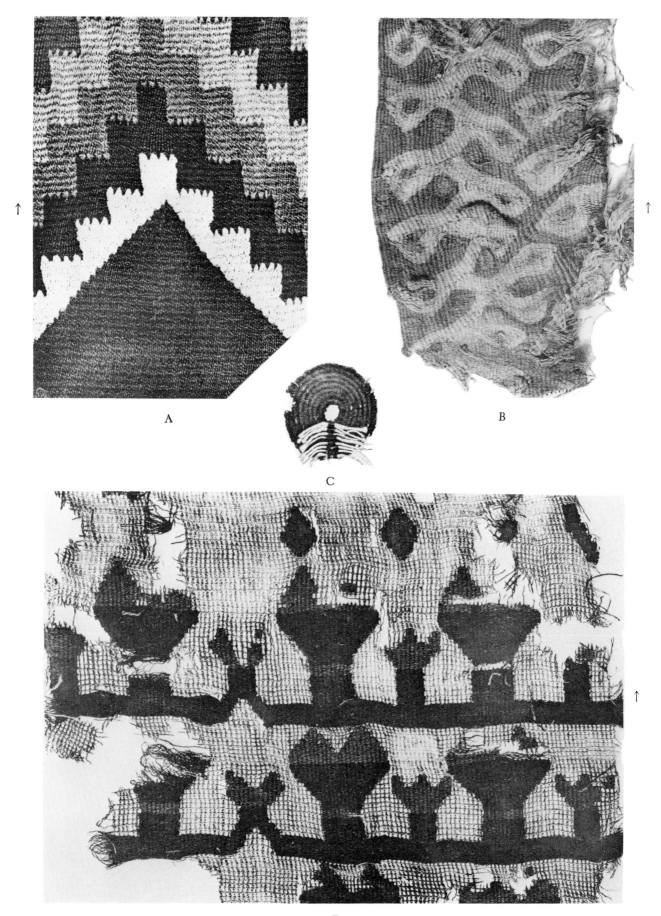

A, fabric with interlocked warp yarns;
B, D, tapestries of various types; C, decorative disk, reverse

PLATE 12

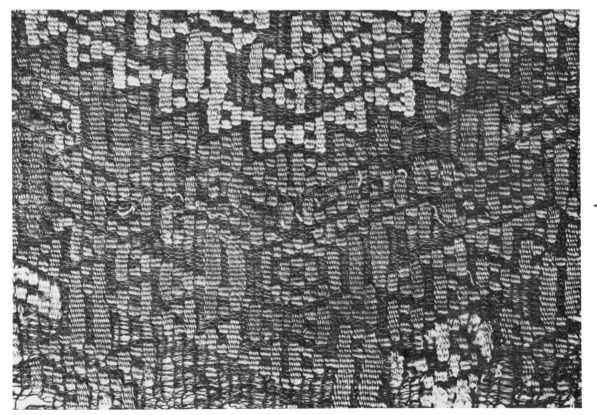

Tapestries on gauze foundation

PLATE 13

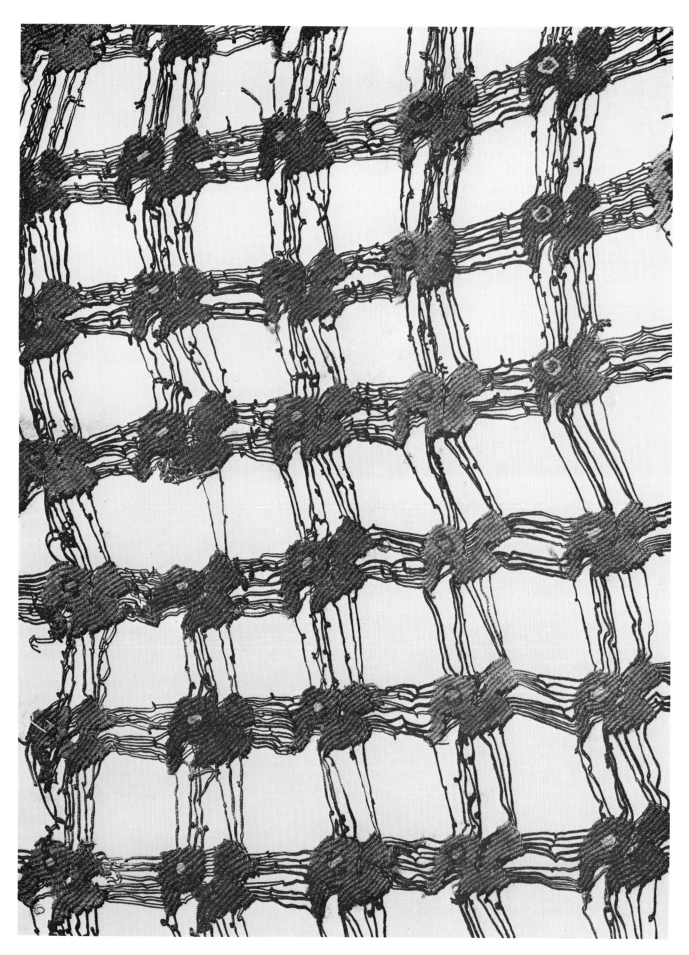

Open-space tapestry

PLATE 14

A

B

→

Open-space tapestries ornamented with pompons

PLATE 15

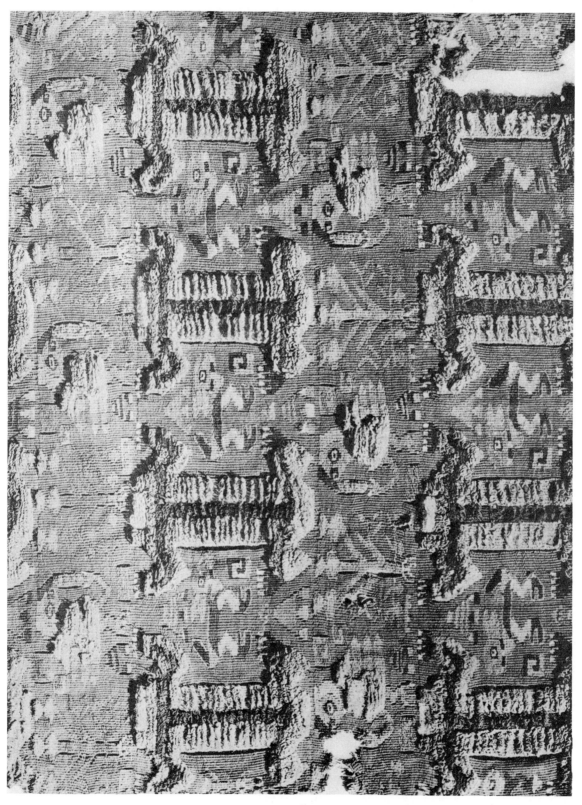

Tapestry with woven loop motives

PLATE 16

Reps and tapestries with loops

PLATE 17

A

B

C

Fabrics with construction subordinated to design

PLATE 18

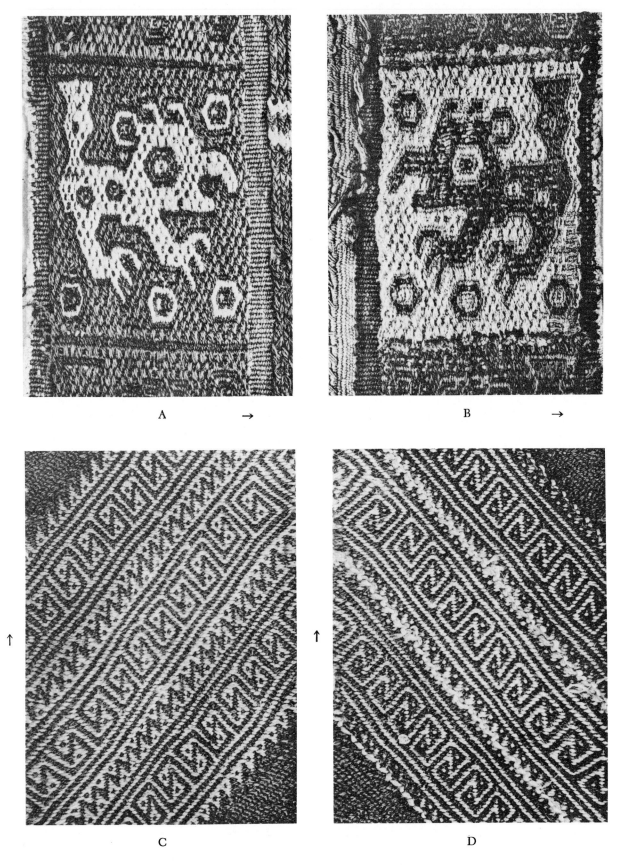

A   →

B   →

C

D

Single-face and double-face weaves with construction subordinated to design

PLATE 19

A   →

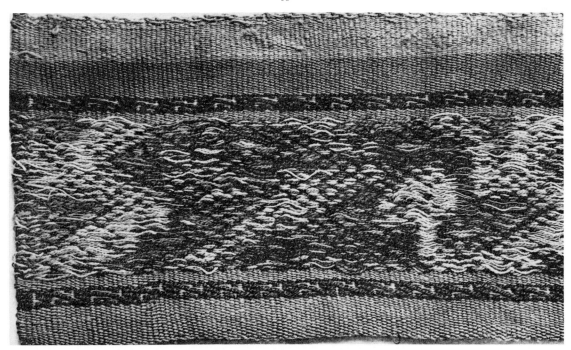

B   →

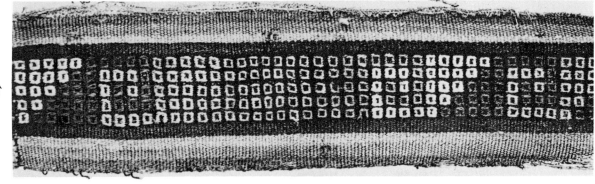

C

Fabrics with construction subordinated to design

PLATE 20

Bag (chuspa) of fabric with construction subordinated to design

PLATE 21

A →

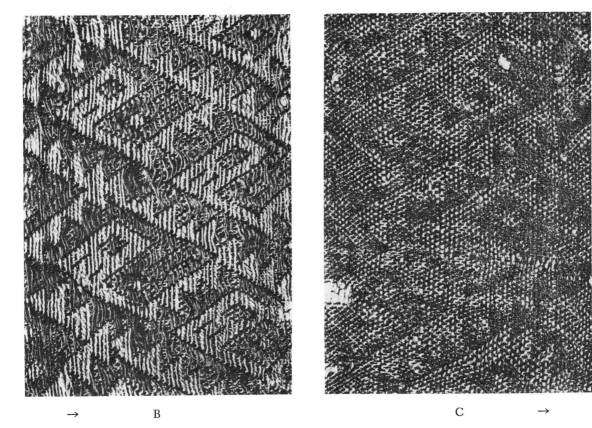

→ B

C →

Fabrics of irregular construction

PLATE 22

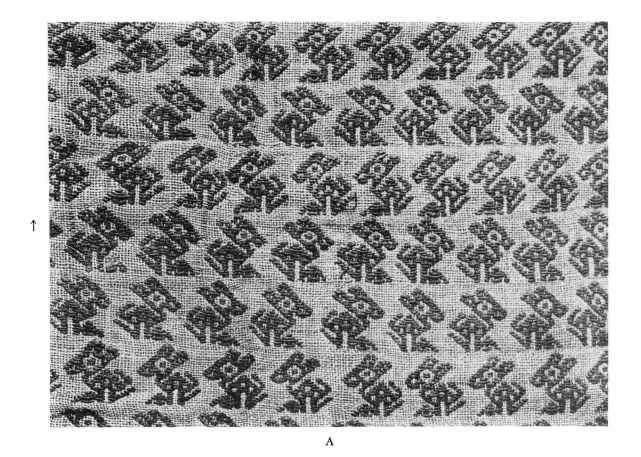

A

B

Fabric with supplementary decorative weft

PLATE 23

Fabric with supplementary decorative weft

PLATE 24

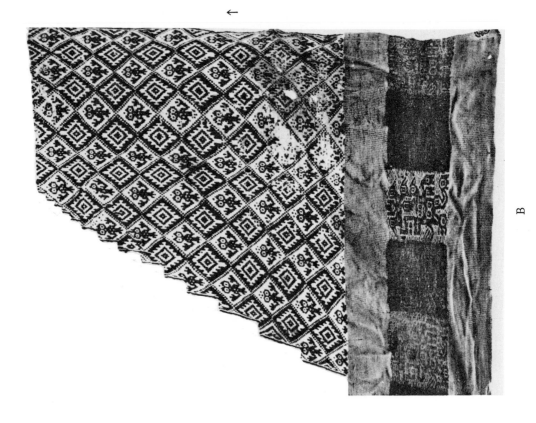

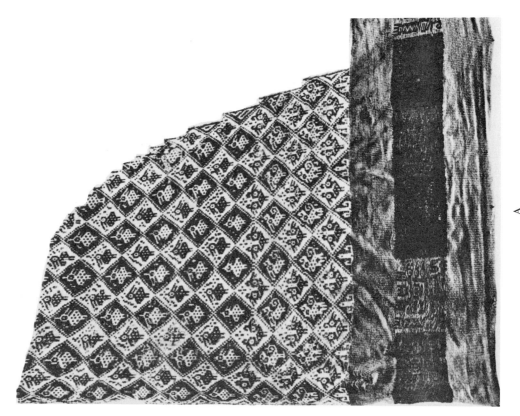

B

A

Fabrics with supplementary decorative weft

PLATE 25

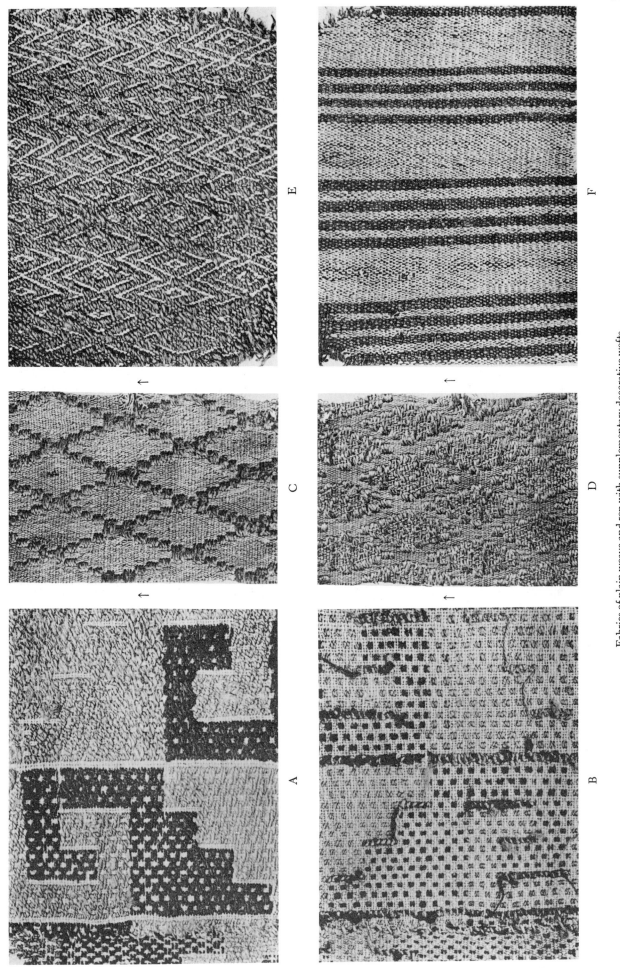

Fabrics of plain weave and rep with supplementary decorative wefts

PLATE 26

A

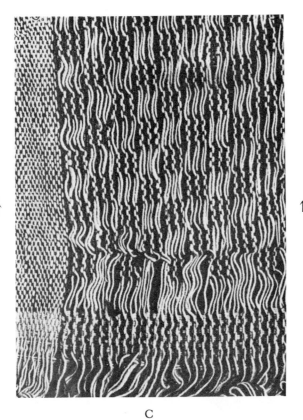

C

B

A, fabric with supplementary warp and weft yarns;
B, C, fabrics with supplementary decorative warp yarns

PLATE 27

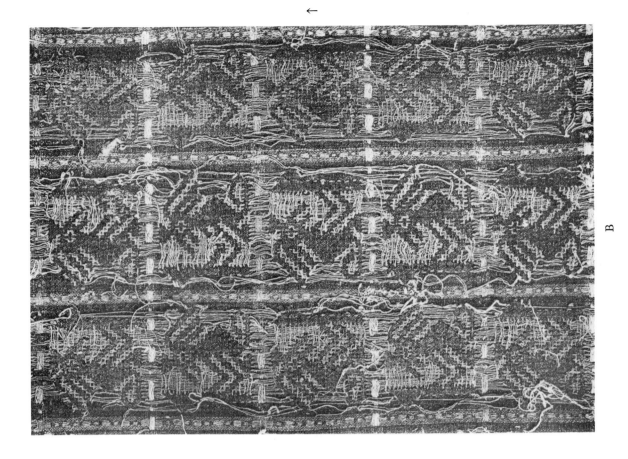

B   Fabric with supplementary warp and weft yarns   A

PLATE 28

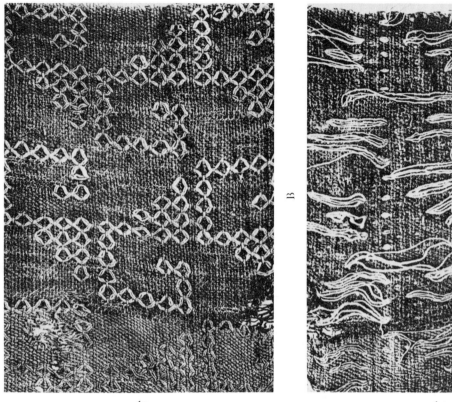

B

C

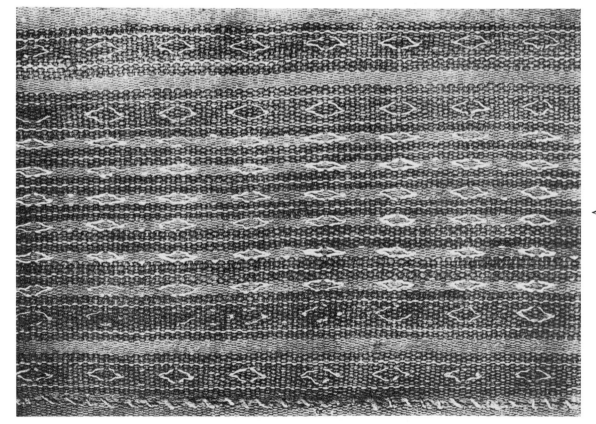

A

Fabrics with supplementary decorative warp yarns

PLATE 29

B

A

Double cloth with plain-weave construction

PLATE 30

B

A, band in double cloth rep, tubular weaving; B, double cloth with embroidery

A

PLATE 31

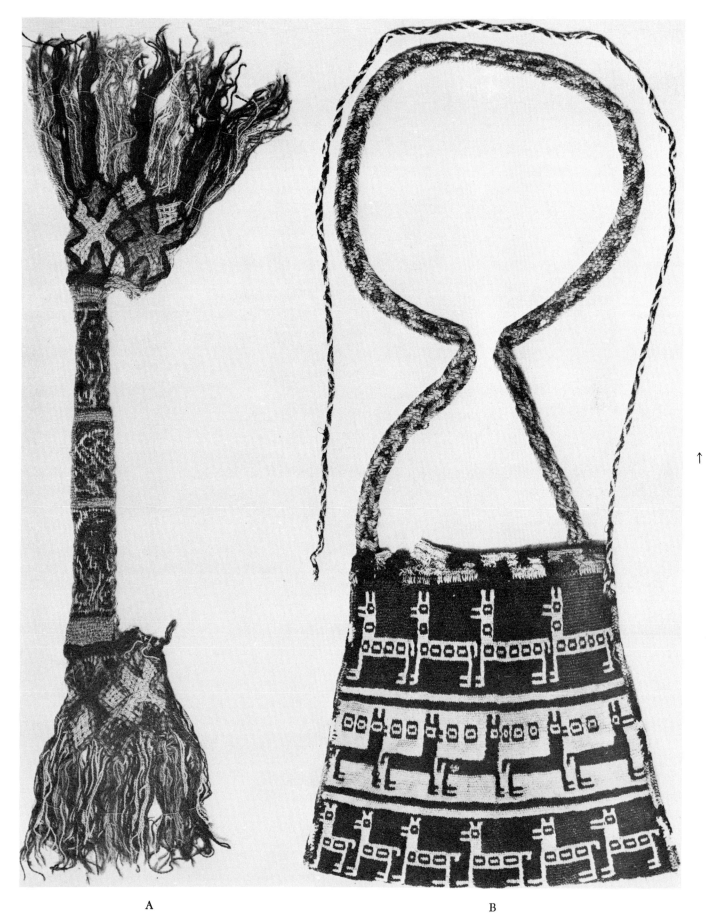

A   B

A, double cloth with double plaiting; B, small bag of double cloth

PLATE 32

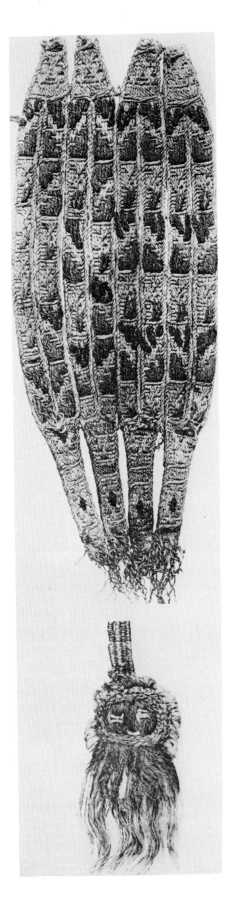

B

A

D

C

A, B, C, central portions of slings; D, small figure embroidered in wool

PLATE 33

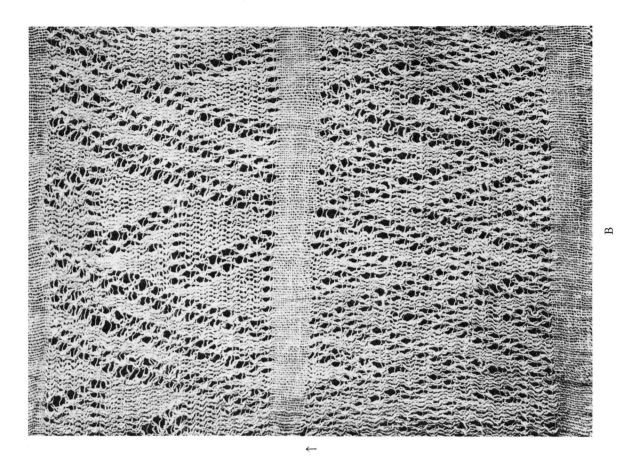

←

B

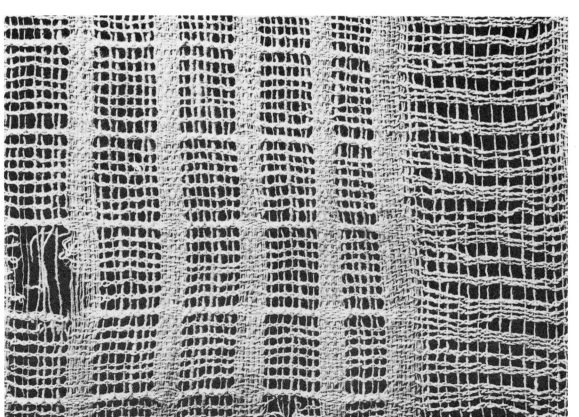

←

A

Fabrics of plain weave and gauze weave

PLATE 34

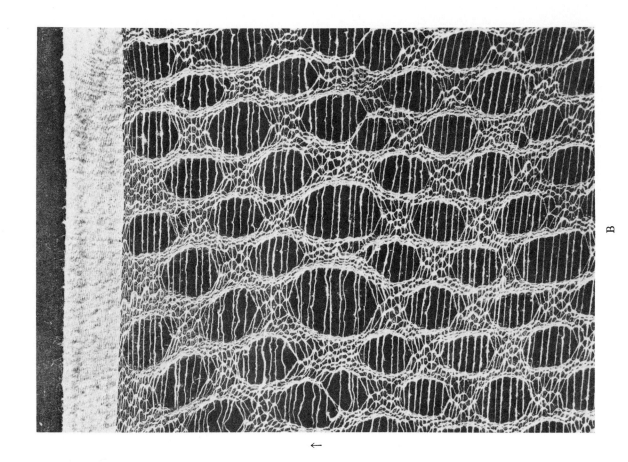

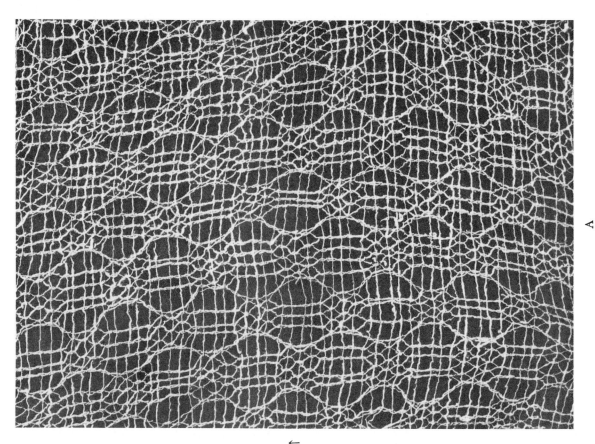

Open-work gauzes

B

A

PLATE 35

↑

Gauze with open spaces and embroidery

PLATE 36

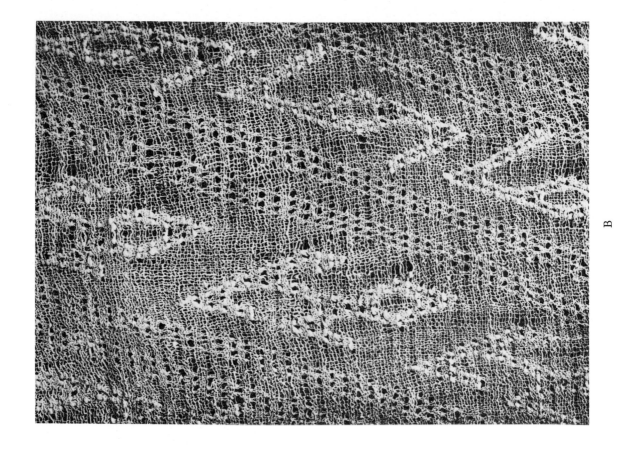

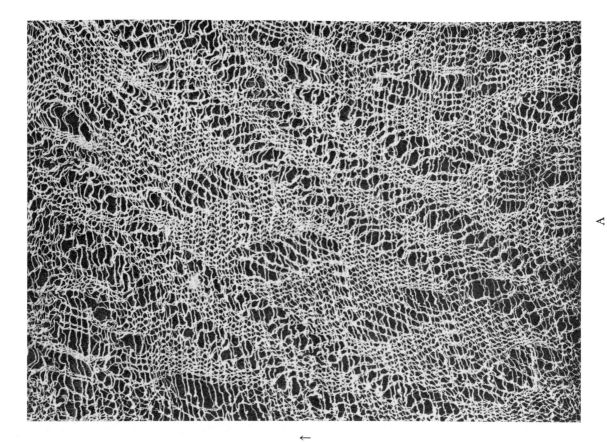

B

A

A, open-work gauze; B, gauze with open spaces and embroidered plain weave

PLATE 37

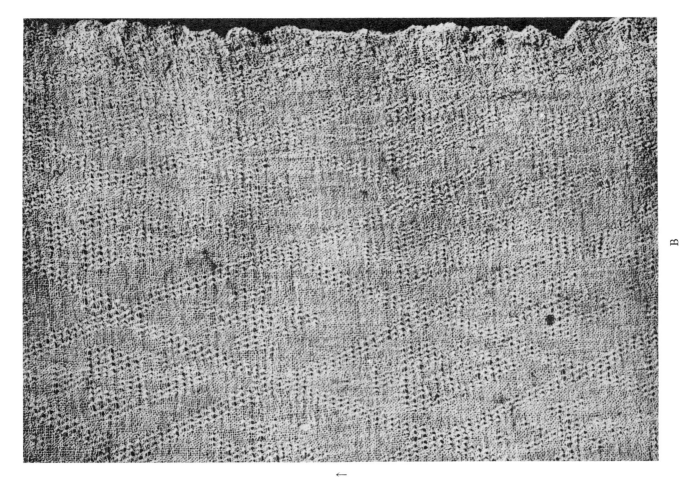

A

B

Fabrics of gauze and plain weave with open spaces

PLATE 38

↑

Fabric of gauze with open spaces and embroidery

PLATE 39

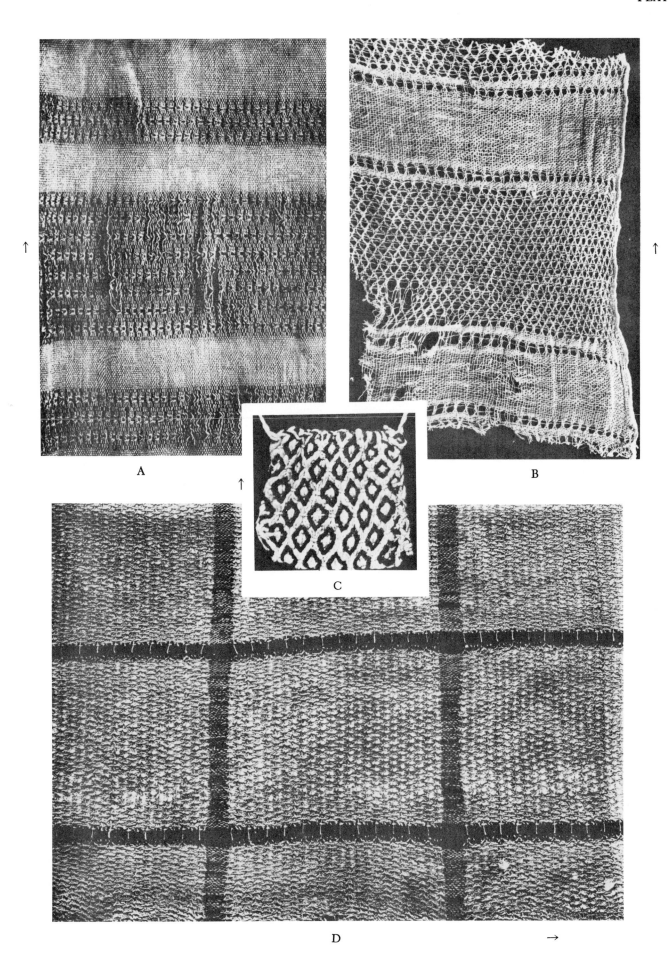

A, B, D, fabrics of open-work gauze and plain weave; C, small bag with gauze construction

PLATE 40

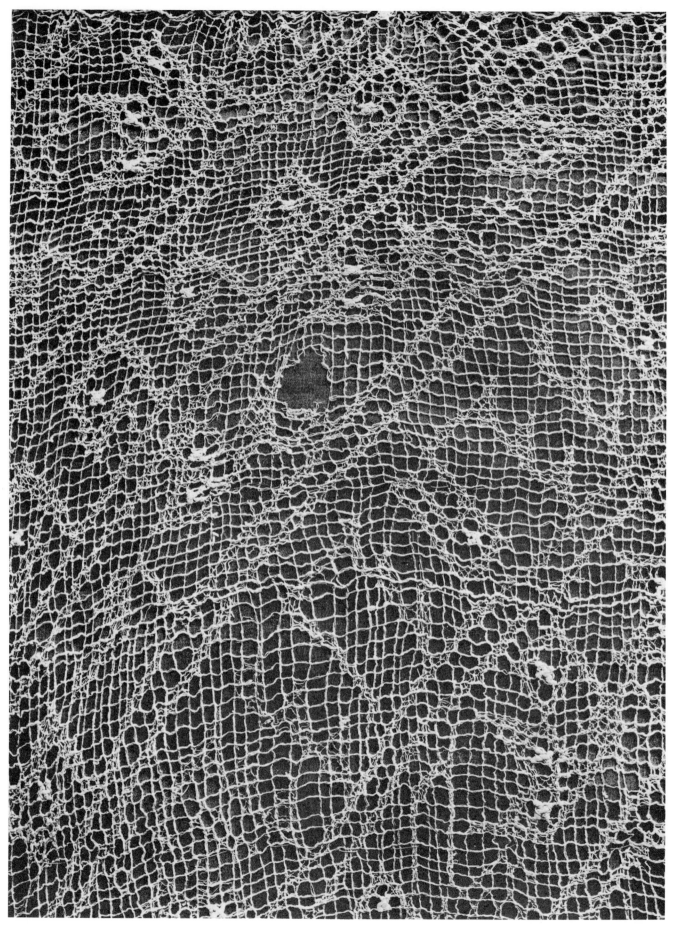

Fabric with square spaces and embroidery

PLATE 41

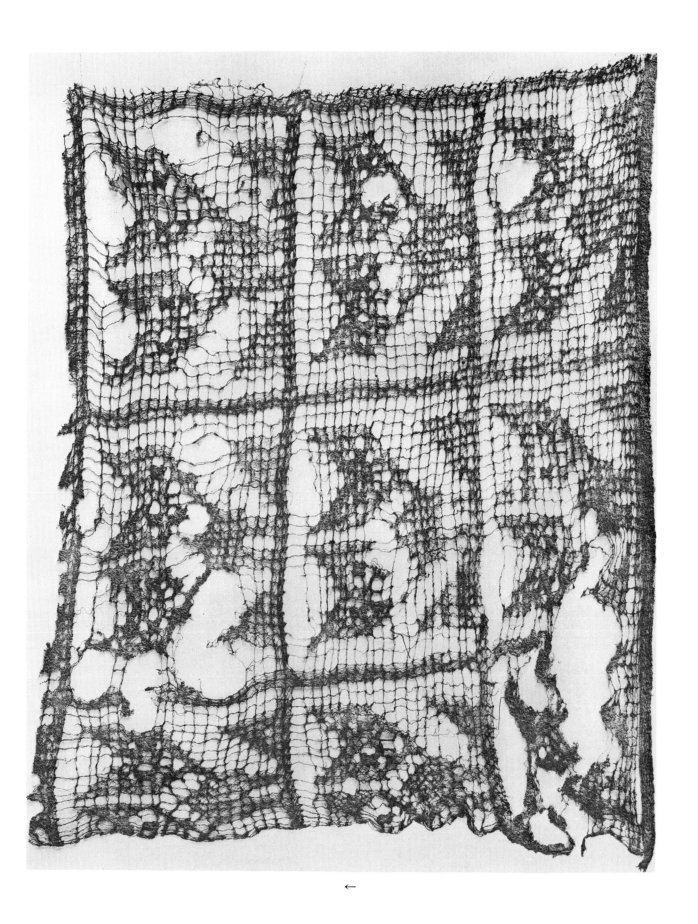

Fabric with square spaces and embroidery

←

PLATE 42

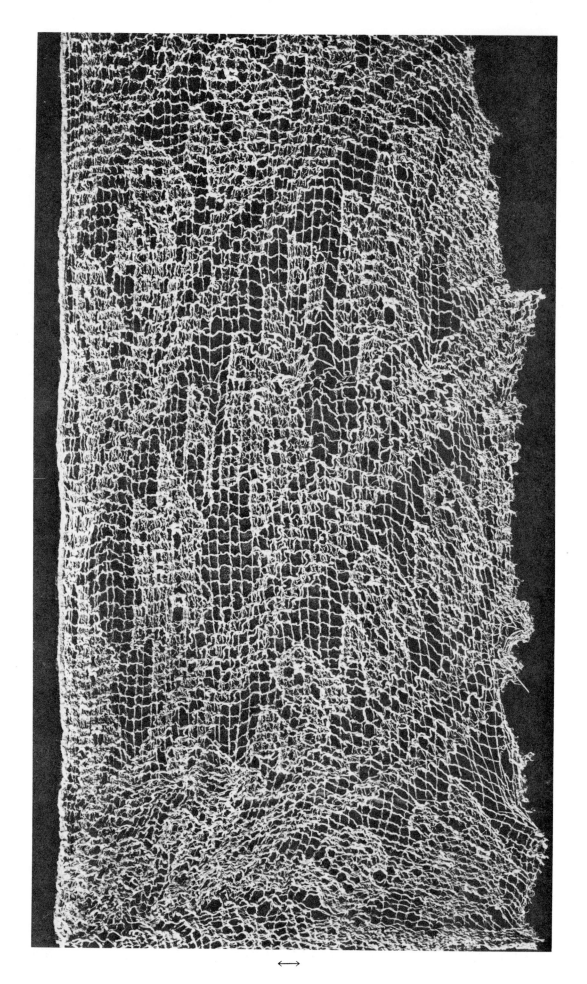

Fabric with square spaces and embroidery

PLATE 43

Fabric with square and triangular spaces and embroidery

←→

PLATE 44

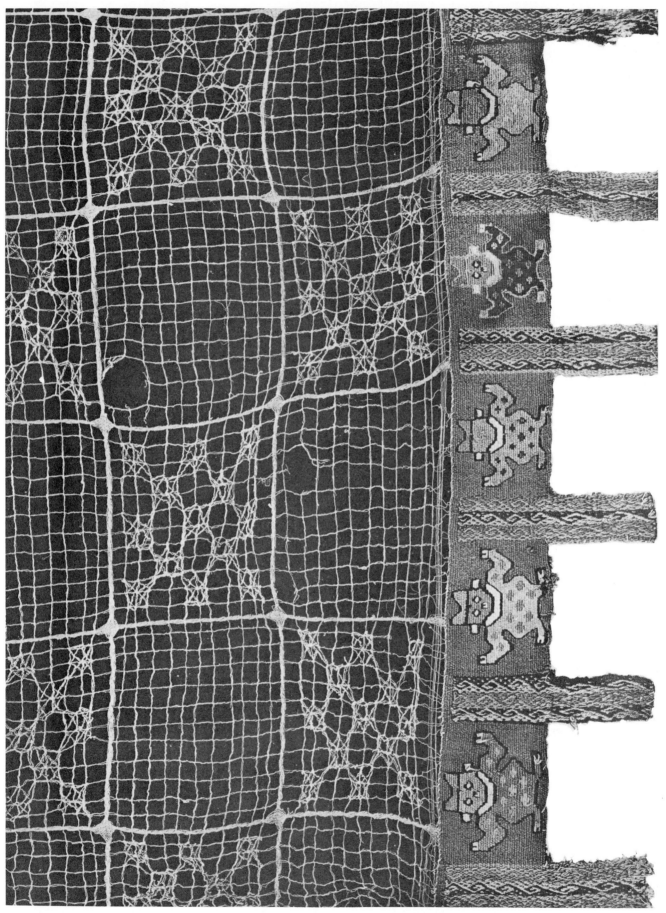

Embroidered fabric with square spaces and tapestry band

PLATE 45

←

B

←

A

Open-space fabrics

PLATE 46

↑

A

↑

B

Fabrics with open spaces in the form of lozenges

PLATE 47

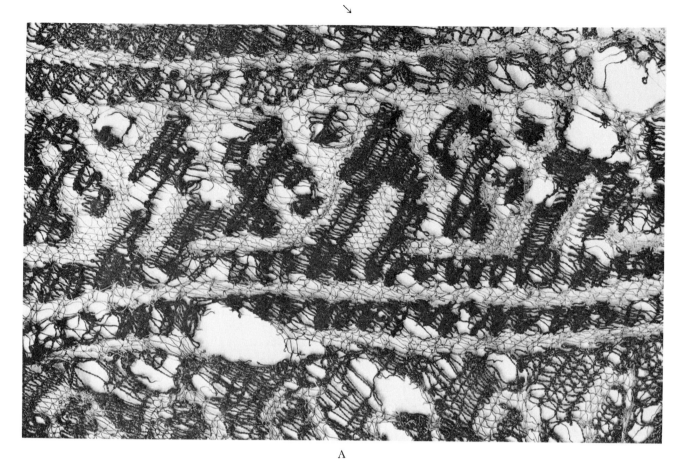

A

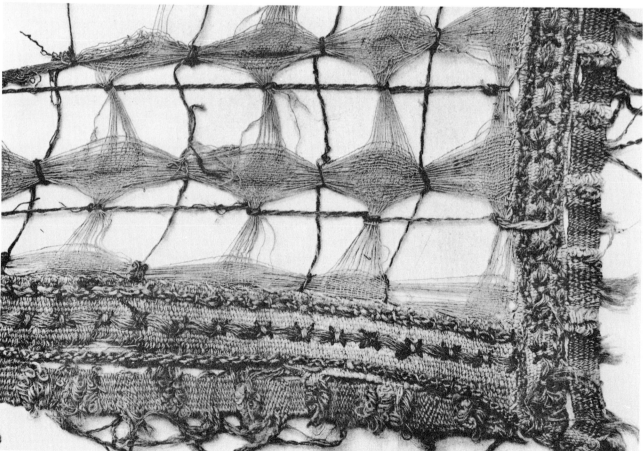

B

A, fabric with interlocked warp and knotted weft; B, open-space fabric
surrounded by a framework of embroidered rep and tapestry

PLATE 48

A

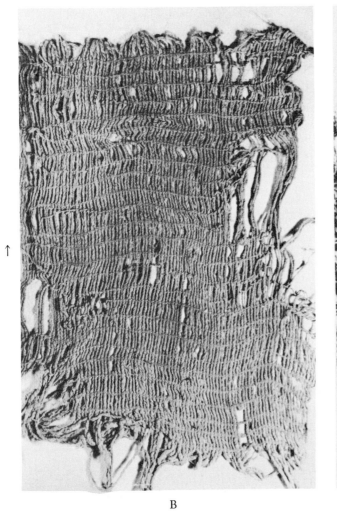

B

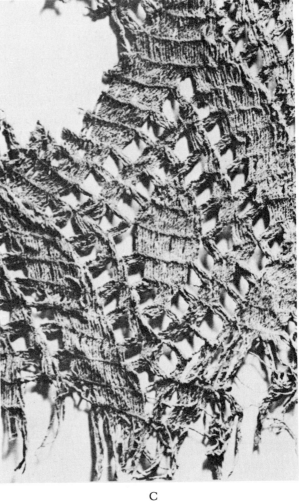

C

A, fragment of cloth with warp yarns twisted in pairs;
B, C, fabrics with weft yarns twisted in pairs (twining)

PLATE 49

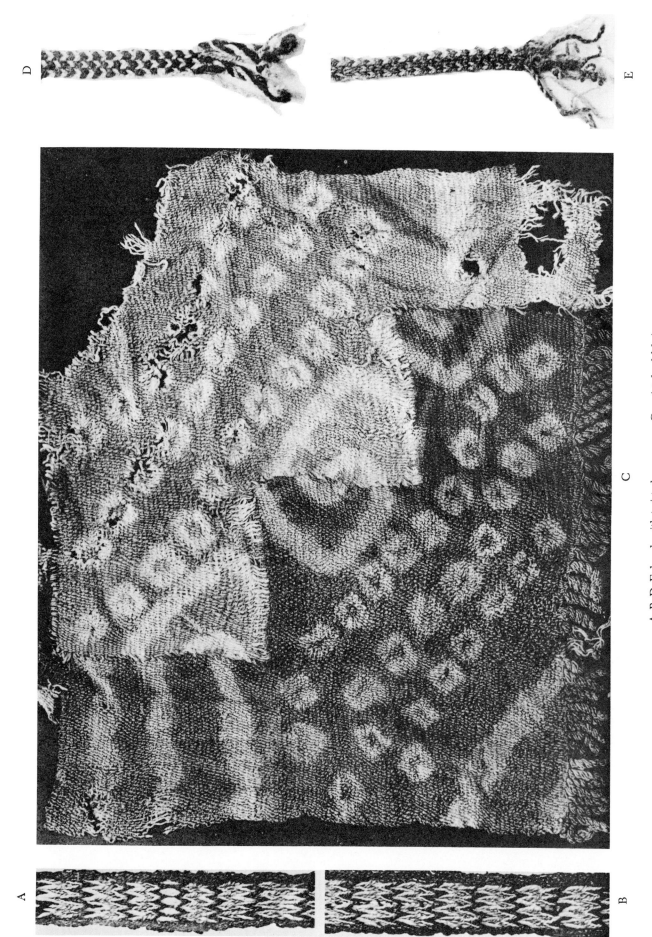

A, B, D, E, bands with twisted warp yarns; C, resist-dyed fabric

PLATE 50

A

B

Painted cotton fabrics

PLATE 51

A

B

Painted cotton fabrics

PLATE 52

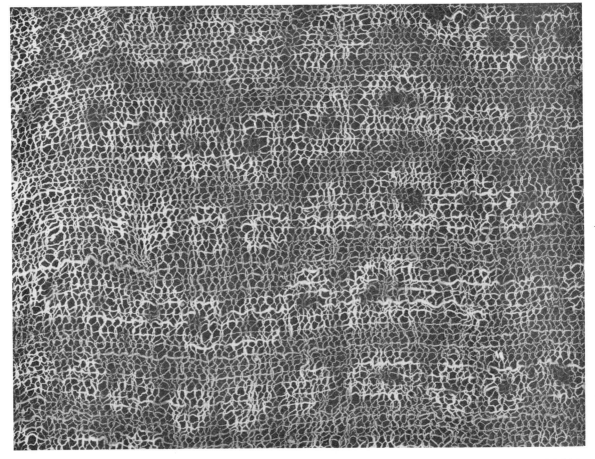

Gauze and sheer plain weave resist-dyed

B

A

PLATE 53

↑

A

↑

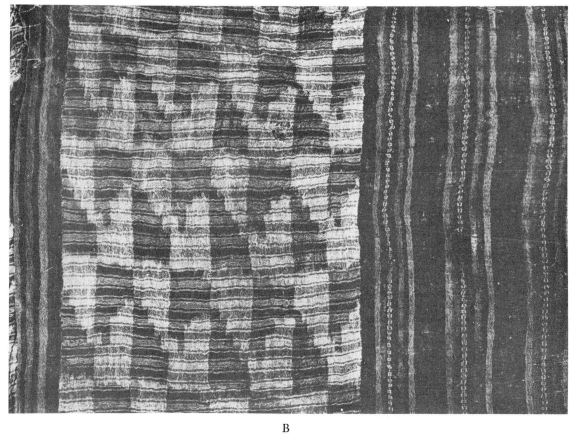

B

Fabrics with warp yarns dyed prior to weaving *(ikat)*

PLATE 54

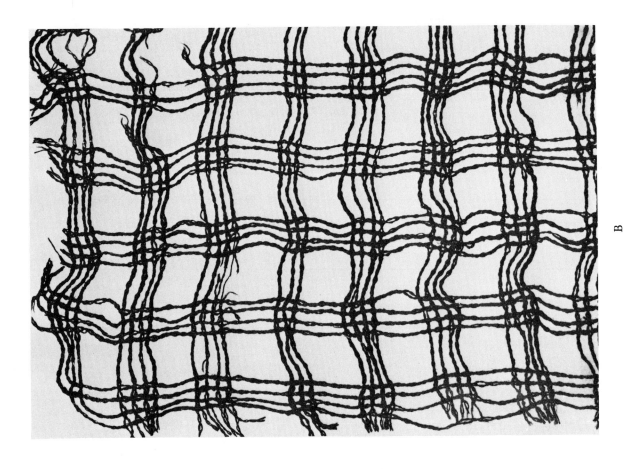

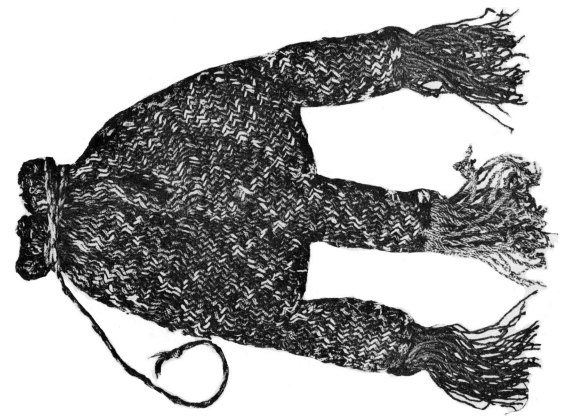

A, small plaited coca bag; B, fabric with yarns twisted in pairs

PLATE 55

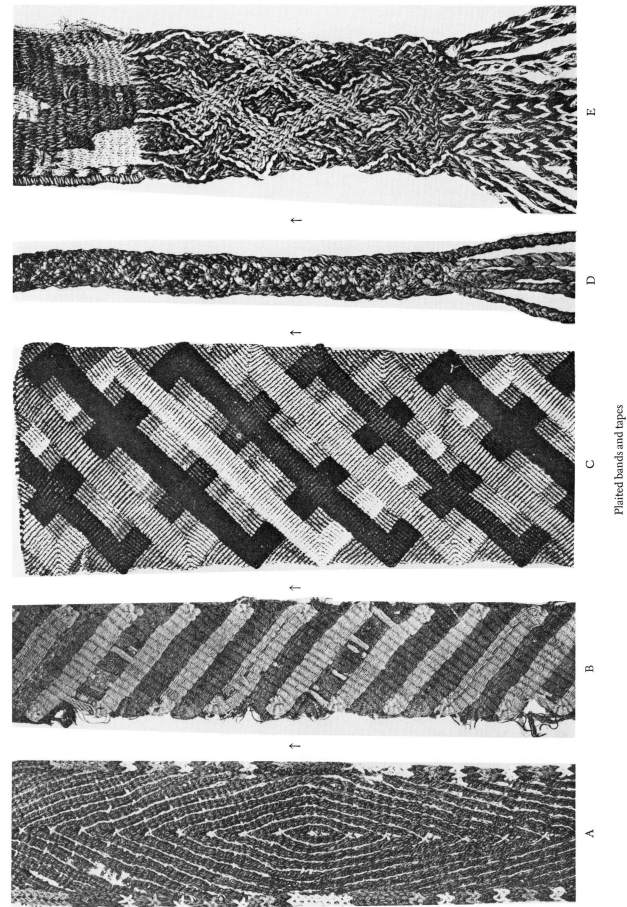

Plaited bands and tapes

PLATE 56

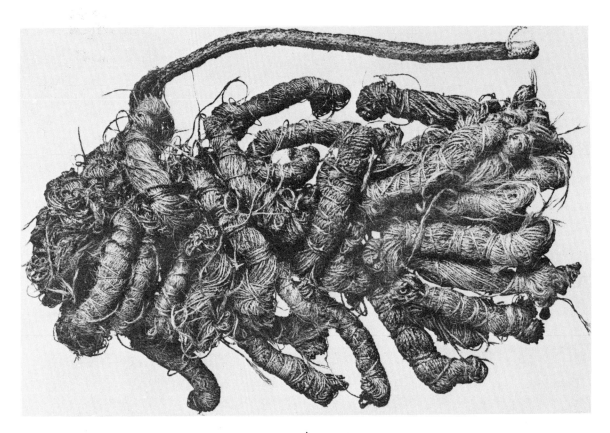

A

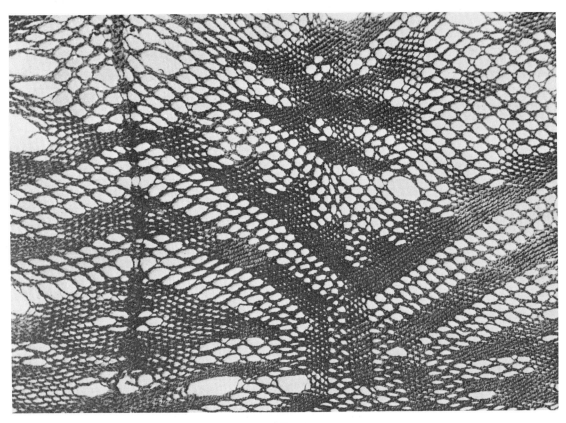

B

A, plaiting with rectangular cross section (in course of construction); B, open-work plaiting

PLATE 57

Neck covering made with double plaiting

PLATE 58

Neck covering made with quadruple plaiting

PLATE 59

A

B

C

D

E

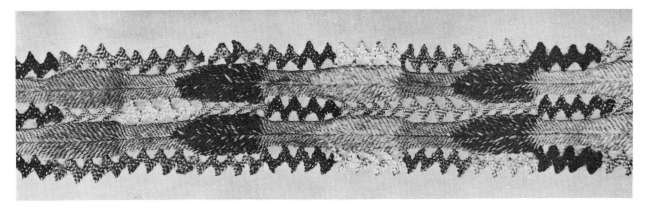

F

A-E, plaited sling cords; F, plaited passementerie

PLATE 60

A   B

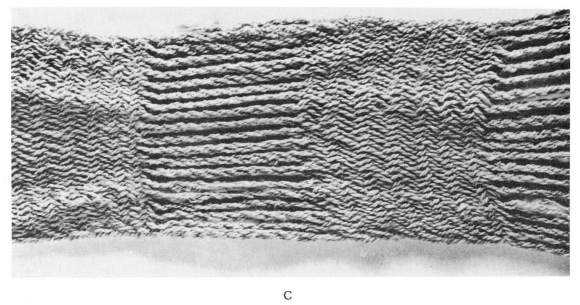

C

D

A, B, sandal soles; C, girth plaited in wool; D, plaited band

PLATE 61

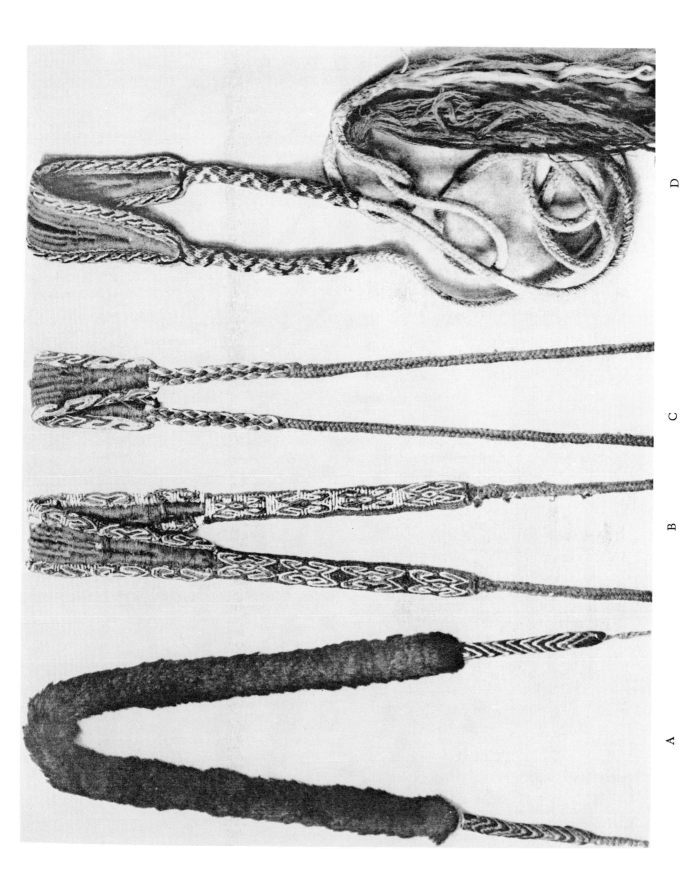

B   C   D

Slings plaited and embroidered

PLATE 62

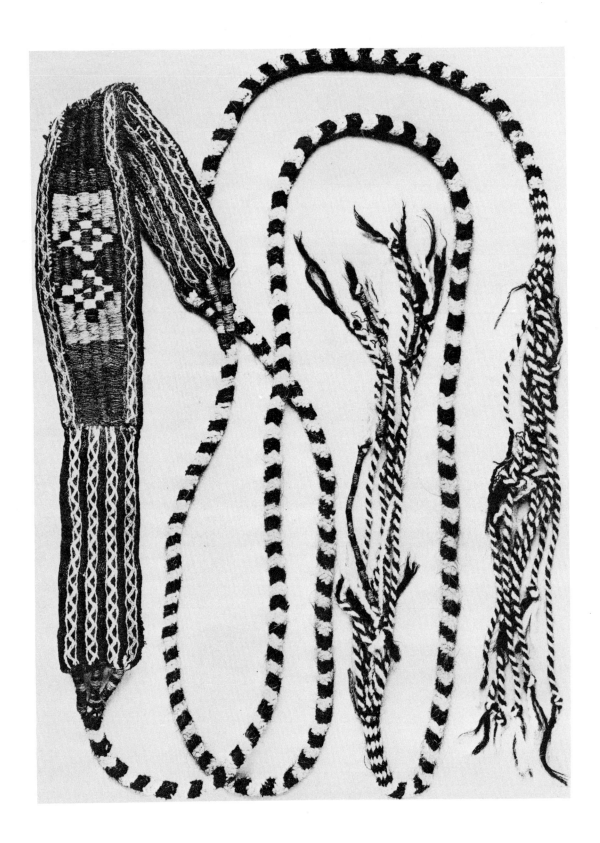

Sling plaited and embroidered

PLATE 63

Ceremonial sling

PLATE 64

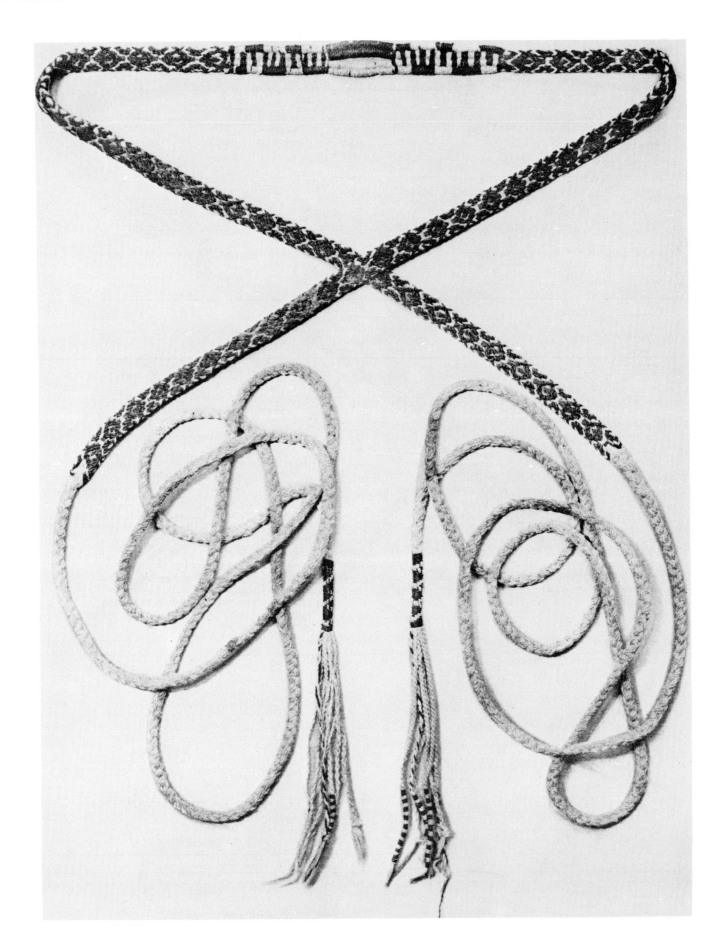

Sling plaited and woven

PLATE 65

D

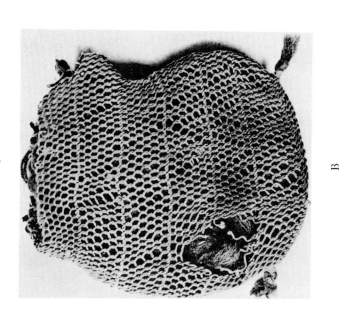

B

C

A

Networks of varied techniques: crown of cap; carrying bags

PLATE 66

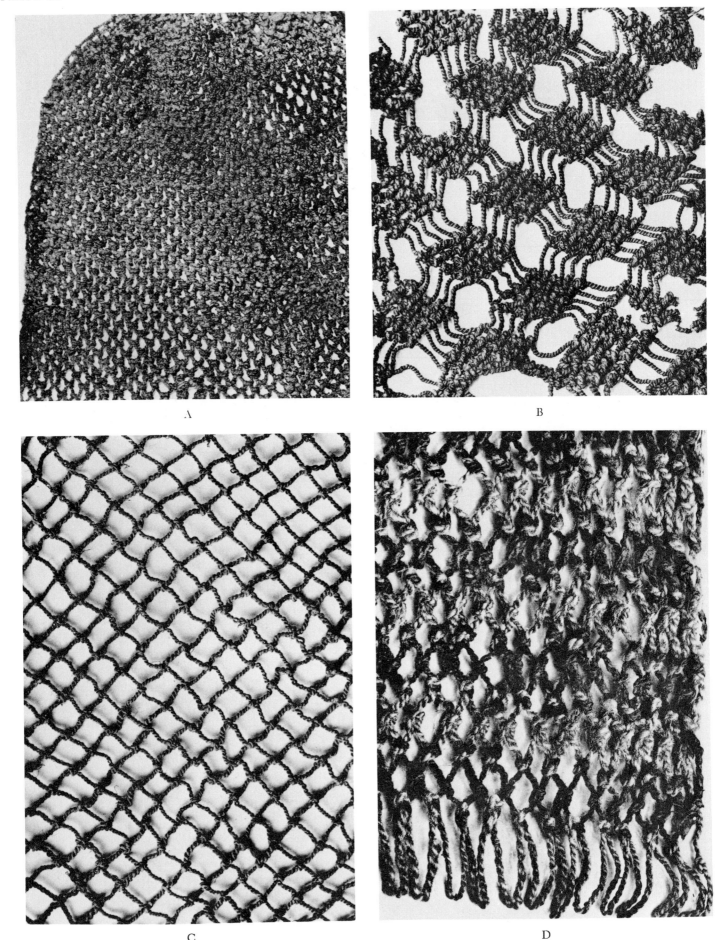

A

B

C

D

Networks of varied techniques

PLATE 67

C

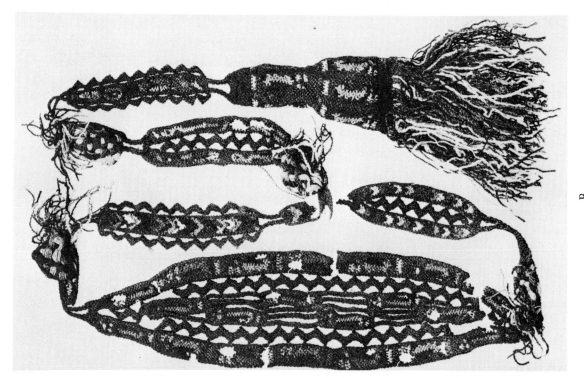

B

Network formed with simple knots

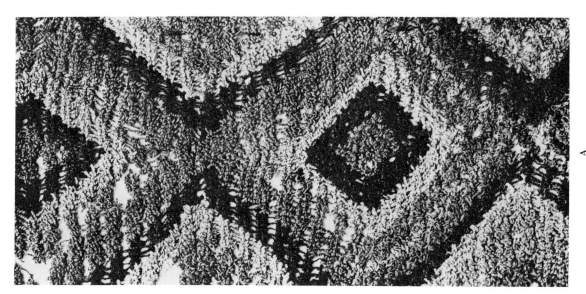

A

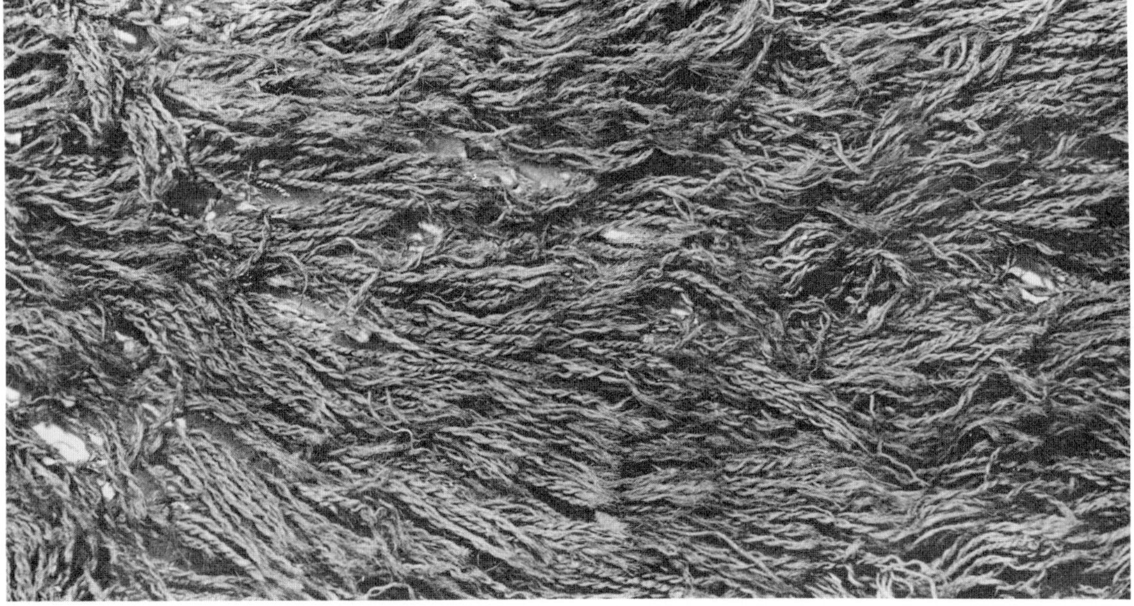

PLATE 68

C

B

A

A, C, network ornamented with wool tassels; B, bird made of network with simple looping

PLATE 69

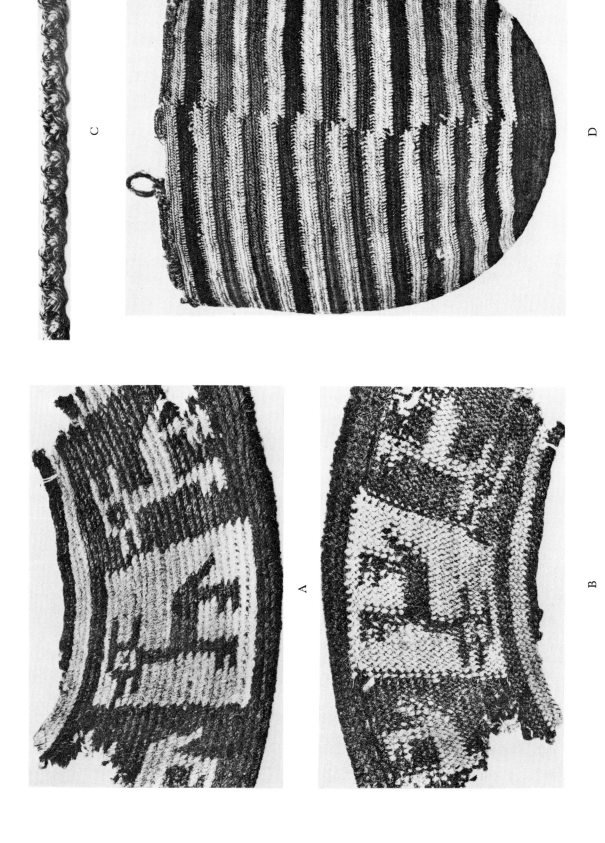

A, B, D, networks of varied construction; C, passementerie (enlarged)

PLATE 70

A

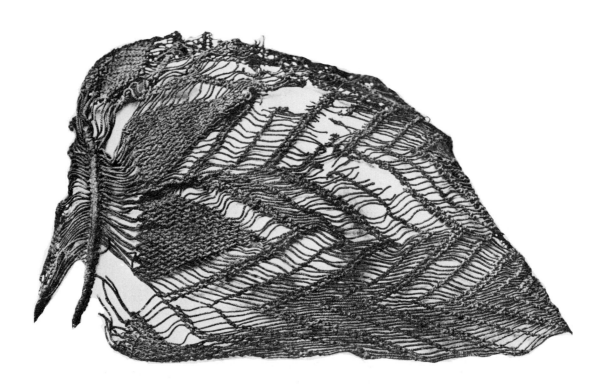

B

A, cap of felted hair; B, network cap of open-space square knot construction

PLATE 71

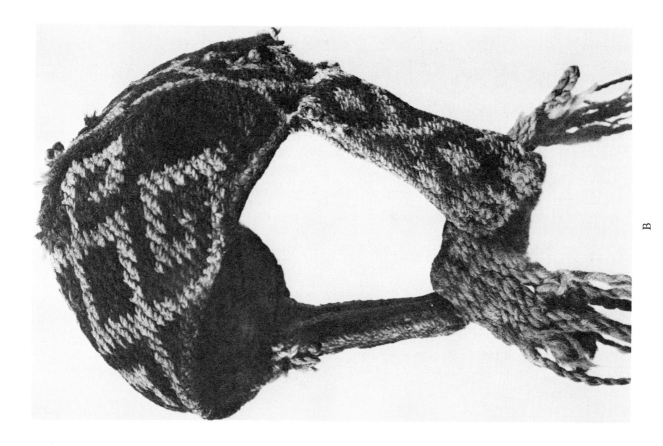

B

A

Caps made with loop stitch

PLATE 72

B

A

Caps made with loop stitch

PLATE 73

A

B

Caps made of "*simili-velours*"

PLATE 74

A, B, D, bandeaux of "simili-velours," right side and reverse; C, furred cord

PLATE 75

A

B

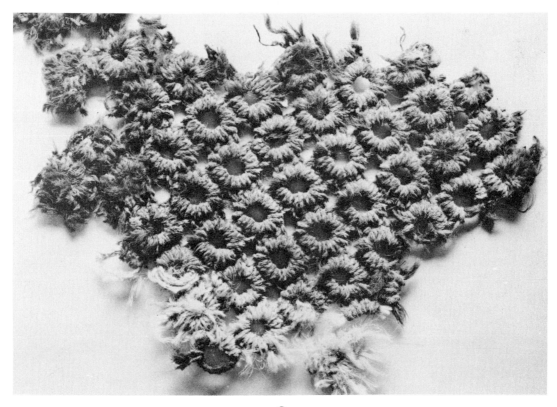

C

A, B, network with small loops, right side and reverse;
C, network made of small rings knotted together by a wool yarn

PLATE 76

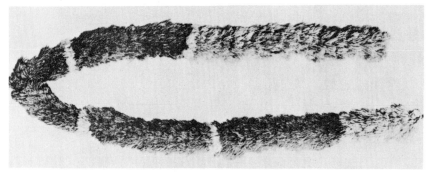

C

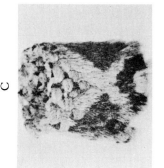

D

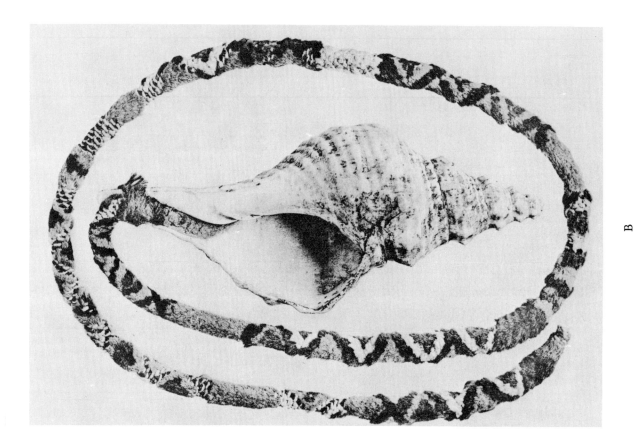

B

A

A, D, cases made of network in peruke stitch; B, C, furred cords

PLATE 77

Wig with wool yarns

PLATE 78

A

B

C

A, C, wigs made of hair; B, wig in cap form made of wool

PLATE 79

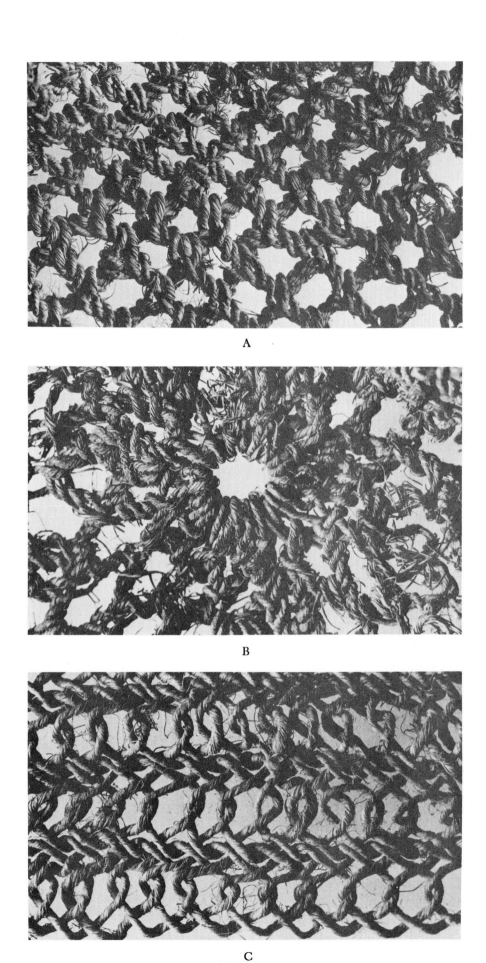

A

B

C

A, B, network with double twisting of yarns (enlarged);
C, network with imbricated loops (enlarged)

PLATE 80

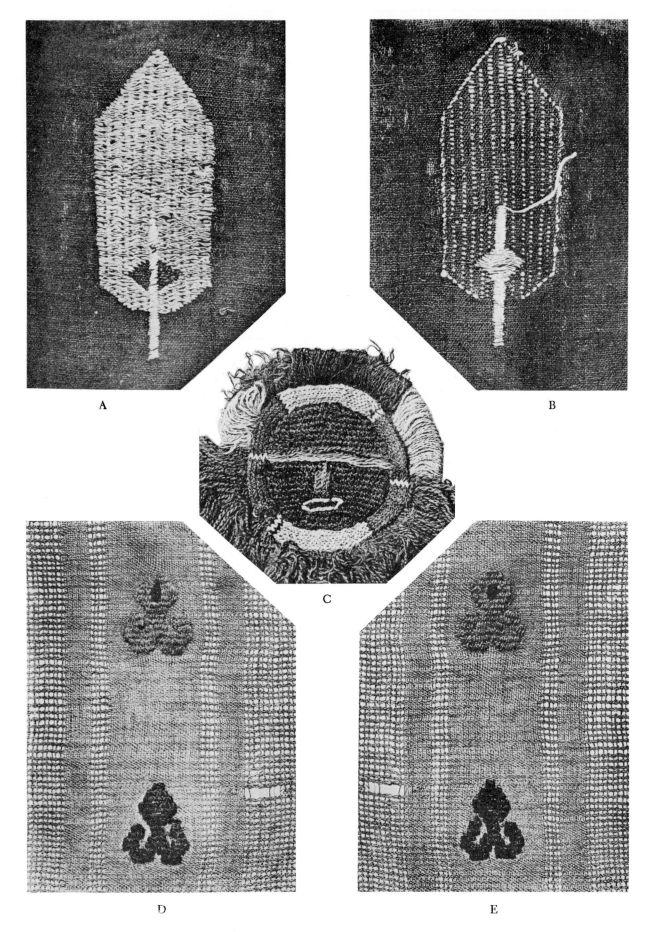

A, B, D, E, embroidered fabrics; C, figurine of network in Venice stitch

PLATE 81

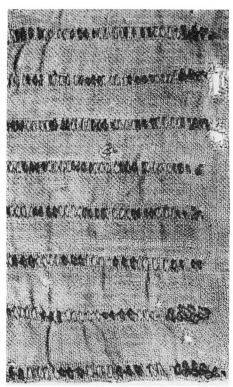

B

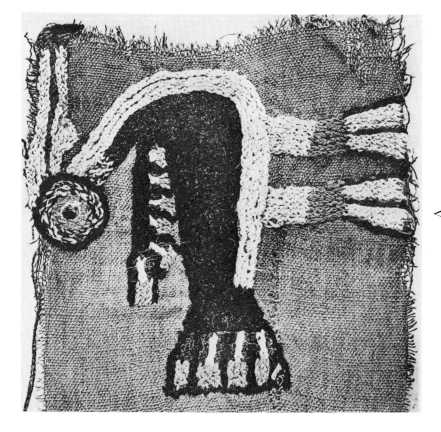

A

C

D

Fabrics embroidered in loop stitch

PLATE 82

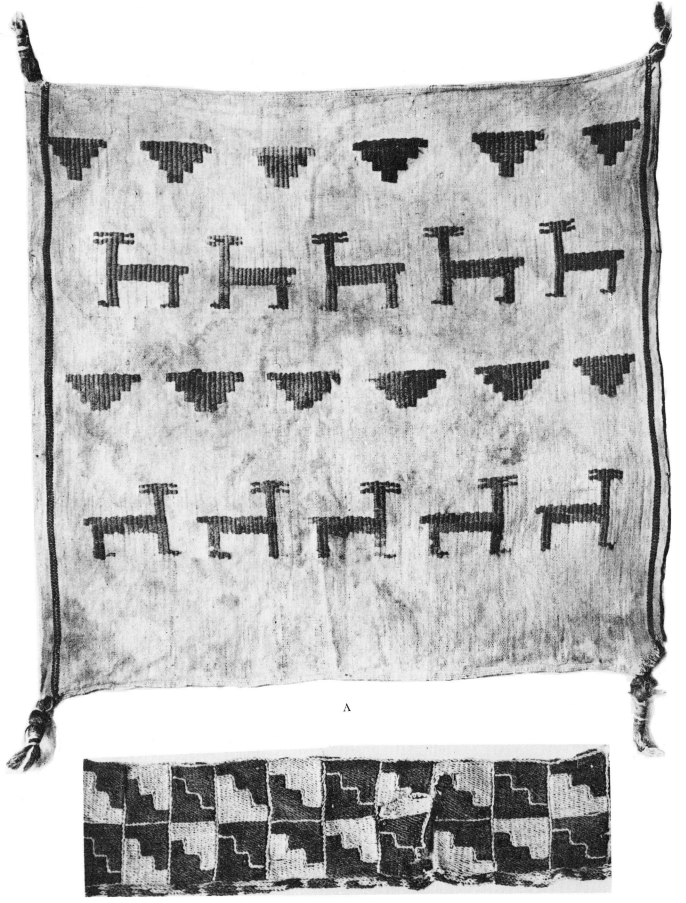

A

B

Fabrics embroidered in flat stitch and stem stitch

PLATE 83

Embroidered fabric and ornament

PLATE 84

A

B

C

D

E

Embroidered fabrics

PLATE 85

A

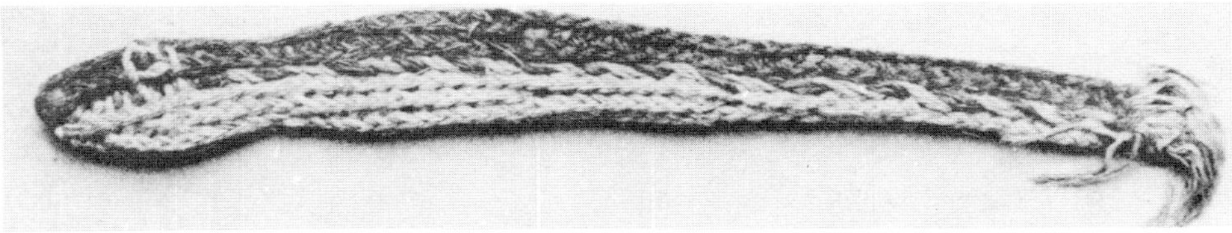

B

A, fabric embroidered in loop stitch;
B, fabric covered with an embroidered network of loop stitch

PLATE 86

A

B

C

Fabrics covered with an embroidered network of loop stitch

PLATE 87

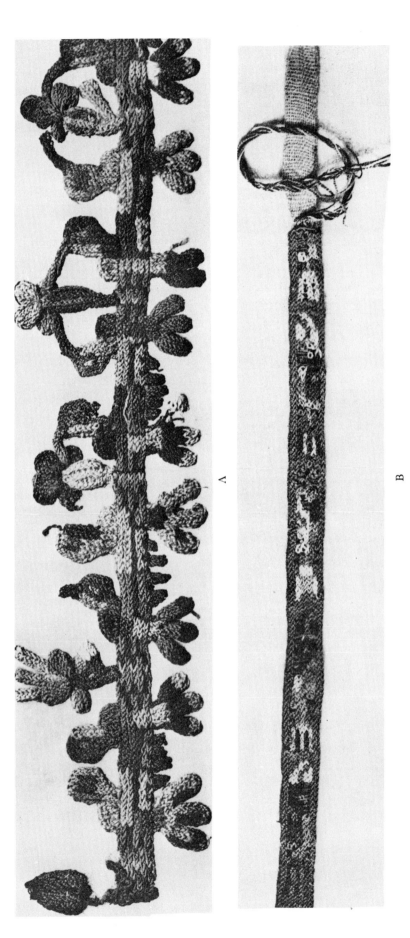

A

B

C

Fabrics covered with an embroidered network of loop stitch

PLATE 88

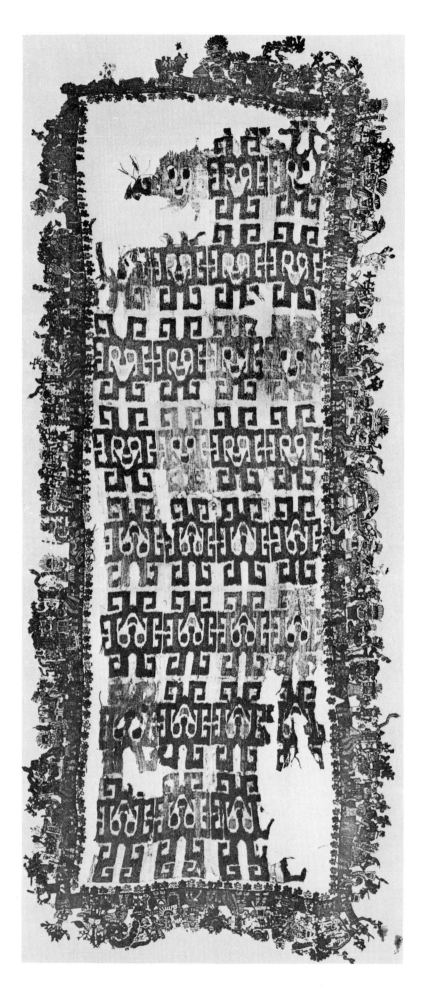

Fabric surrounded with a border of loop stitch figures

PLATE 89

1   2   3

4   5

Details of border of Plate 88

PLATE 90

6 7 8

9 10

Details of border of Plate 88

PLATE 91

11

12

13

14

15

Details of border of Plate 88

PLATE 92

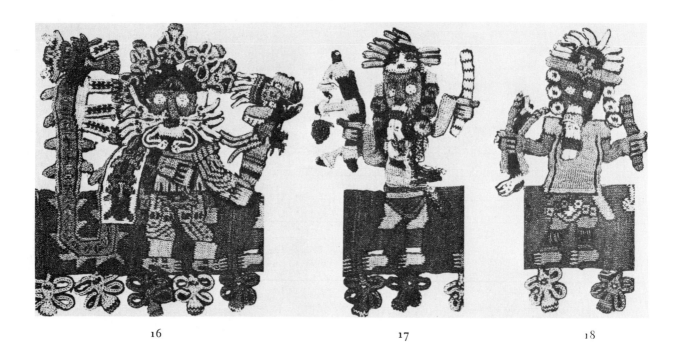

16 17 18

19 20 21

Details of border of Plate 88

PLATE 93

22   23   24

25   26

Details of border of Plate 88

PLATE 94

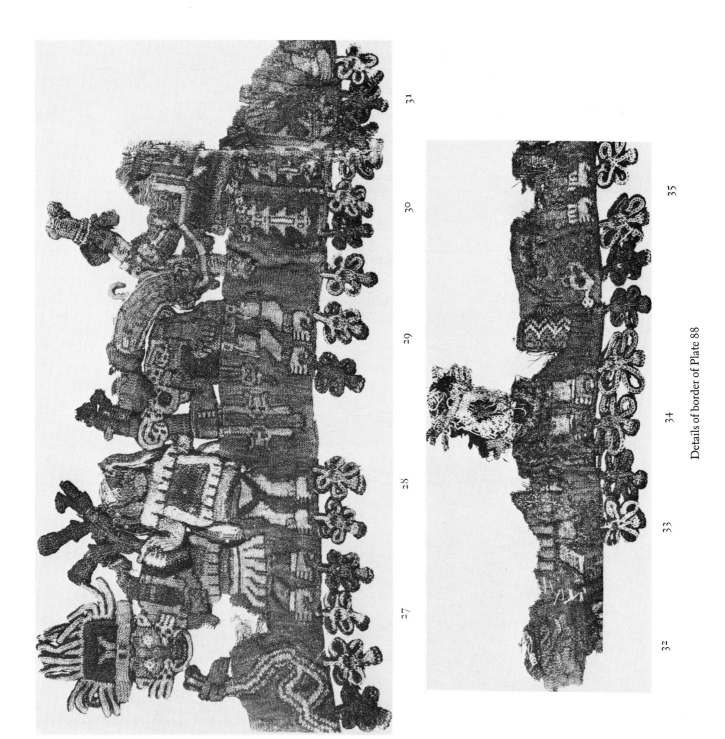

Details of border of Plate 88

PLATE 95

36   37   38

39   40   41

Details of border of Plate 88

PLATE 96

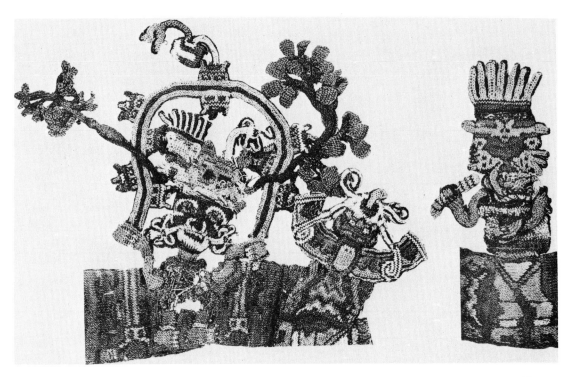

42   43   44

45   46

Details of border of Plate 88

PLATE 97

47   48   49

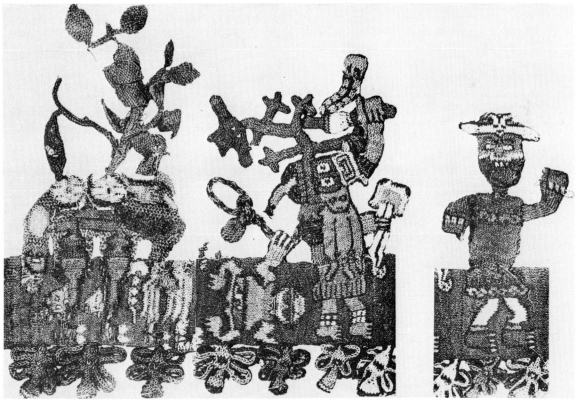

50   51   52

Details of border of Plate 88

PLATE 98

53 54 55 56

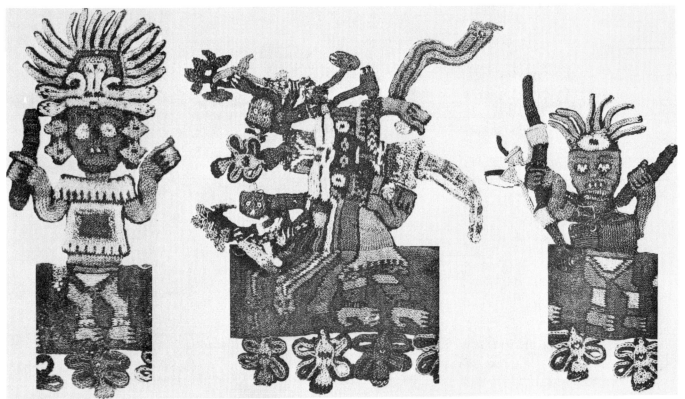

57 58 59

Details of border of Plate 88

PLATE 99

60   61   62

63   64   65

Details of border of Plate 88

PLATE 100

66   67   68

69   70   71

Details of border of Plate 88

PLATE 101

72   73   74

75   76   77

Details of border of Plate 88

PLATE 102

78   79   80

81   82   83

Details of border of Plate 88

PLATE 103

84   85   86

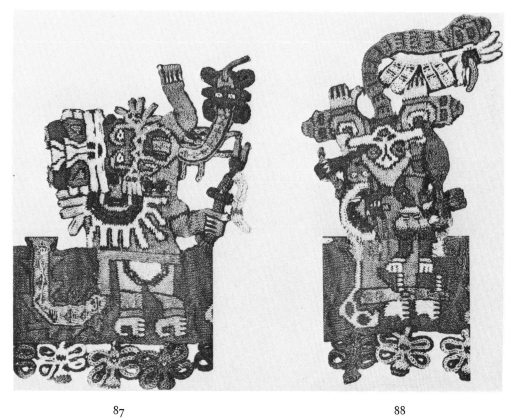

87   88

Details of border of Plate 88

PLATE 104

89   90

Details of border and center of textile of Plate 88

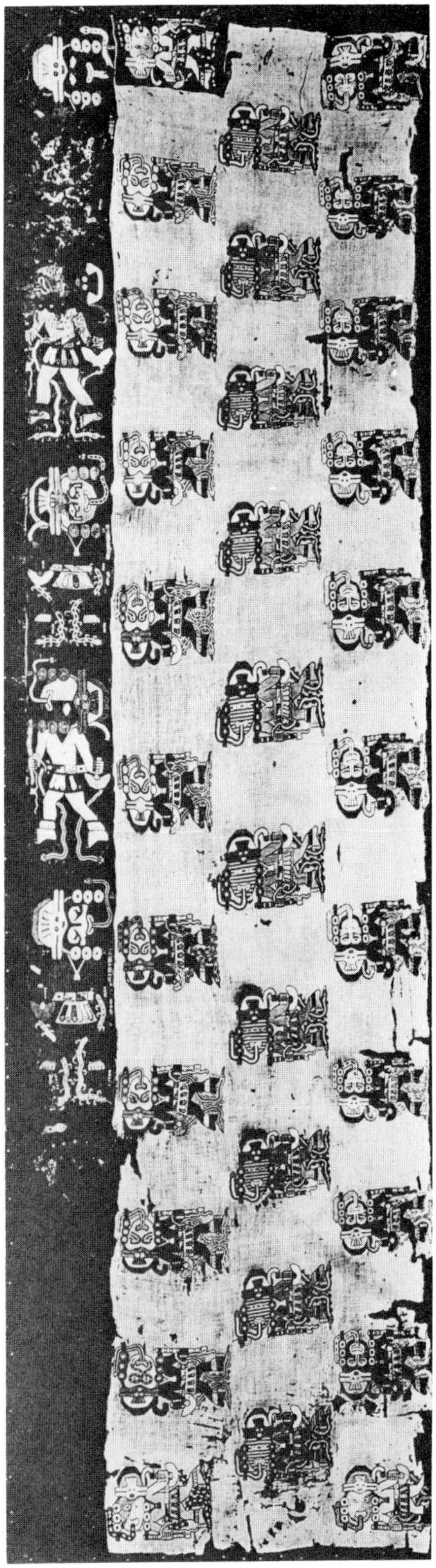

PLATE 105

A

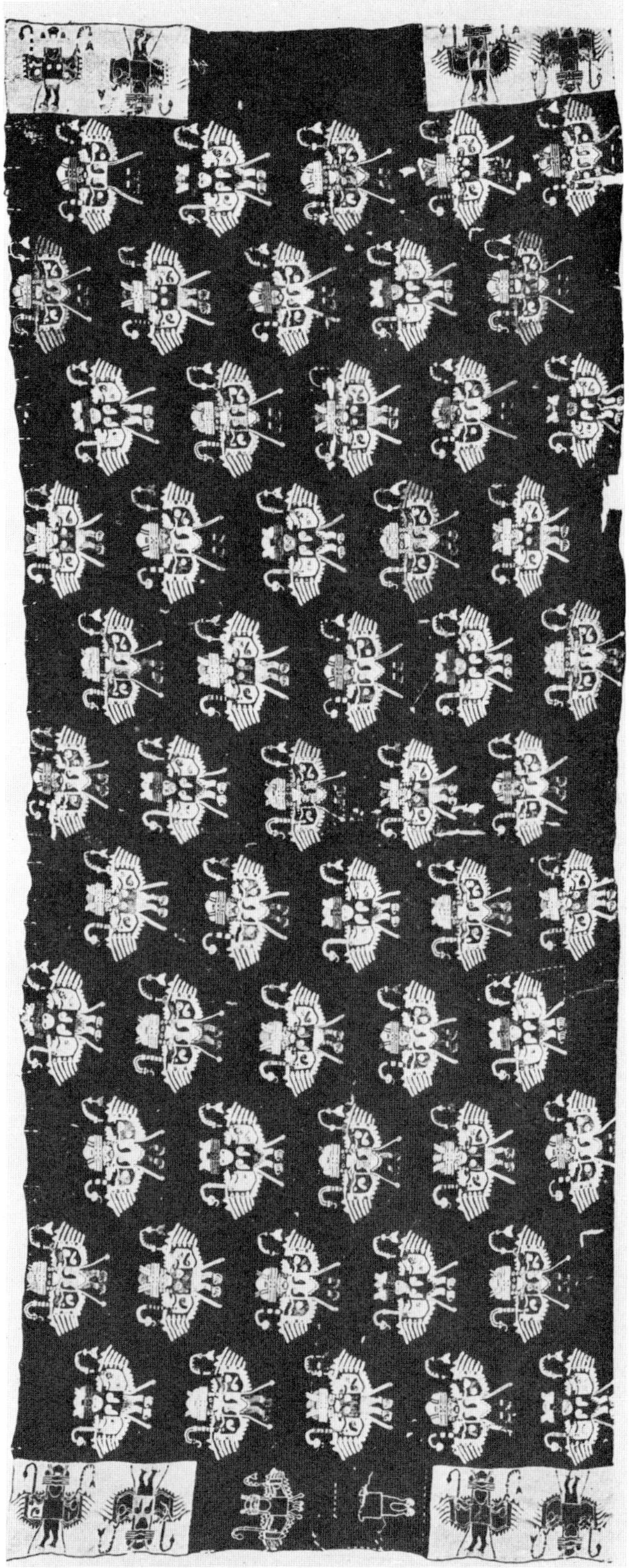

B

Fabrics embroidered in stem stitch

PLATE 106

A

B

Fabrics embroidered in stem stitch

PLATE 107

A

B

Fabrics embroidered in stem stitch

PLATE 108

A

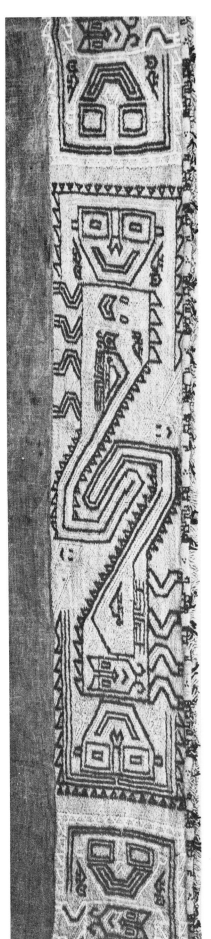

B

Fabrics embroidered in stem stitch

PLATE 109

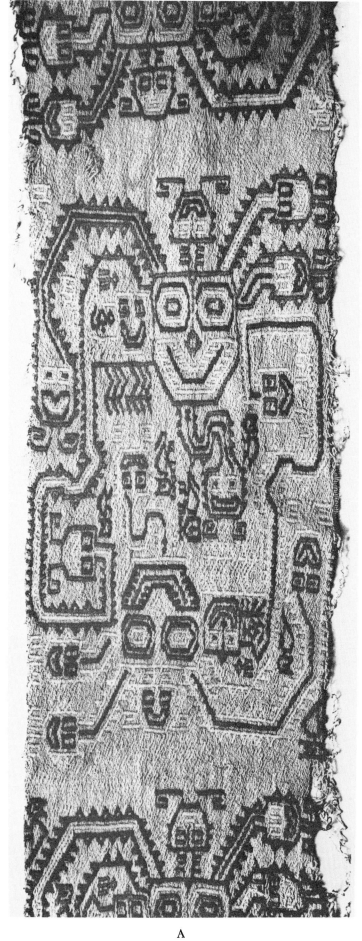

A

B

Fabrics embroidered in stem stitch

PLATE 110

A   C   D

B

Fabrics embroidered in stem stitch

PLATE 111

Small shirt (*cushma*) embroidered in stem stitch

PLATE 112

A

B

Fabrics embroidered in stem stitch

PLATE 113

A

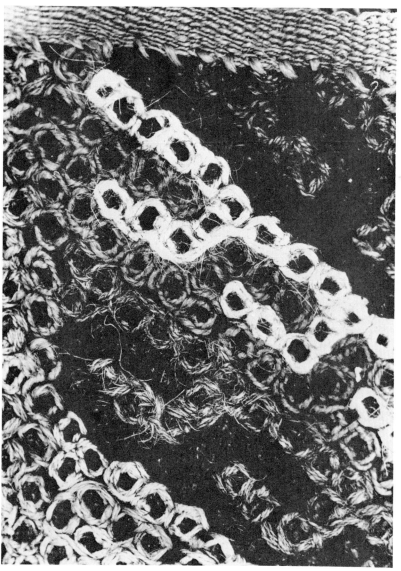

B

Belt of network embroidered in polychrome wool

PLATE 114

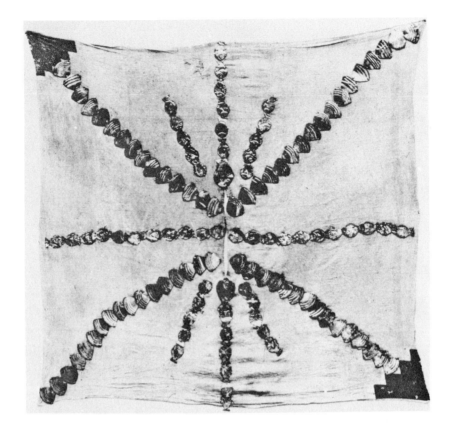

A

B

Fabrics ornamented with pieces of metal or shell

PLATE 115

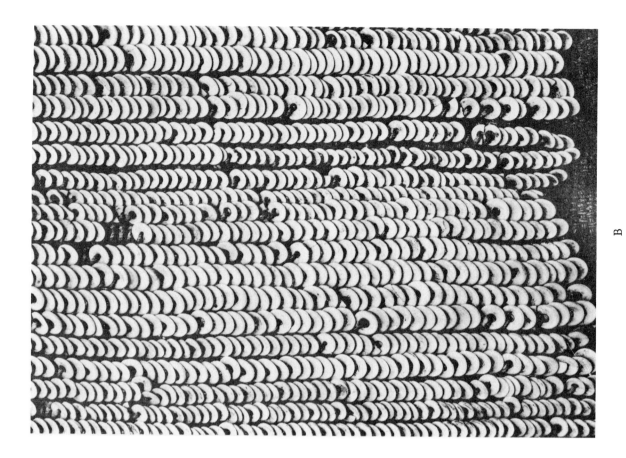

A, fabric ornamented with feathers; B, fabric ornamented with shell disks

PLATE 116

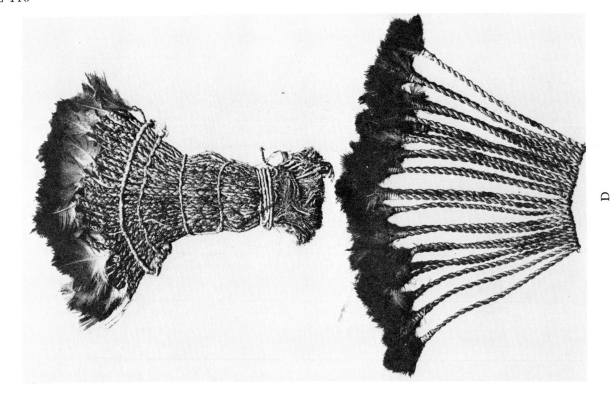

D

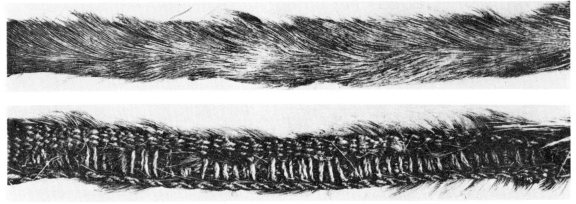

C

B

Feather ornaments

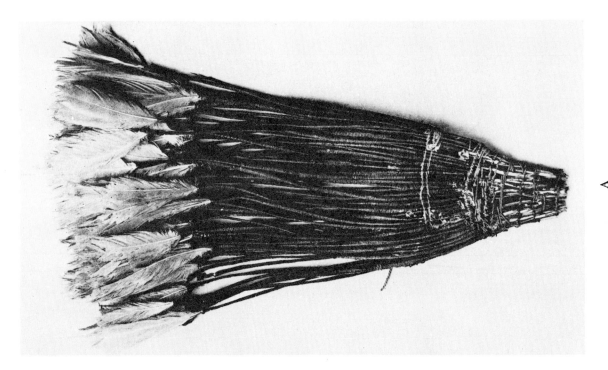

A

PLATE 117

A

B

A, tapestry with shell beads; B, ball of wool covered with embroidery